ART, ETHNOGRAPHY
AND THE LIFE OF OBJECTS

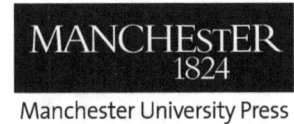

MANCHESTER
1824

Manchester University Press

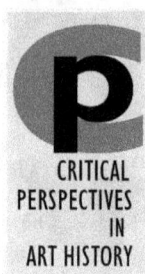

CRITICAL
PERSPECTIVES
IN
ART HISTORY

SERIES EDITORS
Tim Barringer, Marsha Meskimmon
and Shearer West

EDITORIAL CONSULTANTS
Nicola Bown, Robin Cormack, John House, John Onians,
Marcia Pointon, Alan Wallach and Evelyn Welch

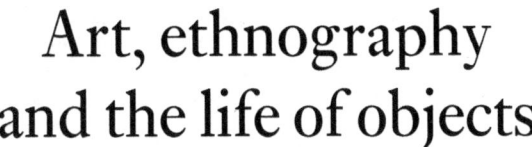

Art, ethnography and the life of objects

Paris *c.* 1925–35

JULIA KELLY

Manchester University Press

Manchester and New York

distributed exclusively in the USA by Palgrave

Published by Manchester University Press
Oxford Road, Manchester M13 9NR, UK
and Room 400, 175 Fifth Avenue, New York, NY 10010, USA
www.manchesteruniversitypress.co.uk

Distributed in the United States exclusively by
Palgrave Macmillan, 175 Fifth Avenue,
New York, NY 10010, USA

Distributed in Canada exclusively by
UBC Press, University of British Columbia, 2029 West Mall,
Vancouver, BC, Canada V6T 1Z2

British Library Cataloguing-in-Publication Data is available

Library of Congress Cataloging-in-Publication Data is available

ISBN 978 0 7190 6941 3 paperback

First published by Manchester University Press in hardback 2007

This paperback edition first published 2013

Printed by Lightning Source

Contents

List of illustrations   *page* ix

Acknowledgements   xiii

Introduction   1

1 Encountering: ethnography, art and the reception of
   non-western objects   12

2 Classifying: the 'irritating' object and its disciplines   40

3 Collecting: fieldwork and its discontents   67

4 Mediating: ethnography through a lens and behind glass   91

5 Making: technologies of the surrealist object   122

   Select bibliography   153

   Index   165

To my late uncle Gustaw Syga

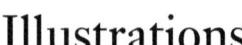

Illustrations

All dimensions are given in cm.

1 Alberto Giacometti, *Spoon Woman*, 1926–27, bronze, 144 x 51 x 23, Kunsthaus Zürich, Alberto Giacometti Foundation, Zurich. Photograph courtesy Kunsthaus Zürich. © ADAGP, Paris and DACS, London, 2005. *page* 17

2 Fang head from the collection of Guillaume in *La Renaissance de l'art français*, 5:4 (1922), p. 225. Photograph courtesy Victoria and Albert Museum. 19

3 'Vengeance fetish', wood, nails, mirrors, rope and charms, in *La Nature* (22 April 1916), p. 258. By permission of the British Library (PP 1614.ca). 20

4 Masks from the Ivory Coast, Senegal and the Gambia, plate XI in Frobenius, *Masks and Secret Societies of Africa* (1898). 22

5 Bangwa mask, Cameroon, wood, 29 x 22, plate 12 in Einstein, *African Sculpture* (1921), formerly collections of Einstein and Tzara. 24

6 Akati Ekplékendo, *Sculpture dedicated to Gou, god of metalwork and war*, Dahomey (Togo), before 1858, iron and wood, 165h, and Baga *nimba* shoulder mask, Guinea, wood, Trocadéro Ethnographic Museum, Paris, in *Cahiers d'art*, 1:7 (1926), p. 180. Photograph courtesy Witt Library, Courtauld Institute of Art. 42

7 Bronze objects from Louristan (Iraq), collections David-Weill, Nazareaga, Pierre, in *Documents*, 2:6 (1930), p. 373. 47

8 Masks and figurines, Tanganyika, Belgian Congo and Angola, patinated ivory and patinated red ivory, collections of Heim, Stora, de Miré, in *Cahiers d'art*, 5:1 (1930), p. 40. 51

9 Peruvian pan scales, Gothenburg Museum, Seri Indian balancing pole and 'Indian' carrying a balancing pole, in *Documents*, 1: 4 (1929), p. 180. 57

10 Detail of Baoule drum, Ivory Coast, wood, 198h x 48d, Trocadéro Ethnographic Museum, Paris, in *Documents*, 2: 1 (1930), p. 47. 58

11 *Bazou*, Dogon, Tiogou, wood, in Desplagnes, *Le Plateau central nigérien* (1907), plate LXXVIII, fig. 152. 69

12 'Used masks, abandoned under a rock', *Minotaure*, 1:2 (1933), p. 51. 74

13 Exhibition of the equipment of the Dakar–Djibouti expedition, Trocadéro, Paris, May 1931. © Photothèque du Musée de l'Homme, Paris, 2005. 77

14 Altar figure (*boli*), Bamana, Mali, wood and encrustation, Musée du quai Branly, Paris (formerly Musée de l'Homme). 83

15 Cylindrical object (population curve), plaster, 34.5 x 17 x 9, private collection
    and Saint-Ouen fleamarket (photographed by Jacques-André Boiffard), in
    André Breton, *Nadja* (1928/1964), pp. 60–1.   *page* 95
16 Roussel's star-shaped biscuit, photographed by Dora Maar, *Cahiers d'art*,
    1–2 (1936), p. 50. Photograph courtesy Witt Library, Courtauld Institute of Art.
    © ADAGP, Paris and DACS, London, 2005.   97
17 Statues and objects in a Birifo funerary chapel, Donko, Gaoua, in Delafosse,
    Haut-Sénégal-Niger (1912), plate XLI, fig. 80.   99
18 The 'Treasury' at the Trocadéro Ethnographic Museum (1932–35),
    photographed in 1934. © Photothèque du Musée de l'Homme, Paris, 2005.   101
19 Dogon 'mothers of masks', Gogoli, Sanga, and shown at the Trocadéro
    Ethnographic Museum, *Minotaure*, 1:2 (1933), pp. 26–7.   103
20 *The potter's daughter holding a doll bought from a Sakyu blacksmith*, Bamako,
    1931, photograph by Marcel Griaule. © Photothèque du Musée de l'Homme,
    Paris, 2005.   104
21 Horn with human head, Nyangaso, San, wood, 45h, Bamana sacrificial calabash,
    Dyabougou, San, 15d, cloudscape, San and Kono ritual mask, Nougna, San,
    84h, for 'Miscellany of the French Sudan', *Minotaure* 1:2 (1933), pp. 22–3. 105
22 Chinese archaic mask, lion, Delos, frieze, Luxor and *Parrot with lizard on its
    back*, Sepik River, New Guinea, 47h, collection of Pierre Loeb, in *Cahiers d'art*,
    4:10 (1929), p. 467.   106
23 *Bazou*, Sanga, 106h, statue with raised arms, Yougo, 45h, *bazou*, Dyamini,
    Sanga, 110h and anthropomorphic statue, Dyamini, 85h, *Minotaure* 1: 2
    (1933), pp. 28–9.   108
24 Gaston Doumergue inaugurating the exhibition *The Ancients Arts of America*,
    Pavillon de Marsan, Louvre, Paris, May–June 1928. © Photothèque du Musée
    de l'Homme, Paris, 2005.   109
25 *Vitrine of the French Sudan*, Trocadéro Ethnographic Museum, Paris, 1934.
    © Photothèque du Musée de l'Homme, Paris, 2005.   113
26 *Black Africa Room. Temporary exhibition of the Dakar-Djibouti expedition*,
    Trocadéro Ethnographic Museum, Paris, 1933 (photograph gift of *Beaux-
    Arts* magazine). © Photothèque du Musée de l'Homme, Paris, 2005.   114
27 *Black Africa Room. Temporary exhibition of the Dakar-Djibouti expedition*,
    Trocadéro Ethnographic Museum, Paris, 1933. © Photothèque du Musée
    de l'Homme, Paris, 2005.   115
28 Pablo Picasso, *Profile*, 1931, flowerpot, roots (fig tree?), horn and red feather
    duster, dimensions unknown, destroyed, in *Minotaure* 1:1 (1933), p. 14.
    © Succession Picasso/DACS, London, 2005.   122
29 *Prey god fetiches*, plate 1 in Cushing, *Zuñi Fetiches* (1883).   127
30 Man Ray, *Aeneus carrying his father*, in *Minotaure*, 1:5 (1934), p. 12.
    © Man Ray Trust/ADAGP, Paris and DACS, London, 2005.   129
31 Alberto Giacometti, *Man and Woman*, 1929 (front left), *Gazing Head*, 1928
    (rear left), *Man*, 1927–28 (rear right) and *Woman*, 1928–29 (front right), in
    Documents, 1:4 (1929), p. 212, photograph by Marc Vaux. Fonds Marc Vaux,
    Bibliothèque Kandinsky, Centre Georges Pompidou, Paris. © ADAGP, Paris
    and DACS, London, 2005.   132

32 Alberto Giacometti, *Man (Apollo)*, 1929 (front left), *Man and Woman* 1929
    (rear left), *Reclining Woman who Dreams*, 1929 (rear right) and *Three Figures
    Outdoors*, 1929 (front right), in *Documents*, 1:4 (1929), p. 214, photograph by
    Marc Vaux. Fonds Marc Vaux, Bibliothèque Kandinsky, Centre Georges
    Pompidou, Paris. © ADAGP, Paris, and DACS, London, 2005.   *page* 134
33 Spoons, Gabon and the Congo, wood and ivory, collections of Moris and
    Rupalley, in Lepage, *La Décoration primitive* (c. 1924), plate XVI.   135
34 Spoon forms in Leroi-Gourhan, *Milieu et techniques* (1945), pp. 189–99.   136
35 Man Ray, *From a little shoe that was part of it…*, 1934, in Breton, *L'Amour
    fou* (1937), p. 48. © Man Ray Trust/ADAGP, Paris and DACS, London,
    2005.   137
36 Pablo Picasso, *Figure*, 1935, ladle, rakes, wood, string and nails,
    112.1 x 61.5 x 29.8, Musée Picasso, Paris. Photograph courtesy RMN/
    © Béatrice Hatala. © Succession Picasso/DACS, London, 2005.   138
37 Installation photograph of the *Exhibition of surrealist objects*, Charles Ratton
    Gallery, Paris, May 1936. Photograph courtesy Archives Guy Ladrière,
    Paris.   145
38 Alberto Giacometti, 'Objets mobiles et muets', *Le Surréalisme au service de
    la révolution*, 3 (1931), pp. 18–19. © ADAGP, Paris and DACS, London,
    2005.   145
39 Alberto Giacometti, *Disagreeable Object to be Thrown Away*, 1931, wood,
    22 x 30 x 30, Scottish National Gallery of Modern Art, Edinburgh.
    Photograph courtesy NGS. © ADAGP, Paris and DACS, London, 2005.   146
40 Alberto Giacometti, *Vide-Poche*, 1930, plaster, 17.5 x 19.5 x 29.5, Kunsthaus
    Zürich, Alberto Giacometti Foundation. Photography courtesy Kunsthaus
    Zürich. © ADAGP, Paris and DACS, London, 2005.   147

Acknowledgements

This book has its origins in a Henry Moore Foundation Post-Doctoral Fellowship that I took up in 2001, to work on the reception of non-western sculpture in 1920s and 1930s France and the critical and artistic discourses this provoked. I am extremely grateful to Tim Llewellyn and the Henry Moore Foundation for the help that made this book possible, as well as providing generous financial support for the illustrations contained within.

This book also has a significant point of departure in my PhD thesis on the art writings of Michel Leiris, and as such it owes much of its approach and intellectual spirit to the guidance of my former supervisor, Chris Green. His support for this project, and his careful reading of the manuscript, has been invaluable.

Much of the research for this book was carried out in the library of the Musée de l'Homme, now sadly no longer in existence, and I am very grateful for the help I received from Catherine Breux-Delmas and others. Some portions of the book relate to earlier research carried out during the completion of my PhD thesis, and I would like to thank in particular in this respect Jean Jamin, Leiris's heir, Sylvie Fresnault and Jeanne Sudour of the Musée Picasso, Paris, Yves Peyré of the Bibliothèque littéraire Jacques Doucet, Paris, Quentin Laurens of the Galerie Louise Leiris, Paris, and Christian Klemm at the Kunsthaus Zürich. Diego Masson and Jacques Dupin kindly shared their recollections of Leiris with me, and I am very grateful to them.

Several individuals have assisted me in sourcing the illustrations to this book and in acquiring picture and textual rights, including Cécile Brunner at the Kunsthaus Zürich; Véronique Wiesinger and Carole Farra at the Fondation Alberto et Annette Giacometti, Paris; Brigitte Vincens at the Bibliothèque Kandinsky, Paris; François Poli at the Galerie Ratton-Ladrière, Paris; Raphäelle Cartier at the Agence photographique de la Réunion des Musées Nationaux; Barbara Thompson at the Witt Library, Courtauld Institute, London; G-Ten in Manchester; Denise Raine and Jackie Howson at the Henry Moore Institute; and Carine Peltier and Sarah Frioux-Salgas at the Musée du quai Branly, Paris.

I would like to thank colleagues at the AHRC Research Centre for Studies of Surrealism and its Legacies, at the University of Manchester and elsewhere for the support and input they have provided over the last few years: David Lomas, Dawn Ades, Jennifer Mundy, Andrew Causey, Mark Crinson, Helen Rees Leahy, Louise

Tythacott, Thomas Dowson, Stephanie Körner, Suzy Butters, Tom Rasmussen, Aris Sarafianos, Natasha Eaton, Sophie Matthiesson, Janet Tatlock, Will Rea, Urszula Szulakowska, Alexandra Parigoris, John Gibson, Alyce Mahon, Jean-Michel Massing, Roger Cardinal, Sophie Berrebi, Mark Dion, Michael Richardson, Donna Roberts, Krzysztof Fijałkowski, Michael Taylor, Michael White, Margaret Iversen, Steven Harris, Gavin Parkinson, Jane Beckett, Fiona Russell, Simon Dell, Matthew Gale, Peter Read, Stacy Boldrick, Richard Williams, Michael Stone-Richards, Sarah Wilson, Richard Wrigley, Martha Buskirk, Sue Malvern, David Hopkins, Maxa Zoller, Yinka Shonibare, Jason Edwards, Sharon Michi-Kusunoki, Penelope Curtis, Stephen Feake, Martina Droth, Alistair Rider, Rebecca Duclos, Elizabeth Kramer, Samantha Lackey, Simeon Hunter, Nikki Merritt-Sudlow, Nick Rogers, Margaret Reid, Emma Berry and Marion Endt. The students of my MA course 'Art and Ethnography' have often served as sounding boards for some of the ideas and material discussed in this book, and I have been always grateful for their responses. Thank you to Charles Miller for his comments on Chapter two, and a special thank you to Anna Dezeuze for many stimulating conversations.

Estelle Karady and her family, and Helen and John Pennant, were welcoming hosts in Paris during research trips, and I am grateful to them. Thanks to members of my family – my mother, father, sister and Barney – for their humour and encouragement, as well as their many years of expertise of a different kind in the 'life of objects'. An additional thank you to my father for his careful proofreading. Most of all, Jon Wood has been and is, an unwavering source of intellectual stimulation, creative energy, love and support.

Manchester University Press has been supportive from the outset, and I am very grateful for the hard work of its staff in producing this book.

Introduction

'Better be imprudent movables than prudent fixtures'
(John Keats, used by André Gide as the epigraph to *Voyage au Congo*, 1927)[1]

The adjectival hybrid 'magical-circumstantial' was first used by André Breton in an essay published in the surrealist periodical *Minotaure* in 1934, where it was part of a complex of ideas and associations that he dubbed 'convulsive beauty'.[2] 'Convulsive beauty' could arouse distinct physical sensations, like 'the feeling of a plume of wind on one's temples wont to cause a real frisson', but it was also marked by a temporal dynamic of the just-passed, of an ungraspable and unfixable lost moment, suggestively situating the 'magic' of 'circumstance' in a putative original and unique context.[3] Denis Hollier, in a 1994 article, elaborated upon the implications of what he now termed 'circumstantial magic' and the properties it could possess: immediacy, anti-narrative qualities of process and the performative, a lack of predetermined outcome, an existential character of one-off personal experience, an inability to be communicated or shared, and a resistance to commodification and redemption.[4] In both cases the term 'magic', through its connotations of non-western systems of belief, also pointed implicitly to the significance of anthropology as an activity highly attuned to 'articulating the work with the context of its reception', as Hollier put it.[5] It was no coincidence, in this respect, that Hollier used as one of his case studies of the workings of 'circumstantial magic' the writer Michel Leiris, in whose career surrealism, autobiography and anthropology overlapped and mutually informed one another.

The work of Leiris will play a significant role in this book, as will that of other surrealist writers and artists like Breton and the sculptor Alberto Giacometti in analysing the encounter between art and anthropology, or more specifically ethnography, in France in the late 1920s and early 1930s. The book's emphasis on three-dimensional art objects and ethnographic objects corresponds to the operation of 'circumstantial magic' at the boundary between the animate and the inanimate (expressing not movement but the 'exact expiration of this movement', in Breton's terms), and between the physical and material thing itself and its representation (often through photography).[6] Magic as a concept might elicit rather negative associations, pointing to a 'fetishistic' overvaluation of objects (including art objects) as well as to an exaggerated sense of power and authority, both in terms of art (the 'magical' ability of the artist) and ethnography (the arrogance of what Bronisław Malinowski called 'the ethnographer's magic').[7] This book, however, looks to the definition of magic in the work of Marcel Mauss and Henri Hubert as a complex technological process of combining and making aimed at a special kind of efficacy, where 'circumstantial' and contextual factors are highly significant, and where on-going procedures are more important than any finished 'product'.[8] 'Circumstantial magic', like the coming together of art and ethnography that this books charts, is by nature slippery, potentially fragmentary or tangential, often fraught, but always compelling.

The encounter at the basis of this book marks out two fields whose relationship to one another is not self-evident. 'Ethnography' and 'art' belong to different orders of experience and interpretation and generate very different results. Ethnography, as the 'observation and analysis of human groups considered as individual entities', or 'the science which deals with the "cultures" of human groups', a process of describing and collecting data in the field, seeks by definition to bring coherence and comprehensibility to its objects of study.[9] Art, on the other hand, does not, in fact it might deliberately prefer to be incoherent or incomprehensible, ambiguous and 'mysterious', although this is not always the case. Ethnography looks to overarching frameworks and patterns of meaning that can be analytically set out in anthropological studies and manuals for fieldworkers as sets of ideas. Art, in our western understanding of it, has often been premised on ideas of singularity and uniqueness (and their associated financial value), and can predominantly be bought and collected in the form of discrete objects, despite the best efforts of artists to resist this.

But these definitions, which immediately raise objections and questions, are clearly not watertight. This book will tease out some of the more fluid aspects of each, in its journey through a particular moment in twentieth-century French cultural history when the discipline of ethnography and the art world in Paris came into close contact through particular forums, events and institutions. Written from an art-historical point of view, this book sets out to chart the complex meanings of 'ethnography' for the art world at this moment: not just artists but art writers, critics, dealers, historians and museum curators. While it will refer to anthropological developments in Germany, Britain and the United States of America, and draw upon materials falling outside the period c. 1925–35, this book's focus on France – and in particular Paris – at this time is intended to situate art's encounter with ethnography very precisely. The unique combinations of interests and activities in the careers of Leiris and Georges Henri Rivière, or the special character of ethnography in the art periodicals *Documents* and *Minotaure*, in the Dakar–Djibouti expedition (1931–33) and in the Trocadéro Ethnographic Museum in the early 1930s, mark out its field. The contextual richness and diversity of these case studies is reflected in this book's close engagement with a range of source materials and texts: from art critical commentaries and ethnographic accounts, to newspaper articles and museum memos.

This book responds in part to two related currents in art and cultural history. One is the delineation of an art-historical field bearing the unhappy title 'primitivism', a term used to describe a wide range of western artistic responses to colonised non-western cultures and their products.[10] The problems inherent in this terminology and the artistic borrowings and appropriations it alludes to have been much discussed.[11] The other derives from the history of anthropology: James Clifford's concept of 'ethnographic surrealism', a process of cultural relativism and questioning of western values with a hard, self-reflexive edge (the acceptable face of 'primitivism', we could say).[12] In both of these scholarly constructions, the discipline and practice of ethnography is pressed into action, respectively, either as a source of inspiration, or as a model of cultural critique. In one, there seems to be an over-emphasis on the creative vision of the artist 'discovering' the blocky masses of the African statue or the intricate patterns of the Oceanic mask (to caricature the ways in which these artistic responses have been categorised). In the other, 'art' is only admitted if it meets the criteria of a generalised modernism: fragmentation, subversion, collage-like juxtaposition. Recent work on the impact of the non-western in France in particular has taken a more nuanced approach to the different forms of visual culture that this might involve, and has examined in greater detail the intellectual concerns it inspired.[13]

One of the key differences in this book's approach, however, is its point of departure in objects and three-dimensional things as they formed the focus of artistic and ethnographic discourses in 1920s and 1930s Parisian culture. This orientation was motivated to some degree by the fact that the reception of non-western material culture in Europe in the early twentieth century was concerned predominantly with three-dimensional forms, around which debates about their status as 'art' or 'artefacts' coalesced. The more neutral term 'object' in this book's title indicates a challenge to this common dichotomy, following recent work in the fields of material culture and the 'anthropology of art'. These have questioned, for instance, the Hegelian bias of western aesthetic categories and looked to anthropological theorists like Mauss to problematise distinctions between western and non-western cultural production.[14] The work of Mauss will be of central importance to this project too, as one of the seminal influences on, and participants in, the development of French ethnography in the inter-war period. Mauss's conception of the interrelationship of human technologies and the production and use of objects, and of the investment of inanimate things with social forces (and agency), plays a significant role in this book. The ways that objects as a point of focus can illuminate and embody networks of reception, collection, reproduction and display, with their own 'biographies' or 'social life', have been taken up in the 1980s and 1990s by cultural theorists whose work equally informs this project.[15]

James Clifford's 1981 article 'On Ethnographic Surrealism' generated a rediscovery of surrealism from the perspective of Anglo-American cultural history, and has been an important inspiration for this book. In its wake, surrealism (in its 'ethnographic' tendencies) was cast as a seminal precedent to what George Marcus and Michael Fischer dubbed the 'crisis of representation in the human sciences', particularly anthropology, in the 1980s.[16] However, despite a series of critiques,

Clifford's notion of 'ethnographic surrealism' has become enshrined in humanities scholarship, and has served to obscure the work of French scholars such as Hollier and Jean Jamin upon which it built.[17] This includes their analyses of the College of Sociology, a loose grouping of intellectuals in Paris in the late 1930s whose lectures examining European culture from an anthropological perspective (using concepts like the 'sacred') were painstakingly reconstructed by Hollier in the 1970s.[18] The work of Hollier and Jamin drew in turn upon the reevaluation of so-called 'dissident' surrealists such as Georges Bataille by Michel Foucault and the Tel Quel group in the 1960s. Leiris, a former 'dissident', played a crucial role in the critical 'recovery' of Bataille, as well as working closely with Jamin.[19] Clifford's 'ethnographic surrealism' drew directly upon these tangled networks of lineages and allegiances, telescoping and contracting them. 'Ethnographic surrealism' was also arguably prefigured in certain aspects of French anthropology itself. Clifford's description of it as 'the fragmentation and juxtaposition of cultural values' in a collage effect can be seen as a variant of Claude Lévi-Strauss's concept of *bricolage* in *La Pensée sauvage* of 1962, particularly in its relationship to surrealist 'objective chance'.[20]

Bataille has dominated the art historical reception of the 'dissident' surrealists and their periodical *Documents* (1929–30). This has led to the relative neglect of other figures involved in the periodical, such as the German art historian and theorist Carl Einstein, or the poet, autobiographer and anthropologist Leiris. Leiris will play a central role in this book, as one of the few figures that could be said to have been specifically involved in the French art world, in surrealism, and in anthropology in a professional capacity. Another of the driving forces behind *Documents*, Georges Henri Rivière, art world impresario and curator at the Trocadéro Ethnographic Museum in the early 1930s, also facilitated in unique ways the encounter between these realms. Einstein, Leiris and Rivière are only slowly becoming the subjects of new research and associated publications, especially in the English-speaking context.[21] My reading of *Documents* in this book will also look beyond these 'avant-garde' figures to the assorted group of ethnologists, art historians, archaeologists and curators that made up its contributors, and the ways in which they brought their own disciplinary expertise to bear upon the periodical's eclectic approach to material culture. The significance of Leiris for this project as a whole lies, moreover, in the ways in which his oeuvre points forward not to 'ethnographic surrealism' in Clifford's sense, but to the theorisation of *practice* in the work of Pierre Bourdieu and Michel de Certeau, among others.[22] This intellectual current has in turn directly informed many of the theorists of material culture and the anthropology of art upon which this book draws. To go back to the early moments of Leiris's engagement with ethnography is to re-engage with the tentative formation of such approaches through their diverse historical contexts.

Ethnography in France in the 1920s and 1930s was a developing discipline, and this book will examine its varied outputs and registers: fieldwork texts and photographs, ethnological theories, quasi-connoisseurial evaluations of artefacts, popularising treatises, exhibition reviews and museum displays. While I will also use the more general term 'anthropology' and the less familiar 'ethnology' (to denote theoretical anthropological approaches not informed by fieldwork practice), my choice of the term 'ethnography' in this book's title is deliberate.[23] It follows Clifford and others who designated ethnography as the aspect of anthropology nearest to the literary text in terms of its self-reflexive and self-critical possibilities.[24] The anthropological historian Robert Lowie as early as 1937 suggested the potential proximity of ethnography and literature, exemplified for him by the work of the late nineteenth-century naval officer and novelist Pierre Loti (Julien Viaud).[25] Ethnography might in this sense be more amenable to the 'creative' impulses of the artist, and might even be prone to a tendentious kind of 'artist envy', as Hal Foster has warned.[26] Indeed, the 'artist as ethnographer' has become a recognised mode of contemporary artistic practice.[27] Whether 'surrealist ethnography' – a seminal example of which has been offered in Leiris's account of the Dakar–Djibouti expedition, *L'Afrique fantôme* – could really exist is questionable. Leiris himself pointed to the contradictions in his professional career that the publication of his fieldwork diary in 1934 initiated, and the ensuing separation of the different aspects of his career as a writer and an anthropologist working for the Musée de l'Homme.[28] When the Trocadéro Ethnographic Museum was reinvented as the Musée de l'Homme in 1937 (and Rivière departed to set up the Musée des Arts et Traditions Populaires), its subsequent infrequent forays into the presentation of ethnographic material as 'art' seemed inevitably awkward and compromised.[29] Moreover, the definition and remit of a 'surrealist ethnographer' are unclear, as Richardson has pointed out: 'No one would ever call Paul Nougé a "surrealist biochemist" or Paul Colinet a "surrealist accountant"'.[30]

But ethnography also carries an important implication within this book's historical project in its function as practice, negotiating the complexity and the ambivalence of collecting and recording data in specific contexts. In this way it can be used to probe the small gestures (what Elizabeth Edwards has called the 'little narratives') in anthropology's historical development: the specific moves of a discipline still very much in the process of institutional formation in 1920s France.[31] While this was certainly true with regard to the Paris Institute of Ethnology founded in 1925, it was also a feature of the ambivalent function of ethnography for figures like Leiris, Rivière and Einstein. Leiris once described the mixture of approaches embodied in *Documents* as a mixture of 'discipline' and 'indiscipline'.[32] Certain moments in his diary give us insights into the realities of 'ethnographic' enquiry for him in the late 1920s. He mentions having 'leafed through' Maurice Besson's *Le Totémisme* at the *Documents* office: a largely superficial though well-illustrated survey of existing theories.[33] He found Lucien Lévy-Bruhl hard going, putting aside his *La Mentalité primitive* for a popularising version of it by Charles Blondel.[34] Einstein, desirous in his second book on African sculpture for a future collaboration between ethnographers and art historians, played down the 'agreeable ethnography' he had included in it in letters to Moïse Kisling.[35] The book was selling well, allowing Einstein to write: 'we have had a great success equally with scientists. Damn'.[36] Leiris's notion of 'indiscipline' might prefigure de Certeau's 'antidiscipline' in his 1974 *The Practice of Everyday Life*, itself indebted to the French sociological and anthropological tradition of Emile Durkheim and Mauss. De Certeau aimed to 'bring to light the clandestine forms taken by the dispersed, tactical and makeshift creativity of groups or individuals already caught in the nets of "discipline"'.[37] The provisional gesture going against the dominant ideology might aptly describe the ways in which 'ethnography' in this book might be the domain both of professional and *unprofessional* ways of writing and behaving.

Ethnographic data, the facts and things encountered, collected, classified, interpreted and sometimes displayed, are raw materials, the beginning point in the construction of theories of what we would now call social or cultural anthropology. This book will be drawn to the lability of the *things* of ethnography as they were open to appropriation, and as they were defined in distinction to other fields and concerns, such as those of art and the art market. When Lowie claimed that the ethnographer 'parts company with the antiquarian who collects odd customs with a philatelist's zeal about his stamps', it seems that he was all too aware of the dangers of ethnographic stamp-collecting – the textual enumeration or literal accumulation of piles of 'stuff'.[38] However, Marcus and Fischer nearly fifty years later referred proudly to anthropology's 'jeweler's-eye view'.[39] When the surrealist set out to find the flea-market 'oddity', the overlooked (and undervalued) detail, how did this sit alongside the ethnographer's quest for material 'evidence' and scientific 'authority'? How might we articulate the possibilities of a kind of 'creative' collection and acquisition, going beyond the 'commodity fetishism' that this book's focus on objects might imply? Alfred Gell once pointed to the television sets purchased by poor, electricity-less Sri Lankan fishermen as 'works of art', marking a 'distinction between dull, unimaginative consumerism, which only reiterates the class habitus, and adventurous consumerism … which struggles against the limits of the known world'.[40]

Karl Marx's analyses of the function of commodities in (western) capitalist societies has been challenged by anthropological theorists like Gell and Appadurai, particularly in relation to Mauss's interpretation of gift exchange in the Trobriand Islands and Northwest Coast America, first published in 1923–24.[41] While the opposition of 'commodity' and 'gift' has been subject to theoretical revisions, it has informed major studies of the reception of non-western objects (as well as discussions of artistic practice), and in turn is important for this book.[42] Such objects might be seen as 'entangled', to use Nicholas Thomas's term, within networks of ideological, institutional and interpersonal interest. Studies of ethnographic collecting and the history of anthropological museums have pulled out and scrutinised some of these threads, especially where they intersect with colonial power structures, notably in the work of George Stocking, Enid Schildkrout and Curtis Keim, or Annie Coombes.[43] Gell has further developed the implications of the 'gift' in an ambitious theory of the art object as the bearer of 'agency', connected to process and doing rather than to semiotic and linguistic models of meaning and communication.[44] Seen in this way, such objects can, as Thomas points out, 'occupy positions in the networks of human social agency that are almost equivalent to the positions of humans themselves'.[45] Gell's work is particularly apposite to this project as it seeks to overcome a bias inherent in the 'anthropology of art' towards an exclusive interest in non-western material.[46] While this bias often continues to promote a division of 'art' from 'craft', it also fails to engage with the possibilities of 'postmodern' art practice. Gell famously compared animal traps in non-western cultures to the function of contemporary art works and installations.[47] This book goes beyond any simple conception of artistic 'modernism' in examining the surrealist object in terms of its embodiment of technological processes, as a variety of art-making which continues to challenge 'modernist' categories.

This book's structure is broadly chronological. Its opening chapter examines the complexities of the reception of non-western material culture in France in the 1920s, as a point of contact between anthropological theories and ethnographic information and the discourses of art criticism, art writing and art history. This serves as a backdrop for the chapters that follow. Chapter 2 looks in detail at the journal *Documents*, particularly in its employment of ethnographic and archaeological material and approaches, and in its dialogue with *Cahiers d'art* and the market in antiquarian 'curiosities'. *Documents* was also the vehicle for the young ethnographers of the Dakar–Djibouti expedition which crossed Africa between 1931 and 1933 collecting objects for the Trocadéro Ethnographic Museum. The tensions inherent in the expedition's collecting principles and the messy transactions it got involved in (within an inescapable colonial framework) form the subject of Chapter 3, particularly as recounted in Leiris's fieldwork diary, *L'Afrique fantôme* (1934). Leiris himself would bring out more strongly his sense of the ethnographer's 'entanglement' in his 1950 essay 'The Ethnographer Faced with Colonialism':

> the acquisition of an object not normally meant to be sold is, in effect, an infringement of common practices and therefore represents an intrusion such that he who is responsible for it cannot consider himself entirely a stranger to the society whose customs have thus been disrupted.[48]

The destabilising of ethnography in Leiris's fieldwork account came not only from his descriptions of the difficult acquisition of objects, but also through his use of narrative strategies borrowed from literature. These in turn found a counterpart in the uneasy accommodation of 'artistic' and 'ethnographic' visual languages in the presentation of the expedition's findings in the art periodical *Minotaure* in 1933. Chapter 4 addresses the ways in which objects collected in Africa were recorded and reproduced through photography, and compares their treatment to the 'documentation' of surrealist found objects. The differing strategies for displaying non-western material at the Trocadéro in the early 1930s will also be examined in this chapter, an important and overlooked moment in its history before its apparent adoption of 'stricter' anthropological principles in the late

1930s, when it was rebuilt as the Musée de l'Homme. The final chapter pursues some of the implications of the ethnographic approaches outlined in the other chapters for the production and reception of surrealist objects and sculpture in the late 1920s and early 1930s. It reads three-dimensional works by Giacometti and Picasso in particular in relation to the processes of human techniques and technology, and explores the potential of anthropological theory (in the work of Mauss and Lévi-Strauss in particular) to open up fresh interpretations of surrealist object-making and its legacies.

This book sets out to show that the significance of ethnography for artists and writers in the late 1920s and early 1930s in Paris went beyond any simple appreciation of objects from Africa, Oceania or Northwest Coast America, through an admiration of their unfamiliar forms and functions. At this historical moment of rich exchanges between different writers, scholars, artists, theorists, collectors and curators, disciplines and institutions could learn from each other, and ethnography played a crucial role in this process. Surrealism too was dedicated to the fundamental flexibility and permeability of ways of knowing, interpreting and making, seeing scientific research and artistic experimentation as part of the same continuum of surrealist activity. In 1935, the art historian Jean Cassou, contributing to an extensive survey of recent artistic developments, made the observation that surrealism 'exceeded', or could not be contained by, art history.[49] This book is an art historical study, operating within the limits of its discipline as a scholarly analysis of a particular historical period. But it also points to the ways in which art history can be enriched and its own boundaries extended, blurred and complicated by an encounter with ethnographic history and theory.

Notes

1 Keats, letter to Fanny Brawne, 5 and 6 August 1819, in Robert Gittings (ed.), *Letters of John Keats* (Oxford: Oxford University Press, 1990), p. 275.
2 Breton, 'La beauté sera convulsive', *Minotaure*, 1:5 (1934), pp. 9–16.
3 *Ibid.*, p. 10.
4 Hollier, 'Surrealist Precipitates: Shadows Don't Cast Shadows', *October*, 69 (summer 1994), pp. 111–32.
5 *Ibid.*, p. 117.
6 Breton, 'La beauté sera convulsive', p. 12.
7 On the too-easy dismissal of 'fetishism' and 'magic' in relation to material culture, see Cardoso, 'Putting the Magic Back into Design: from Object Fetishism to Product Semantics and Beyond', *Art on the Line*, 1:2 (2004), pp. 8–15. Malinowski's phrase has served as the title of a volume of essays examining anthropology's difficult history, Stocking (ed.), *The Ethnographer's Magic* (Madison: University of Wisconsin Press, 1992).
8 Henri and Mauss, 'Esquisse d'une théorie générale de la magie', *L'Année sociologique*, 7 (1902–3) (Paris: Alcan, 1904), pp. 1–146, translated by Brain, *A General Theory of Magic* (London: Routledge and Kegan Paul, 1972).

9 These definitions are from Lévi-Strauss, *Structural Anthropology* (1958) (Harmondsworth: Penguin, 1979), p. 2, and Lowie, *The History of Ethnological Theory* (London: Harrap, 1937), p. 3. Lowie's use of inverted commas for the term 'culture' also points to the difficulties of its anthropological definition since Tylor's seminal *Primitive Culture: Researches into the Development of Mythology, Philosophy, Religion, Art and Custom* (London: John Murray, 1871). See Williams, *Keywords* (Glasgow: Fontana, 1976), pp. 80–1.

10 The classic articulations of this field are Goldwater, *Primitivism in Modern Art* (1938) (London: Belknap Press, 1986) and Rubin (ed.), *'Primitivism' in Twentieth-Century Art: Affinity of the Tribal and the Modern* (New York: Museum of Modern Art, 1984). The same term has been used for a recent anthology of primary source materials, Flam and Deutch (eds), *Primitivism and Twentieth-Century Art* (Berkeley: University of California Press, 2003).

11 The now famous responses to MoMA's 1984 exhibition by Thomas McEvilley, James Clifford and Hal Foster are reprinted in Flam and Deutch, *Primitivism and Twentieth-Century Art*, pp. 335–50, 351–68 and 384–95.

12 Clifford, 'On Ethnographic Surrealism', *Comparative Studies in Society and History*, 23 (1981), pp. 539–64, revised and reprinted in *The Predicament of Culture: Twentieth-Century Ethnography, Literature and Art* (Cambridge, MA: Harvard University Press, 1988), pp. 117–51.

13 See Green, 'Zervos, Picasso and Brassaï, ethnographers in the field: a critical collaboration' in Gee (ed.), *Art Criticism since 1900* (Manchester: Manchester University Press, 1993), pp. 116–39, Archer-Straw, *Negrophilia* (London: Thames and Hudson, 2000), and Tythacott, *Surrealism and the Exotic* (London: Routledge, 2003).

14 See Danto, 'Artifact and Art', in *Art/Artifact: African Art in Anthropology Collections* (New York: Center for African Art, 1988), pp. 18–32, and Alfred Gell's response in 'Vogel's Net: Traps as Artworks and Artworks as Traps", *Journal of Material Culture*, 1:1 (1996), pp. 15–38. Gell discussed his debt to Mauss in *Art and Agency: An Anthropological Theory* (Oxford: Clarendon Press, 1998), p. 9.

15 See Appadurai, 'Introduction: Commodities and the Politics of Value', and Kopytoff, 'The Cultural Biography of Things: Commoditization as Process', in *The Social Life of Things* (Cambridge: Cambridge University Press, 1986), pp. 3–63 and pp. 64–91, and Thomas, *Entangled Objects: Exchange, Material Culture and Colonialism in the Pacific* (Cambridge, MA: Harvard University Press, 1991).

16 Marcus and Fischer, *Anthropology as Cultural Critique: An Experimental Moment in the Human Sciences* [1986] (Chicago: Chicago University Press, 1999), p. 7.

17 See Jamin, 'L'ethnographie mode d'inemploi', in Hainard and Kaehr (eds), *Le mal et la douleur* (Neuchâtel: Musée d'ethnographie, 1986), pp. 45–79, Slaney, 'Psychoanalysis and Cycles of "Subversion" in Modern Art and Anthropology', *Dialectical Anthropology*, 14 (1989), pp. 213–34, and Richardson, 'An Encounter of Wise Men and Cyclops Women, Considerations of Debates on Surrealism and Anthropology', *Critique of Anthropology*, 13:1 (1993), pp. 57–75.

18 Hollier (ed.), *The College of Sociology* (1979), trans. Wing (Minneapolis: University of Minnesota Press, 1988, and Jamin, 'Un sacré collège ou les apprentis sorciers de la sociologie', *Cahiers internationaux de sociologie*, 68 (1980), pp. 5–30. See also the volume edited by Lecoq and Lory, *Ecrits d'ailleurs: Georges Bataille et les ethnologues* (Paris: Maison des Sciences de l'Homme, 1987).

19 See Leiris, *A Propos de Georges Bataille* (Paris: Fourbis, 1988).

20 Clifford, 'On Ethnographic Surrealism', p. 539, and Lévi-Strauss, *La Pensée sauvage* (Paris: Plon, 1962), pp. 26–47.

21 See for example Hand, *Michel Leiris, Writing the Self* (Cambridge: Cambridge University Press, 2002) and Joyce, *Carl Einstein* in Documents (Philadelphia, PA: Xlibris, 2003). Studies of Rivière exist so far only in French and German, of which the most comprehensive is Gorgus, *Der Zauberer der Vitrinen: Zur Museologie Georges Henri Rivières* (Münster: Waxmann, 1999).

22 Bourdieu, *Outline of a Theory of Practice* (1972) (Cambridge: Cambridge University Press, 1989) and de Certeau, *The Practice of Everyday Life*, trans. Steven Rendall (1974) (Berkeley: University of California Press, 1988). See also Blanchard, '"N stuff…": Practices, Equipment, Protocols in Twentieth-Century Ethnography', in *On Leiris, Yale French Studies*, 81 (1992), pp. 111–27.

23 The term 'ethnologie' in French carries this more specific meaning, separating the data-gathering of 'ethnographie' from its theoretical analysis. In English, though, 'ethnology' is rather archaic and rarely used, seen as either a synonym for 'ethnography' or for 'social' (rather than 'physical') anthropology more broadly.

24 See for instance Clifford and Marcus (eds), *Writing Culture* (Berkeley: University of California Press, 1986) and Geertz, *Works and Lives: The Anthropologist as Author* (Stanford, CA: Stanford University Press, 1988).

25 Lowie, *The History of Ethnological Theory*, p. 3.

26 Foster, 'The Artist as Ethnographer', *The Return of the Real* (Cambridge, MA: MIT Press, 1996), p. 180.

27 See Coles (ed.), *Site-Specificity: The Ethnographic Turn* (London: Black Dog, 2000) and Highmore, 'Ethno-Graphics', *Art History*, 24:1 (February 2001), pp. 132–9.

28 Price and Jamin, 'Entretien avec Michel Leiris', *Gradhiva*, 4 (1988), pp. 29–56.

29 See *Chefs-d'oeuvre du Musée de l'Homme* (Paris: Musée de l'Homme, 1965) and *Arts primitifs dans les ateliers d'artistes* (Paris: Musée de l'Homme, 1967).

30 Richardson, 'An Encounter of Wise Men', p. 72, note 3.

31 Edwards, *Raw Histories: Photographs, Anthropology and Museums* (Oxford: Berg, 2001), p. 3.

32 Leiris, 'De Bataille l'impossible à l'impossible *Documents*', *A Propos de Georges Bataille*, p. 27.

33 Leiris, *Journal, 1922–1989* (Paris: Gallimard, 1992), p. 186, and Besson, *Le Totémisme* (Paris: Rieder, 1929).

34 Leiris, *Journal*, p. 188, and Blondel, *La Mentalité primitive* (Paris: Stock, 1926).

35 Meffre (ed.), 'Lettres de Carl Einstein à Moïse Kisling (1920–1924)', *Les Cahiers du MNAM*, 62 (winter 1997), p. 86.

36 *Ibid.*, p. 105.

37 De Certeau, *The Practice of Everyday Life*, pp. xiv–v.

38 Lowie, *The History of Ethnological Theory*, p. 4.

39 Marcus and Fischer, *Anthropology as Cultural Critique*, p. 15.

40 Gell, 'Newcomers to the world of goods: the Muria Gonds', in Appadurai, *The Social Life of Things*, p. 115.

41 Appadurai, 'Introduction: Commodities and the Politics of Value', in *The Social Life of Things*, pp. 6–16, and Mauss, *The Gift* (1923–24), trans. W. D. Hall (London: Routledge, 1993).

42 See Gregory, *Gifts and Commodities* (London: Academic Press, 1982), and Thomas, *Entangled Objects*, pp. 7–34. For the use of gift theory in relation to contemporary art, see *Il Dono, The Gift: Generous Offerings, Threatening Hospitality* (Milan: Charta, 2001).

43 Stocking, *Objects and Others: Essays on Museums and Material Culture* (Madison: University of Wisconsin Press, 1985), Schildkrout and Keim (eds), *The Scramble for Art in Central Africa* (Cambridge: Cambridge University Press, 1998), Coombes, *Reinventing Africa: Museums, Material Culture and Popular Imagination in Late Victorian and Edwardian England* (New Haven, CT: Yale University Press, 1994).

44 Gell, *Art and Agency*.

45 Thomas, 'Introduction', in Pinney and Thomas (eds), *Beyond Aesthetics: Art and the Technologies of Enchantment* (Oxford: Berg, 2001), p. 5.

46 See Coote and Shelton, 'Introduction' in *Anthropology, Art and Aesthetics* (Oxford: Clarendon Press, 1992), pp. 1–11.

47 Gell, 'Vogel's Net'.

48 Leiris, 'The Ethnographer Faced with Colonialism' (1950), in *Brisées* (San Francisco: North Point Press, 1989), p. 114.

49 Cassou, 'Le Dadaïsme et le Surréalisme', in Huyghe (ed.), *Histoire de l'art contemporain: La Peinture* (Paris: Alcan, 1935), p. 337.

1

Encountering: ethnography, art and the reception of non-western objects

Some time in the early years of the twentieth century, art historian Wilhelm Worringer felt it his duty, while on a study trip to Paris, to visit the Trocadéro Ethnographic Museum.[1] The experience was not immediately stimulating, as Worringer recalled: 'A grey forenoon destitute of all emotional atmosphere. Not a soul in the museum. The solitary sound: my footsteps ringing in the wide halls in which all other life is extinct'.[2] Suddenly, however, he spied another visitor to the museum across the echoing halls: the Berlin-based philosopher Georg Simmel, whose lectures he had attended. Without exchanging a word with this figure whose 'spiritual personality' he admired, Worringer was inspired to produce the doctoral thesis that he completed in 1907 and published in 1908, *Abstraction and Empathy*. In it, Worringer would challenge the prevailing tendency to equate the history of art with 'the history of the imitation impulse'.[3] Instead, he proposed a theory of art's development that attempted to account for the kinds of things he might have found at the Trocadéro at that time: African sculptures, decorative Oceanic wood-carvings, Stone Age artefacts, fragments of Romanesque monuments.

In a famous conversation with André Malraux in 1937, during the preparations for the opening of the new Musée de l'Homme, Pablo Picasso recalled the effect of its former incarnation: 'When I went to the old Trocadéro, it was disgusting. The Flea Market. The smell. I was all alone. I wanted to get away'.[4] Dark and fusty, crammed with a jumble of strange artefacts, the old Trocadéro for Picasso acted as the site of dark revelation, a place of witchcraft. His attention would be held most of all by objects which he understood as 'weapons', 'tools' or 'intercessors' which could protect against 'spirits' and unconscious emotions: 'I always looked at fetishes', the artist recalled. Picasso claimed that *Les Demoiselles d'Avignon* was inspired that day, as his first 'exorcism-painting' arising from the intensity of his experience: 'All alone in that awful museum, with masks, dolls made by the red-skins, dusty manikins'.[5] Scholars and historians have used Picasso's statement extensively in examining his awareness of African and Oceanic objects as early as 1907. Some have suggested that Picasso's references to magic practices reflect knowledge he could only have picked up later, stressing the retrospective nature of his comments, reported in any case via Malraux.[6] Moreover, Picasso's dramatic 'recollections' built upon an already well-established set of tropes about the Trocadéro as a shabby and rather sinister place of memory.

Picasso's friend Guillaume Apollinaire had made several references to the Trocadéro's sorry state in his press reviews of the 1910s, describing the dwindling collections, 'too vast' spaces and limited opening hours of this most important but 'most sacrificed' of Parisian museums.[7] The appeal of the objects to be found there, some of which for Apollinaire were undiscovered masterpieces 'piled up pell-mell in the vitrines', appeared to be limited to Sunday visitors, 'servicemen on leave and nannies out for a stroll'.[8] Picasso's famous commentary certainly echoed familiar clichés about the museum. More directly, it reflected the images of darkness, dustiness and 'exotic' fear that permeated reminiscences about the Trocadéro in the 1930s, as it was undergoing its first major transformation. The museum's renovation inevitably led journalists to recall its former state: 'full of dust, it was nothing but a monsters' lair with which garden wet-nurses frightened children when they wanted to prove that the bogeyman existed'.[9] The wastes of the 'awful museum', according to another account, would inspire only a desire to leave:

> When, thirty or so years ago, you took a schoolchild on a Sunday in winter to the rooms of the ethnographic museum, you brought back with you (after having seen nothing but the accumulated objects that a dusty and apparently endless cave hid from your eyes) a bent back, a moral nausea, a 'desert of boredom'.[10]

These negative commentaries about the Trocadéro served to point up what was seen as its miraculous transformation in the early 1930s. This important period in the museum's history has been largely overlooked, overshadowed by its reincarnation as the Musée de l'Homme a few years later. Already by 1933, for instance, one newspaper marvelled at the fleet of luxury cars and the crowds of elegantly dressed women that the museum was now attracting.[11] It was widely perceived that the revamping of the museum had succeeded in making ethnography fashionable and popular. The opening of one of its hit shows in the early 1930s, of Benin 'bronzes' and ivories in June 1932, was held at night and coincided with the opening of Picasso's retrospective at the Galerie Georges Petit. As an evening event, it drew in the *beau monde*, attracting roughly the same audience as for Picasso's show according to one press report:

> a handful of past, present and future Ministers, so many princesses born in Moscow, Chicago or in the Faubourg Saint-Germain, so many more or less surrealist poets and more or less avant-garde artists, all the habitués of the Ballets Russes and the Coupole … critics, dealers, museum curators, art lovers, all of them in tails and dresses cut as low as can be.[12]

'Celebrities' present at the Benin opening included Georges Braque, Max Ernst, Man Ray, Henri Matisse, André Derain, Salvador Dalí, Joan Miró, Le Corbusier, Daniel-Henry Kahnweiler, Max Jacob, Jean Cassou, Waldemar George, Darius Milhaud, Georges Wildenstein, Marcel Mauss, Lucien Lévy-Bruhl, the de

Noailles, Georges Hardy, Julius Lips, Paul Valéry, Natalie Barney, Julien Green, René Crevel and Jean-Martin Charcot.[13]

Despite the evident hyperbole of journalistic accounts, the reversal in fortunes of the Trocadéro, from a place of dusty confusion to a potential playground of the fashionable avant-garde, marked its long-awaited rebirth as an institution on a par with anthropological museums world-wide. This was not only a matter of wider public perception: the inadequacies of the museum had also long been a matter of concern for ethnologists and ethnographers.[14] The way that this change was brought about in the early 1930s owed much to the leadership of the ethnographer Paul Rivet, but also to the work of the untrained curator, jazz pianist and art-world aficionado Georges Henri Rivière as assistant director. Part of the transformation of the old museum was purely physical, involving an internal restructuring of the building, and an overhaul of display and storage facilities. The old and unloved display mannequins alluded to by Picasso were amongst the first to go, in what Rivière described as a 'massacre of the innocents'.[15] But the changes at the Trocadéro were also a conscious reflection of the values of the discipline of ethnography. New approaches to material culture necessitated the kinds of display and research facilities that had been available elsewhere in Europe and the USA since the turn of the century. Its perceived success also arguably marked the coming of age of ethnography in France, both in the eyes of academe and of the public.

The problems suffered by the Trocadéro reflected the late development of ethnography as an institutionally-sanctioned university discipline in twentieth-century France.[16] France was not quick to exploit the support that ethnography could give to colonial aspiration, although this connection might not be as determining as we might assume, as H. Glenn Penny has shown with regard to German ethnographic museums.[17] Certainly in France, although there were societies of anthropology and ethnography, there was no major state funding for specifically ethnographic (rather than broadly 'scientific', natural history or even archaeological) expeditions before 1930, and there were no university-trained ethnographers before the generation of Marcel Griaule.[18] Victor Karady has suggested that one of the reasons for this neglect was the persistence of 'a paradigm of erudition' ('un paradigme lettré') in the French education system, which valorised Latinate, text-based 'civilisations' as the object of scholarly study.[19] Studies of African culture at the beginning of the century, he argues, focused on 'elevated' subject matter, while some of the first ethnography university courses in the 1920s and 1930s concentrated on comparative religion as an area with suitably 'high' cultural implications.[20] To set out to collect and study a wide range of objects representing both special rituals and humble everyday functions, as the Dakar–Djibouti expedition was to do, was a late development in the French context.

One of the repercussions of this delay was the complexity of the reception of non-western material culture in early twentieth-century France. Its discovery as 'art' has often been attributed to artists such as Maurice de Vlaminck, in a now canonical story of modernist assimilation. This mythic history was already well in place by the 1930s, allowing Rivière to state baldly in a 1931 catalogue preface that 'one day, certain artists and critics discovered *art nègre*'.[21] Robert Goldwater, in his seminal 1938 study *Primitivism in Modern Art*, while providing an excellent overview of the development of ethnographic museums, saw them as essentially backward in their 'low opinion' of non-western 'art'.[22] To judge them from this perspective, however, is to misunderstand their aims, and, crucially, to divert our attention as historians away from ethnological and ethnographic discussions of non-western material in the late nineteenth and early twentieth centuries, particularly in France. In Britain, for example, as Annie Coombes has shown, the 'punitive' acquisition of the Benin 'bronzes' in the 1890s provoked loaded debates which combined 'scientific' theory with considerations of artistic merit.[23] France had its own equivalent of Benin, the kingdom of Dahomey, pillaged pieces from which were shown in the Trocadéro. A series of articles in *La Nature* in 1894 by the colonial anthropologist Maurice Delafosse examined the large Dahomean figures that are now very well known (the *Gou* god of metalwork, the ancestor statues of kings Guézo, Gléglé and Béhanzin), studying in detail their construction and iconography.[24] The same figures were shown not as great 'works of art', but as ethnological examples in Maurice Besson's 1929 popularising study of totemism, a book available in the office of the 'dissident' surrealist periodical *Documents*.[25] Further research into the reception of such material in the 1890s in France may well challenge the *idée fixe* of the sudden 'discovery' by artists of African culture, a narrative enshrined not only in art historical accounts, but also in the work of French ethnologists.[26]

By the 1920s and 1930s in France, as this chapter will show, discussions of non-western objects from an ethnographic perspective often overlapped with judgements of their 'artistic' nature and implicit considerations of market value. It has often been repeated that a major reevaluation of non-western material took place during the early twentieth century, to allow it to be considered for the first time as 'art' (a shift encouraged by the development of the art market in this period). Clearly this formed part of a broader agenda of critics like Apollinaire, who called for the reappraisal of what had formerly been seen as 'curiosities' or 'documents'.[27] The persistence of this terminology into the 1930s can be gauged from the response of the Liège-based art historian Paul Fierens to the Trocadéro's Benin exhibition: 'The object of curiosity, presented as it ought to be and isolated from the crush of secondary, documentary pieces, takes on all of its value as an art object, an art work.'[28] The drive for the 'acceptance' of non-western objects and their perceived 'ascent' of a scale of value and interest – from 'curiosity', to ethnographic 'document', to 'art work' – was and is still a complex problematic. The fact that early calls by Apollinaire and others for the representation of non-western material in the Louvre were only realised in 2000 might be an example of this. Nevertheless, this emphasis on admittance into the artistic canon, which was such a strident voice within the discourse around non-western objects, has obscured the ways in which ethnographic information did feed into these, even in small ways.

The uneasy tensions between ethnography and the art world also played a part in responses to the Trocadéro, as a prime repository of ethnographic material. While it might act as a place of potential intellectual inspiration, for Picasso or Worringer, even if accidentally so, this was in spite of its lack of success as a means of informing or educating. This paradox found its logical outcome in the commentaries that appeared after the Trocadéro's renovation, and its re-emergence as the Musée de l'Homme in 1938, which suggested that its new 'scientific' ethnographic organisation had led to sterility and lack of imaginative appeal. The poet and former member of 'Le Grand Jeu' René Daumal, writing for the *Nouvelle revue française*, while reluctantly praising the changes made by Rivière, also felt nostalgia for the old Trocadéro: 'The heroic days when, in this chaotic and dusty place, you could make sensational searches and discoveries, are surely over. It is now a big luxury store.'[29] The old museum had been described as a 'pirate's cave', with mannequins guarding their treasure, a place of adventure and discovery.[30] The Trocadéro's new chic 'Treasury', on the other hand, conceived by Rivière and designed with the help of Jacques Lipchitz, imitated a shop window display, with its recessed niches back-lit in pink and its sleek black plinths. Daumal's desire for a lost 'authentic' experience echoed a wider modern tendency: non-western cultures and their objects could function as a means of escaping from or alleviating the alienation of western commodity society. Georg Simmel in his *Philosophy of Money*, first published in 1900 and then reworked in 1907, had mapped out this theme in relation to the distance maintained between modern people and things, apprehended as fragments or through tentative contact. 'Reality is touched not with direct confidence but with fingertips that are immediately withdrawn', Simmel wrote, and related this modern malaise to an increasing interest in 'far removed' artistic styles.[31] The tensions between resisting or accommodating commodification and the taming of the unexpected 'fragment' will be important themes in this book in relation to ethnographic practice, and in the responses of art critics, art historians and artists. But before ethnography in France could begin to develop its own discourses of classification, collection or display, and before art could draw upon these, it would have to negotiate the 1920s reception of non-western objects by the art world and the complex encounters that this involved.

Ethnographic function and the challenge to sculptural form

The work of sculptor Alberto Giacometti in the 1920s and his engagement with non-western material provides a good example of such an encounter. Besides drawing upon the cubist sculpture of Henri Laurens and Lipchitz (who collaborated with the Trocadéro in installing its 'Treasury' as well as lending pieces from his collection to the 1932 Benin exhibition), Giacometti also looked to the kind of combination of sources (African, Oceanic, Sumerian, Cycladic) that were becoming a signature of avant-garde artistic practice. Without being an artist-collector in the manner of Derain or Jacob Epstein, Giacometti did acquire in c.1926 a Bakota reliquary figure,

1 Alberto Giacometti, Spoon Woman, 1927, bronze, 144 x 51 x 23,Kunsthaus Zürich, Alberto Giacometti Foundation.

and scholars have been tempted to draw connections between this object and con-temporaneous works by the sculptor, such as his *Spoon Woman* of 1926–27 (figure 1).[32] This sculpture – 1.5 metres high, a rendering of a woman's body as a hollowed-out 'spoon' abdomen surmounted by an angular wedge-like torso and a small geo-metricised and incised head – has been discussed particularly in relation to African Dan grain spoons, and other works like *The Couple* (1926) have also prompted formal comparisons with African objects.[33] But these works are also seen, importantly, to resist and complicate such comparisons, by transposing small, wooden carved pieces (the Dan spoons) into larger-scale bronze, for example, and by combining and styl-ising supposed African motifs and elements into a syncretic and distinctly 'modern' whole.

If a dynamic of formal 'borrowing' cannot easily account for the relationship between Giacometti's 1920s works and non-western material, in what then might this relationship consist? One scholarly approach has been to posit instead a con-ceptual internalisation of the principles of African sculpture, as exemplified in Yve-Alain Bois' reading of Picasso's 1912 *Guitar* in relation to the Grebo mask that the artist owned, based on a connection first made by his dealer Kahnweiler.[34] The pro-truding sound-hole of the cardboard or metal guitar, at first sight bearing no apparent reference to any non-western source, is 'like' the protruding eyes of the Grebo mask in terms of an understanding of the interplay between plane and sculptural volume. A different, but related, conceptual connection is made in the accepted reading of the two figures in Giacometti's 1926 *Couple* as recapitulations of their characteristic sexual features: the woman as a large vulval shape and the man as a phallic cylinder, although their respective eyes reverse this logic (the man's eye as vulva, the woman's as penis).[35] Although it is difficult to pin down any specific non-western source for this sculpture, this correspondence between body and sex appears to strengthen the work's potential connection to African sculpture (through western assumption and projection). In both of these examples, it is really western conceptions of sculpture that are at stake, with non-western objects reduced to convenient props and triggers.

However, the growth of ethnographic information about these objects and the discourses that developed around them in the 1920s, allowed for different readings to emerge. In 1929, the surrealist poet Michel Leiris published an article on Giacometti's recent work in the periodical *Documents*.[36] In it, he discussed a series of small-scale plaster heads and bodies, variously configured as flattened plaques, sharpened points and skeletal grid-like forms, associating them with moments of 'crisis', extraordinary images of bodily contact, and the processes of 'fetishism'. To align Giacometti's sculptures implicitly with 'fetishes' was extremely suggestive. It proposed ritual and magical practices as well as loading the sculptor's works with social and psychological connotations.[37] On a more literal level, Leiris's text implied that Giacometti's works were in some way like African or Oceanic objects, the groups of things that had become a studio staple for the artistic avant-garde. However, this 'likeness' was not based on visual resemblance, but on function: Giacometti's small

sculptures as special touchable and move-
able things, implicitly compared, in Leiris's
article, to tools and utensils such as sieves,
spatulas and griddles.

Leiris's interpretation of Giacometti's
work was a crucial example of the applica-
tion of ethnological and ethnographic concepts to art works for the Parisian
avant-garde in the late 1920s, particularly in
the development of the surrealist object, as
chapter five will discuss. Notably, it sought
to reorient sculptural discourse away from
an emphasis on autonomy and towards a
conception of a sculptural object implicated
in the viewer's experience of it. 'Do not
expect that I will positively speak *sculpture*',
Leiris wrote: 'I prefer to DIVAGATE; as
these beautiful objects that I have been able
to observe and palpate activate in me the fer-
mentation of so many memories'.[38] To
follow Leiris's deliberately diversionary
path would be to go beyond the equivalences
of certain shapes or formal concepts connecting, for example, the hollow of
Giacometti's *Spoon Woman* to the concave
back plane of a Bakota reliquary, or the rectangular incised hands of the *Couple* to the
striations of African masks, to complicate
the notion of sculptural form itself. Leiris's
striking text, in turn, would not have been
possible without earlier discussions of non-
western objects, both in France and
Germany, which mapped out the terrain of
European contact with this unfamiliar
material. The formal coherence and sculptural autonomy of African and Oceanic
objects was a significant aspect of their
reception within the competing claims
of 'art' and 'ethnographic' function,
often mediated through their physical and
material qualities.

The complex perception of non-Western
objects in the 1920s, which Giacometti and

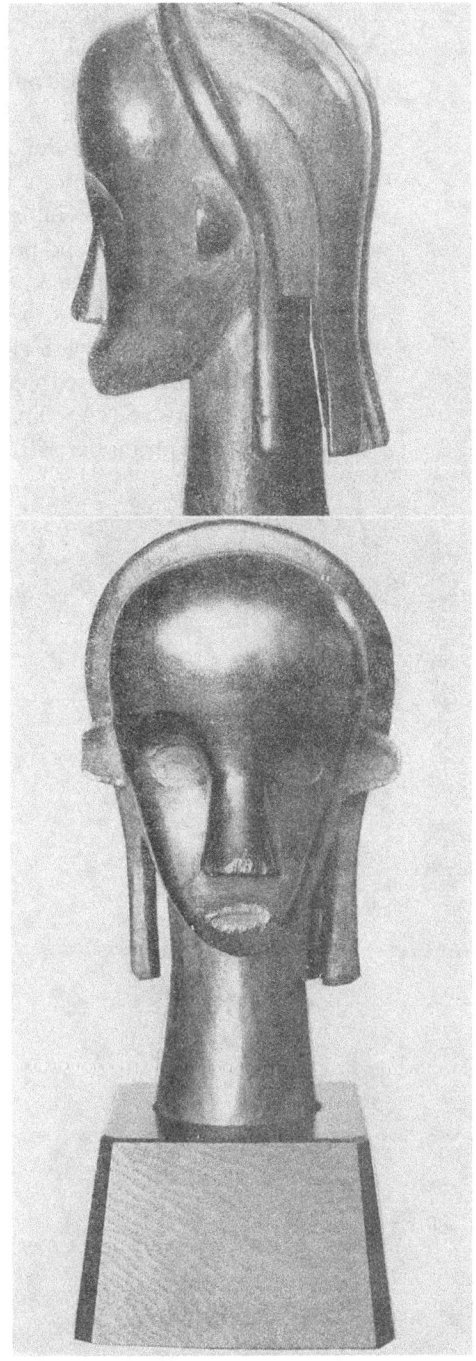

2 Fang head from the collection of Guillaume
in *La Renaissance de l'art français*, 5:4 (1922).

Leiris's responses reflect, built upon a set of often conflicting ideas, which it is worth reviewing here in some detail. The first significant French publication presenting non-western material to a broad public was the product of a collaboration between a critic and a dealer: Apollinaire and Paul Guillaume's *Sculptures nègres* of 1917, the catalogue of an exhibition at Guillaume's gallery.[39] The problems of defining and categorising non-western objects were already apparent in this book, despite its ostensible emphasis on 'art'. Guillaume in his contribution to the catalogue singled out certain African regions and population groups that he felt had produced 'the most significant and unexpected works', including the Baoule, the Pahouin (Fang) and the Bakotas.[40] The pieces to which his preference implicitly referred were mainly in dark carved wood with a high polish, like the Fang heads that he collected (figure 2). Guillaume dismissed objects from Dahomey, rejecting the term 'fetish' as a synonym for 'curiosity'.[41] Apollinaire, on the other hand, provided a lively description of the material properties of 'fetish' objects, whose ephemeral, replaceable elements he listed: 'cotton loin-cloths, large plumes, resin pellets, necklets, earrings, little iron bells, creepers, handfuls of grasses, shells, swine's teeth, mirrors, nails, all kinds of bits of scrap metal'.[42] These parts which were easily broken or worn out, and whose changing nature hindered the task of ascribing dates to these sculptures, were seen by Apollinaire as the result of the artist's 'fancy', choosing and combining simple materials that were to hand.

Apollinaire's list of heterogeneous materials echoed his championing of the new possibilities of cubist collage, made of ephemeral everyday things, in his famous assessment of Picasso's work in 1913.[43] But it was also an almost direct quotation from an ethnological text published by the Trocadéro's then director, René Verneau, in 1916. Verneau had described the components of Congo fetish figures as: '…cotton loin-cloths, large plumes, necklets, earrings, little iron bells, creepers, handfuls of grasses, etc.', and had illustrated his text with examples of these (figure 3).[44] This source, upon which Apollinaire undoubtedly drew, was concerned not with distinct 'art works', but with religious and magical practices, 'cabalistic operations' which employed 'equipment

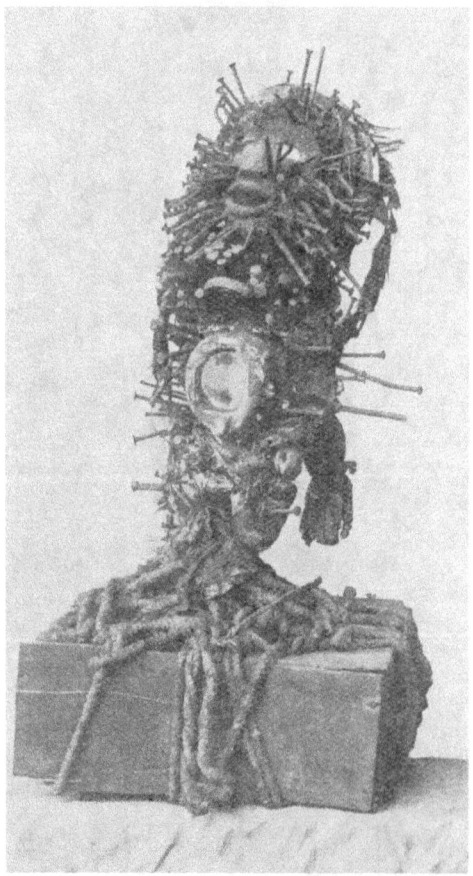

3 'Vengeance fetish', wood, nails, mirrors, rope and charms, in *La Nature* (22 April 1916).

made up of the most disparate objects'.[45] Even though the kind of materials described by Apollinaire did not appear in the catalogue's plates, with the exception of the Trocadéro's *nimba* shoulder mask complete with grass costume, the catalogue's presentation of a coherent body of 'sculpture' was certainly problematised by its contradictory texts.[46] The 'ethnological' implications of certain objects worked against the 'artistic' coherence of others.

The fault-line that the juxtaposition of Apollinaire and Guillaume's texts exposed in this 1917 publication corresponded to an implicit division of different types of non-western objects in texts of the 1920s. While more 'refined' and stylistically homogenous pieces could begin to accrue in value as 'great art', works in mixed media of an impermanent nature, or works seen to be lacking clear formal composition, continued to be thought of as ethnological artefacts. The Fang heads collected by Guillaume, often mounted on special pedestals and reproduced widely, had clearly delineated volumes and glossy surfaces, lending themselves to formal sculptural analysis. Guillaume's 1926 book with Thomas Munro, *Primitive Negro Sculpture*, drawing on the Barnes collection and eschewing ethnological information as a 'distraction', pursued just such close formal readings.[47] The outlines of the Congo nail figures, on the other hand, were obscured by the proliferation of small metal blades embedded in their wooden bodies, allowing for no coherent grasp of their volumes (quite literally, if one were to touch them). The kinds of judgement made about non-western objects in this period had important ramifications for their market value. For instance, in a 1930 study of the art of New Guinea, the eminent medic Dr Stephen Chauvet tried to stem the rise in value of what he saw as mediocre pieces, setting out a distinction between 'real' sculpture and the 'minor arts'. Here, one of Guillaume's Fang figures represented the former, while functional objects like cups, bobbins, stools and spoons as well as 'small wooden fetishes' made up the latter.[48]

While the taste of collectors like Guillaume and Barnes fuelled distinctions between what was seen as 'art' and what as mere 'artefact', such dichotomies, as recent anthropological historians have shown, were by no means clear-cut in late nineteenth-century and early twentieth-century discussions of non-western material.[49] Some of the most influential ethnological sources for critics, historians and artists working in Paris in the 1920s came from the German context, where ethnographic expeditions and museum collections had developed significantly in the 1880s and 1890s.[50] A key example of this was Leo Frobenius's seminal book *Die Masken und Geheimbünde Afrikas* (*The Masks and Secret Societies of Africa*, 1898).[51] This book contained a wealth of extraordinary illustrations, including photographs of masks that previously would only have been known through artists' impressions, if at all, and these were cut out and isolated against neutral backgrounds. At the same time, the book's text was interspersed with drawings and photogravures that showed costumes in use. This ambivalent mixture of different kinds of presentation both suggested the serious anthropological study of 'masks' in their contexts, *and* allowed their 'artistic' qualities to be appreciated – Frobenius devoted one of

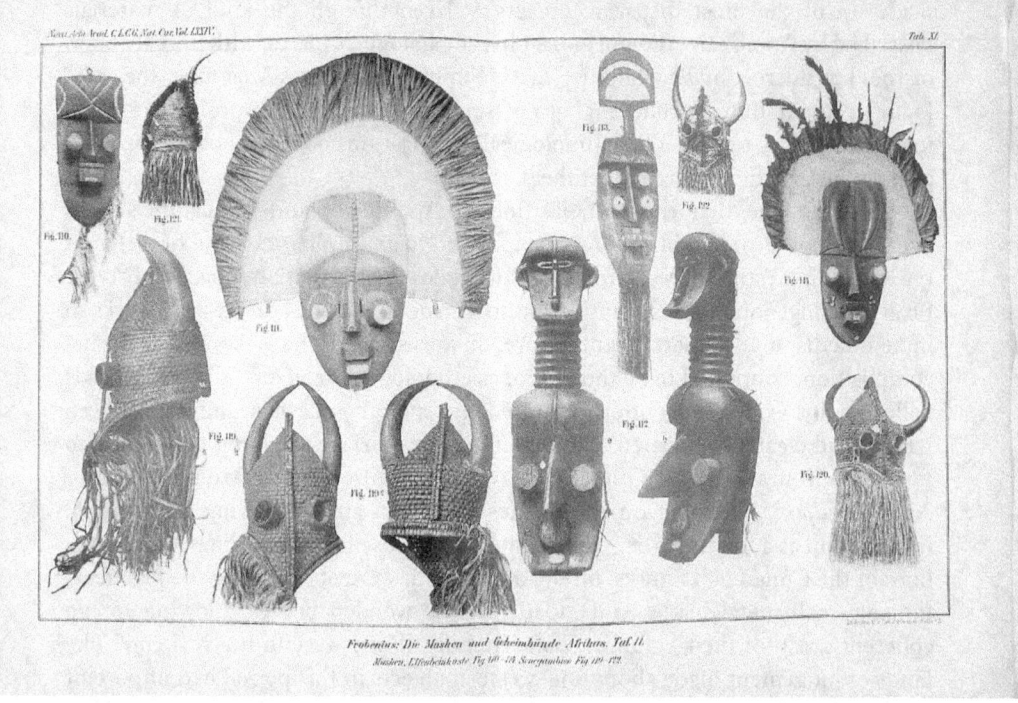

4 Masks from the Ivory Coast, Senegal and the Gambia, plate XI in Frobenius, *Masks and Secret Societies of Africa* (1898).

the sections of his book to an 'Art-critical comparison of forms'.[52] Importantly, the photographs of mask series largely included the raffia and feather extensions that were integral parts of the original costumes, for example, in the reproduction of Ivory Coast Grebo masks (figure 4). At the same time, however, Frobenius interpreted Kota reliquary figures as 'masks', read as sets of transposed human features. Despite the fact that he included a drawing after Jacques de Brazza in his text, showing similar pieces in use surmounting bundles of ancestral bones, he failed to make the connection between these and his Kota figures.[53] The misreading of Kota and Hongwe reliquary figures as either free-standing or as masks was common: Apollinaire and Guillaume's 1917 book reproduced one as a 'guardian of the home' mounted on a rectangular pedestal.[54] A Hongwe figure belonging to the Trocadéro was reproduced in Charles Ratton's 1931 book on African *masks*, cropped to conceal its base, which consisted of a wooden ring and the remains of fibres used to attach its ritual bundle.[55]

The tendency to isolate non-western objects and divest them of their 'appurtenances' was epitomised by Carl Einstein's influential 1915 *Negerplastik*.[56] Einstein reproduced over 100 pieces without identifying them, as a foil for his 'aestheticising' agenda. We might see his 1915 text as primarily a treatise of modern and especially cubist sculpture, arguing for an anti-pictorial conception of sculpture as self-contained and autonomous, in response to the theories of Adolf von Hildebrand, amongst others.[57] Non-western sculpture could serve as a crucial model for this, for Einstein, due to its independence from its creator and viewer. In distinction to the interpersonal dynamic of western sculpture, conceived as a 'topic of conversation between two people', African and Oceanic art transcended this interactive dimension through its religious function: 'The work of art striving for effect is meaningless here, as idols were often revered in the dark'.[58] Einstein's discussion was clearly aided by the perceived anonymity of his illustrated works, reinforcing his assertion of sculpture's transpersonal function.

Einstein's 1915 study had a mixed reception, including a positive response from the ethnologist Eckart von Sydow, who compared him to Frobenius, and who did not seem unduly worried by his apparent 'aesthetic' bias.[59] It has been suggested, though, that Einstein himself conceived *Negerplastik* in conjunction with a further publication that would provide more specific ethnological information: his 1921 book *African Sculpture*.[60] This second book is often overlooked, appearing in French in 1922 and yet to be translated into English, and presenting a more obscure and ambiguous argument than *Negerplastik*.[61] While reasserting the difficulties of discussing African art in the absence of historical evidence and of knowledge about its creators, Einstein sought in this second book to distance his tentative commentary from developments in the art of his time. Warning against what he called the 'alexandrianism' of the artistic appropriation of 'exotic' African sculpture, Einstein called for the future collaboration of 'ethnographers and art historians' in treating this material.[62] His discussions of individual works in this book presented them not as definitive 'artistic' statements, but as something more ambiguous. Of Benin 'bronze' heads, for example, Einstein claimed that their ancestral and totemic symbolism (as portraits of the dead) could outweigh their aesthetic effect: 'one becomes tightly entangled in the wish for the sculpture's magical or religious suggestiveness and demands a work which is more magical means than image'.[63] This was a striking reversal of the trend to valorise Benin pieces aesthetically, given their antiquity, their more familiar naturalistic qualities, and the permanent and 'precious' nature of their material make-up. Einstein's 1921 book pointed to a web of associations that might surround the non-western object, complicating the viewer's reception of it as something discrete and self-contained, 'entangling' them in its implications. A wooden Cameroon head-dress from Einstein's own collection that was used as a plate depicted a man with a spider on his head, and was interpreted by him as a complex combination of proto-cubist volumes and ancestral symbolism (figure 5).[64]

If these German sources had intimated ways in which the functions of non-western objects went beyond their formal qualities, 1920s writings in France brought out more strongly their tactility and the implications of physical contact with them. Ethnological theories of the late nineteenth and early twentieth centuries had already stressed the centrality of 'contagion' to the supposed 'primitive'

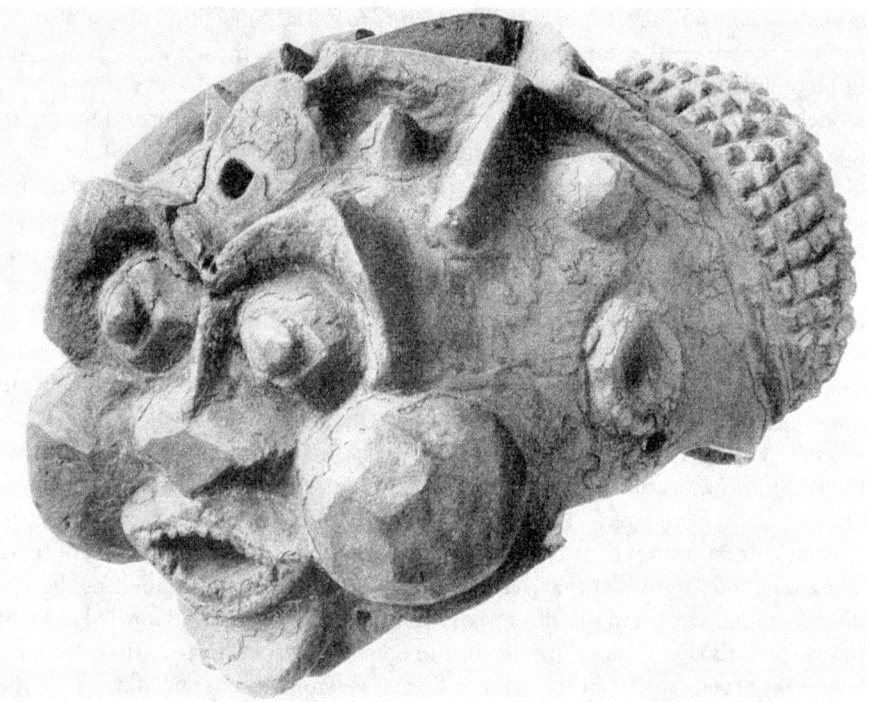

5 Bangwa mask, Cameroon, wood, 29 x 22, plate 12 in Einstein, *African Sculpture* (1921).

mind, a concept which fed into Lucien Lévy-Bruhl's 'law of participation', for instance.[65] The continuity between the objects and their makers and users could also extend by association to their viewers and collectors. Arguably the high valorisation of the patinated Fang and Ivory Coast pieces preferred by Guillaume and attracting the highest prices was in part due to connotations not only of age and 'antiquity', but also of frequent physical contact, suggestive of ongoing reverence. A Fang figure from the collection of Georges de Miré was sold in 1931 for the sum of almost 30,000 francs.[66] The marks of a long history of use could also be detected in much less 'acceptable' pieces. In a 1924 book, Henri Clouzot and André Level discussed not only Fang objects in terms of their finish, but also pieces from Dahomey, considered by them as possibly the most 'savage' and alien to the Western mentality. Small-scale Dahomean objects, for them, carried with them the history of years of domestic use: 'little family cult effigies summon us to them by a polish that they owe to the household attentions of devout descendants'.[67]

    Hand-held objects could also have a transcontinental function, transmitted over large spaces over great periods of time. Elie Faure, in the fifth volume of his massive *Histoire de l'art*, first published in 1927, described a generic 'idol' as a crucial carrier of artistic civilisation. This was due to its communicative potential, to its portable nature, and to its involvement in everyday practices, as the following passage set out:

Taken everywhere, from town to town, from shore to shore, across mountains and deserts, the idol has insinuated its spirit everywhere … Having its own reality independent of the conventions that govern articulated language, it translates into a concrete, immediate, living, existing and insisting form the abstractions and relations which reveal the solidarity of things between themselves and of things with us.[68]

Faure did not give any explicit examples of the 'idols' he discussed, but his passage was illustrated with a Nigerian Yoruba figure from the collection of Felix Fénéon. His assertion of the 'idol's resistance to language threw into relief his striking imagery of its 'insinuation', presumably by non-verbal means like sight and touch. Fellow art historian Henri Focillon, in his study *L'Art bouddhique*, evoked a small-scale object as the product of a universal and originary impulse: 'To touch a cared-for object, squeeze it warmly in one's palms, to caress it to bring out its polish: that is a disinterested instinct, as ancient as human consciousness.'[69] Focillon's image of the tactile joys of the object to some degree destabilised the anthropological principles of his study, by questioning his own emphasis on the importance of cultural rituals. Of this touching, squeezing and stroking, he claimed: 'In it there is pure desire, whose magical utilitarianism does not give us its key'.[70] In both his and Faure's accounts, the non-western object was a means of communication between itself and its maker, but also between itself and those who used and handled it. Here, the 'conversation between two people' that Carl Einstein had dismissed in favour of sculptural autonomy, was a defining aspect of the function of the 'idol'. This kind of 'primary' object could also bypass hierarchies. From the point of view of those who encountered it, the 'idol' could mediate between 'high' and 'low', serving as a unique artistic epitome of spiritual expression, as well as being a functional and changeable object. An 'idol' in these terms could be both the shiny Fang figures that were so revered in 1920s and 1930s Paris, and the 'crude' nail fetishes that the public largely dismissed. As an 'art' object, it could occupy an intermediate position, determined most significantly through its relationships with its makers, users and viewers.[71] For Leiris writing on Giacometti in 1929, having just read a popularising version of Lévy-Bruhl's *La Mentalité primitive* with its discussions of bodily contagion, his physical encounter with the sculptor's works brought about their symbolic dissolution as distinct and discrete objects.[72] Not merely 'in conversation' with Giacometti's sculptures, Leiris in the conclusion of his article imagined them as edible, things to be consumed and absorbed into the body in an ultimate form of contact.[73] Maintaining a 'safe' conceptual and cultural distance from non-western objects, however, was a key point of contention in the 1920s.

Art nègre in the service of the irrational

It might be assumed that by the 1920s, given the fashion for so-called *art nègre*, and the prominence of dealers like Guillaume and also Ratton (a crucial supporter of the Trocadéro), the attempt to raise the artistic profile (and market value) of non-western objects had completely succeeded. As a corollary, the promotion and discussion of such material as 'art' was the dominant discourse. In fact, neither of these things was true. Public prejudice against non-western cultures was still to be reckoned with in the 1930s. Reviewing the 1931 Colonial Exhibition, Henri Classens attributed the public's interest in *art nègre* to a declining interest in virtuosity, and claimed that what were regarded as 'masterpieces' in fact lacked skill, were technically rudimentary, and by no means intended deliberately as 'art'.[74] One of the reviewers of the Trocadéro's Benin show in 1932, a certain Irénée le Doré, identified African art with crude child-like carvings and 'scribbles', and claimed to be extremely surprised at the Benin brass works: 'I admit without too much shame to not have suspected that a different kind of *art nègre* could exist'.[75] Some artistic appreciations of non-western objects, conversely, implied the racist consequences of not accepting this new 'art', as Apollinaire had done in 1917 by condemning as outdated the evolutionist theories of Joseph-Arthur de Gobineau.[76] But alongside these wrangles over non-western 'art' or 'not art', there were also discussions which took a broader view of cultural production. The most prolific writers on non-western objects in France in the early 1920s were joint authors Henri Clouzot, curator at the Musée Galliéra, and André Level, critic and dealer (and former member of the Peau de l'Ours investors), who were at pains to provide their readers with anthropological information. This period also saw the publication in France of 'serious' anthropological studies by authors like Georges Hardy. For these writers, the *interest* of non-western objects, and even their status as 'art', was already assumed. Rather, it was the ideological implications of these objects' functions and contexts that were in play.

French ethnography, as we have seen, was slow in developing, and some of its more progressive aspects, like the ethnological work of Emile Durkheim, had focused not on French colonial territories, but on Australian culture.[77] Compared to Britain or Germany, in France there were fewer explicit discussions of the material that was arriving back in Europe (and a greater emphasis on physical anthropology rather than a culturally oriented ethnology). The colonial lieutenant Louis Desplagnes who explored the French Sudan (including an encounter with the 'Habbé' or Dogon), collected and photographed ritual objects, but did not appear to view them as worthy of detailed analysis.[78] One of the most prolific French anthropologists of the 1910s and 1920s, colonial administrator Maurice Delafosse, examined aspects of France's African colonies, but made virtually no specific reference to objects or art works. The British anthropologist R. S. Rattray, for instance, had famously begun to address these areas in particular as part of studies of Ashanti culture.[79] Frobenius too in Germany, after his youthful 1898 book on African masks, led a series of expeditions whose published results included discussions of objects, particularly as considered in their contexts. His *Das unbekannte Afrika* ('Unknown Africa') of 1923 was highly influential, cited in the bibliographies of several French accounts of non-western culture.[80] The photographs included in this book showed objects in situ and in use, such as Congolese men kneeling in homage to carved figures mounted on temple posts, a very different presentation than that common in books and periodicals in France.[81]

Clouzot and Level's writing combined aspects of the 'artistic' appreciation of non-western culture with ethnological information and broader cultural speculation. In the catalogue for the 1919 exhibition at the Galerie Devambez, *L'Art nègre et l'art océanien*, they were explicit about the difficulty for the European viewer of understanding the pieces on show.[82] Stressing the problems of dating works, a commonplace in discussion of non-western objects in this period, they briefly discussed Africa's past empires (in Ghana and Mali), echoing Frobenius's work on great former African civilisations.[83] This historical agenda was significant, as the two authors related the conditions of production of African and Oceanic works to the European Middle Ages, as a collective art created to satisfy religious needs. Medieval pre-Gothic art of the twelfth century, previously considered as 'barbarous', had undergone a revaluation in French art history at the beginning of the twentieth century, and it was no coincidence that Clouzot and Level were relating their discussion to this art-historical trend.[84] Thus they were able to present the 'grotesque' proportions of African figures as a reflection of religious beliefs, and as equivalent to medieval figures created in relation to architectural settings.[85] Focillon would take up precisely this issue in his study of Romanesque sculpture of 1931, based on lectures at the Sorbonne in the 1920s, but he would see its strangely proportioned figures as a logical, coherent part of an architectural scheme.[86] That Clouzot and Level considered non-western objects as anti-rational, by contrast, was reflected in their avowed interest in, as they put it, 'the most transposed art ever, the most surrealist, to use a fashionable word in its broadest sense'.[87]

One of the types of African object that were of particular interest to Clouzot and Level were the so-called 'nail' figures of the Congo and Dahomey. In their 1919 catalogue essay, they pointed to the Trocadéro's collection of a dozen 'Loango' figures punctured with nails and metal blades.[88] They drew explicitly upon the essay by Verneau on the 'fetish' that Apollinaire had also used, quoting directly his speculative assessment of the fear motivating the (often violent) production of these figures.[89] For the authors, 'civilised' peoples shared the same motivation in periods of strong religious belief.[90] In their article of 1922 for *La Renaissance de l'art français*, they made this connection more explicit, comparing an African figure with a mirror in its stomach concealing its consecrated object, from Level's own collection, to medieval reliquaries.[91] Clouzot and Level's implicit defence of the 'fetish' in these texts was made explicit in their 1924 book *Sculptures africaines et océaniennes*, which corresponded to the 1923 exhibition of colonial 'native art' at the Pavillon de Marsan. The show's visitors had demonstrated a marked, and in their view misguided, preference that they were seeking to counter:

> Seduced by the unexpectedness, the beauty, and the perfect craft of the masks and functional objects, some people have continued to dismiss the idols as repellent, without wanting to examine them, or, we should say, the fetishes, more difficult works, but sometimes greater and yet more significant.[92]

Clouzot and Level's deliberate shift in focus away from objects that were considered as 'high' art was partly in keeping with the interest of Clouzot in particular in interior decoration and textiles.[93] But their appeal to medieval art history was significant as it marked an attempt to shift the discourse around non-western objects away from 'aesthetic' judgements not only with reference to anthropological ideas but also by comparing systems of religious thought. Focillon's *L'Art bouddhique* of 1921 opened with a reflection on religious art as something foreign to the twentieth-century mind, accustomed to thinking of art as individualistic, Kantian play.[94] New areas available to the art historian, Focillon argued, citing the art of Asia, Africa, America and Polynesia, presented a concept of art with a social and religious function.[95] He used the example of Japanese tea ceremonies as crucial to an understanding of Japanese ceramics and landscape painting.[96] Underlying Focillon's text was the equivalence of medieval culture, as an 'other' in Europe's past, with non-western cultures and their unfamiliarity. Clouzot and Level's elevation of the 'fetish', as strikingly implicated in religious practices, and their comparison with the function of medieval art, echoed this art-historical approach.

However, Clouzot and Level's attachment to the small-scale ritual object was at odds with the dominant understanding of medieval sculpture in the 1920s. Emile Mâle, in his extensive 1922 study of twelfth-century art, disputed earlier theories about the origins of eleventh-century figurative monumental sculpture in the reliquary statues of saints, claiming instead that their iconographic inspiration lay in manuscript illustrations.[97] The significance of sacred objects was here discarded in favour of a pictorial genesis. Romanesque sculpture was also an important reference point in critical discussions of the work of Emile-Antoine Bourdelle, Giacometti's teacher in Paris, where it served as a model for the renewal of France's sculpture tradition (spearheaded, naturally, by Bourdelle himself).[98] Monumentality was perceived to be a crucial aspect of this renewal, just as national museums in the period continued to pursue archaeological finds of monumental sculpture as part of a tacit hierarchy of artefacts.[99] The other significant divergence in the perception of non-western and medieval art that developed in the 1920s concerned their relative 'rationality'. Focillon's 1931 book on Romanesque sculpture famously diverted attention away from its perceived 'monstrosity', instead emphasising its geometric order and architectural coherence. In this way he imputed to Romanesque art the 'Occidental' and also specifically French virtues of order and rationality that surfaced in intellectual discourse in 1920s France in many different forms.[100] In Focillon's case, his interest in a national cultural heritage has to be seen as relatively liberal and humanist in intent, but it was a shift in position from his earlier study of Buddhist art, with its implicit acceptance of cultural difference within a European past.[101]

To allow unfamiliar cultures their 'foreignness', however, could have both positive and negative results in critical accounts of non-western objects. Focillon's *L'Art bouddhique* inaugurated a series of studies under the rubric 'Art et Religion', with Focillon as overall editor, including in 1927 Georges Hardy's book *L'Art nègre: L'Art animiste des noirs d'Afrique*.[102] Hardy was the head of the Ecole Coloniale and a former student of leading French anthropologist Delafosse.[103] In this sense his book carried an implicit weight of authority which other studies did not have. It was an ostensibly full account of African art, divided into analytical sections and illustrated by plates from the collections of the Trocadéro, the British Museum, Berlin's Museum für Völkerkunde and the Royal Congo Museum in Brussels among others, as well as from the private collections of Guillaume and Level. However, Hardy's study, with all of its institutional sanction, carried a subtle but significant message: the distinct separation of African culture from European concerns. At some level, this took the form of a careful sensitivity to terminology: Hardy expressed concern about the term 'nègre' and its pejorative connotations as well as its generalising potential, comparing it to the insufficiency of the imagined term 'art blanc'.[104] He went on to outline the impossibility of ever knowing about the animistic beliefs on which this art was based, and to posit what he saw as the African's lack of 'our' sense of the 'good' or the 'true'.[105] His assessment of African art was negative, as 'a repressed art' that had taken refuge in the creation of small-scale sculptures, made by artisans whose activity was indistinguishable from that of magicians.[106] On his terms, such an art was 'trapped' by its religious context, unable to renew itself: '*art nègre* is very much a sacred slave ... constrained in the bindings of the ethnic spirit'.[107]

A similar distinction between non-western art-making and the activities of European artists was apparent in the writings of Adolphe Basler at the end of the 1920s. Basler's 1928 book on the sculpture of his time, *La Sculpture moderne en France*, was premised on his assessment of its degenerate state.[108] A superficial concern with the archaic, in his view, had distracted sculptors from the more profound aim of creating monumental works, and of reaching back to France's own medieval tradition.[109] In his summary of the development of sculpture in France in the early twentieth century, Basler described in terms of near contempt the interest taken by painters and sculptors in African sculpture: 'They familiarise themselves with the horrific examples of this primitive statuary, with its puerile and very architectural simplifications, its gauche foreshortenings, its tortoise-like legs and arms stuck to cylindrical trunks'.[110] Basler's terms would be echoed by Waldemar George, another critic obsessed with the 'degeneration' of French art, in his survey of the early 1930s.[111] In 1929, however, Basler published a serious study of non-western art with over 100 plates.[112] In the book's introduction, he repeated his negative judgement of the contribution of non-western art to current artistic practice, arguing that the interest in a form of liberation from European civilisation had led only to a deleterious 'exotic folklore'.[113] Basler's way of dealing with the 'problem' of non-western art and its unhappy impact was to place his study under the aegis of 'ethnography'. 'The aim of these pages is not at all, in order to flatter a certain snobbery, to integrate into the history of art the Negro, Indian or Oceanic arts', he opined.[114] Instead he would draw upon 'science' to shed light on his subject matter, in order to make clear to the artists and other interested parties drawn to his book that: 'only ethnography and Palaeolithic science are capable of shedding light on the origins of art'.[115]

The sleight of hand that allowed Basler to coerce the discipline of ethnography into a thinly veiled disavowal of non-western cultures showed that the ramifications of their 'acceptance' were complex. Although lavishly illustrated with works from major European museums and private collections, presented as isolated 'precious' objects, like the Trocadéro's Baoulé mask, Basler's text relegated them to a non-art status, which was less threatening to western artistic culture. Basler's book arguably played an important role in reintroducing to the public works that had long been languishing in the Trocadéro's store, a significant piece of publicity prior to the museum's renovation in the early 1930s. This aligned him in part with the project of its new socialist director Paul Rivet. The humanist values of French anthropology, however, did not necessarily stand in opposition to the humanist defence of the western tradition in art critical discourse, as Christopher Green has shown.[116] The necessary 'distance' that Basler's use of ethnography imposed between western and non-western cultures reflected to some extent the French colonial policy of 'association' (rather than an earlier principle of 'assimilation'): the preservation of 'difference' that implicitly relegated colonised cultures to an inferior status.[117] Arguably, what was probably the most well-known anthropological concept in the 1920s, the philosopher Lévy-Bruhl's notion of a distinct 'primitive mentality', carried within it the same ambiguity of identification and difference, capable of interpretation as either completely unfamiliar to western thought, or structurally similar.[118] Ethnography's colonialist agenda, and the ethnographic valorisation of non-western systems of belief, were crucial points of tension in the avant-garde reception of non-western culture in the late 1920s and early 1930s, particularly in relation to surrealist activity.

Objects from the colonies and their surrealist subversion

By 1931, the ethnologist Marcel Mauss, nephew of Durkheim and one of the founders of the Paris Institute of Ethnology, could celebrate a progressive shift away from formerly held ideas:

> Indigenous art objects were 'curiosities', 'cheap stuff', 'knick-knacks', 'fetishes', 'grotesques' … Only ethnographers and sociologists began to see, if not to really understand, the interest of these things and of these civilisations. We can even fear that the cause is not yet completely won … But victory is close because young people are on our side.[119]

A new generation could provide a new perspective, like the group of writers collecting around the periodical *Documents*, including one of the Institute of Ethnology's first students, Marcel Griaule. This generation could question the tendencies of the French establishment, hence Griaule's dig at the Sorbonne in one of his articles for the journal.[120] The position that Focillon, as a Sorbonne professor, had begun to assume by the late 1920s, as a champion of 'Occidental' values, was implicitly challenged by the alternative intellectual lineage constructed in *Documents*. This drew upon currents in German art history as well as recent ethnological and archaeological theoretical developments in several European countries. But the 'new' generation to appreciate non-western cultures also included the writers and artists associated with surrealism, whose approaches to them were not always consistent with the aims of ethnography. Indeed, in the context of the major 1931 Colonial Exhibition in Paris, surrealists and ethnographers were apparently in direct opposition.

The surrealist interest in non-western objects seemed to add fuel to some of the less progressive critical stances of the period, such as that of Waldemar George (an admirer of Focillon).[121] An antipathy towards surrealism was used in order to question the relative worth and intellectual interest of the kinds of objects the group was drawn to: primarily Oceanic, South East Asian and North West Coast American material. Henri-A. Lavachery, reviewing the 1930 exhibition of African and Oceanic art at the Galerie Pigalle in Paris, ranked the former over the latter precisely for this reason:

> African art is very much greater than that of the Oceanians because it has a human tone that the works of the Pacific Isles hardly have at all. The latter frequent a realm of the imagination where the fear of the unknown has given rise to a kind of madness and we understand why the surrealists, who believe themselves to be liberated from so many contingencies of earthly logic, have chosen this art as inspiration and friend.[122]

The often-noted surrealist preference for non-western material other than African has been attributed to several factors, not least the vagaries of avant-garde one-upmanship (marking a break with cubism and its alleged 'African' inspiration).[123] The fact that the first most prominent public outcomes relating to the new Institute of Ethnology in the early 1930s – the Dakar–Djibouti expedition and exhibitions at the Trocadéro – predominantly focused on Africa may well have played a role in the split between surrealists and ethnographers. *Documents* was already being published when Breton initiated the surrealist 'crisis' in February 1929, edited by Georges Bataille, who had been taking Mauss's courses since the autumn of 1925. Griaule returned from fieldwork in Abyssinia in August 1929 to join the journal's team. Breton and Paul Eluard, on the other hand – while collecting material from Oceania, the Americas and Asia, as well as Africa in the late 1920s – did not engage seriously with ethnographic theory in its presentation in *La Révolution surréaliste* and elsewhere.

A similar problem arose in the staging of the surrealist 'counter-colonial' exhibition in 1931, timed to coincide with the huge Colonial Exhibition that year. This vast showcase for France's colonial holdings, which drew in over 33 million visitors, had in fact been in the planning since 1913. This may have accounted for the fact that it did not reflect more recent developments in French ethnography, consisting instead of a now notorious phantasmagoria of replicas and 'interpretations' of buildings from Africa and elsewhere, such as Angkor Wat in Cambodia.[124] A virulent response was inspired in a group of surrealist writers and artists, who felt compelled to produce their own alternative exhibition and two condemnatory pamphlets. Both of these phenomena have been analysed in detail.[125] However, readings of this moment predominantly suggest a sharp divide between the politically 'radical' surrealist protestors and a 'retrograde' colonialist anthropology, and this simplification is misleading. The Trocadéro Ethnographic Museum put on its own display to coincide with the Colonial Exhibition, which had a considerable success. Central to the main display were the Dahomean statues that had been in the Trocadéro's collection since the 1890s, which attracted much press attention.[126] But the Trocadéro and its staff cannot be wholly aligned with the ideals of the Colonial Exhibition, whose 'scientific' principles were largely generated by the right-wing establishment anthropologist Louis Marin. The Institute of Ethnology had a clear socialist bias, and Rivet, the Trocadéro's director, had been a member of the 'League against colonial oppression and imperialism' since 1927. Lebovics has charted the uneasy power relations between Marin and Rivet in the promotion of their different variants of ethnography.[127] Former surrealists and contributors to *Documents* such as Leiris, Griaule, musicologist André Schaeffner and Rivière were active as part of the Trocadéro team, and its display set out, as its co-curator Jacques Soustelle insisted, to place the 'art work … back into its milieu'.[128]

The surrealist section of the 'counter-colonial' exhibition and accompanying tracts, authored by a group including Breton, Eluard, Louis Aragon, René Crevel, René Char, Benjamin Péret and Yves Tanguy, set out to attack colonialism in the guise of Western missionaries imposing their religious beliefs on non-western cultures.[129] One of the two photographs of the 'counter-colonial' display published in *Le Surréalisme au service de la révolution* famously showed a series of 'European fetishes'.[130] Intended as 'ironic', the display according to original plans for it would show: 'all of the propaganda gear of the Church, the numerous colour images of piety, then the ingenious adaptations of Christianity for each race: a black baby Jesus and virgins'.[131] As Hodeir and Pierre have pointed out, it is not at all clear from the photographs or from other evidence whether the statuettes displayed were actually produced in Africa under missionary influence, or created in Europe for missionary use.[132] A Dahomean wooden virgin and a Benin copper crucifixion scene, for instance, were shown in the 'Pavillon des Missions' during the exhibition, and reproduced in an article by Jean Gallotti.[133] The display included non-western objects from the collections of Breton, Eluard, Tzara, Aragon and Georges Sadoul, but the way in which these were discussed in the two surrealist tracts was ethnographically naïve. African or Oceanic objects could be great art, but could not be seen to have a religious function, the authors implied. Aragon recalled the presence in the display of 'fetish statuettes' and of funerary masks.[134] Exactly how the organisers of this display understood the functions of artefacts like this is unclear. The 'fetish', for example, had negative connotations within this display (as the 'European fetishes' show), presumably in keeping with

Marx's notorious conception of 'commodity fetishism'.[135] However, Marx's formulation had clearly implied a negative evaluation of non-western systems of belief (as 'primitive' superstition).[136] The political principles behind the 'counter-colonial' display led to impasse: intending to assert the superiority of non-western cultures it simultaneously undermined them.

The surrealist 'counter-colonial' display implicitly valorised and 'rescued' non-western objects predominantly from an artistic standpoint and to the detriment of ethnography. The role of religion, implicitly rejected by the surrealist display, was a major concern and subject of study for French ethnology. The antipathy of this surrealist group towards the ethnography of the Paris Institute of Ethnology might be gauged by the inclusion of Durkheim and Lévy-Bruhl in their 'Do not read' anti-pantheon of 1931, rejected in favour of Paul Lafargue, Marx's son-in-law. However, the 'cultural problems' section of 'The Truth about the Colonies' – the display of non-western 'art' objects organised by Aragon, Eluard and Tanguy – was already at odds with the principles of the French Communist Party, who were ultimately behind the 'counter-colonial' exhibition. Tanguy was not actually a party member. Breton and Eluard, signatories of the tracts, were at the same time collectors of, and sometime dealers in, non-western material.[137] Indeed, Breton and Eluard took full advantage of the increased public interest in African, Oceanic, Precolumbian and North West Coast American objects by timing the sale of their collections for July 1931, coinciding in fact with the opening of the 'counter-colonial' display.[138] Ratton probably advised them on the timing of this sale, which raised 285,000 francs. Crevel, another signatory, was spotted in June 1932, just a few months after the close of 'The Truth about the Colonies' in February, at the opening of the Trocadéro's hit exhibition of Benin bronzes.[139]

Ethnography in 1920s France was inevitably yoked to colonial interests. But the positions taken against this were not necessarily as clear-cut as they might seem. The intricate relationships between ethnography and discourses in the art world – art writing, art criticism, art history – also served to complicate its role in presenting and analysing objects and artefacts, particularly where these were already fast acquiring a market value and a status as collectors' pieces. The surrealist response to the 1931 Colonial Exhibition suggested a distinction between 'authentic' non-western objects and those corrupted by colonial contact and market forces (the figurine of a child with a begging bowl). Ethnography too was being mobilised to counter the claims of the market, playing down the 'artistic' value of individual pieces, with its financial connotations, in favour of contexts of practice and technology. But it would also seek to question western assumptions about the 'purity' of non-western objects in relation to the complications of the ethnographic encounter. In association with disciplines like archaeology and pre-history, ethnography would have to draw upon specific, concrete and recent findings to counter and destabilise the powerful recuperative pull of the market for autonomous and 'authentic' things.

Notes

1   Worringer, *Abstraction and Empathy* [1908], trans. Michael Bullock (London: Routledge and Kegan Paul, 1963), 1948 foreword, pp. vii–xiii.
2   *Ibid.*, p. viii.
3   *Ibid.*, p. 21.
4   Malraux, *Picasso's Mask* [1974] (New York: Da Capo Press, 1994), p. 10.
5   *Ibid.*, p. 11.
6   See for example Green, '"Naked Problems"? "Sub-African Caricatures"?', in Green (ed.), *Picasso's* Les Demoiselles d'Avignon (Cambridge: Cambridge University Press, 2001), p. 158.
7   Apollinaire, 'Sur les musées' (*Le Journal du soir*, October 1909), in *Oeuvres en prose complètes*, Vol. II (Paris: Gallimard, 1991), p. 123, and 'Le Musée du Trocadéro' (*Paris-Journal*, July 1914), *ibid.*, p. 833. Unless otherwise stated, all translations are my own.
8   Apollinaire, 'Exotisme et ethnographie' (*Paris-Journal*, September 1912), in *ibid.*, p. 475 and p. 474.
9   Anon, 'Les bronzes et les ivoires du Bénin', *Le Mois* (1 July–1 August 1932), p. 247, Archives of the Muséum National d'Histoire Naturelle, Paris – Laboratoire du Musée de l'Homme, hereafter MH/ 2 AM 1 B4a.
10 Anon, 'Au Musée d'Ethnographie du Trocadéro', *L'Europe nouvelle* (25 June 1932), MH/2 AM 1 B4a.
11 Anon, 'L'exposition d'ethnographie au Trocadéro', *Excelsior* (13 June 1933), MH/2 AM 1 B4f.
12 'Ch', 'La saison de Paris', *Nouvelles littéraires* (25 June 1932), MH/2 AM 1 B4a.
13 This selection is made from a list of those attending the Trocadéro's Benin show in *Comoedia* (19 June 1932), MH/2 AM 1 B4a.
14 See Verneau, 'Le Musée d'ethnographie du Trocadéro', *Anthropologie*, 29 (1918–19), pp. 547–60, and Dias, *Le Musée d'ethnographie du Trocadéro (1878–1908)* (Paris: CNRS, 1991), pp. 251–4.
15 C. M., 'Renaissance merveilleuse du Musée d'Ethnographie', *L'Oeuvre* (26 December 1931), MH/2 AM 1 B9e.
16 See Karady, 'Le problème de la légitimité dans l'organisation historique de l'ethnologie française', *Revue française de sociologie*, 23:1 (1982), pp. 17–35.
17 Penny has argued against the common assumption that colonialism was the driving force behind the development of ethnography, claiming that German anthropology pre-dated any significant colonial expansion, *Objects of Culture: Ethnology and Ethnographic Museums in Imperial Germany* (Chapel Hill and London: University of North Carolina Press, 2002), pp. 11–13.
18 Griaule was the first holder of a university chair in ethnology in 1943. The Institut d'Ethnologie, founded in 1925, was funded by local authorities in the colonies, Karady, 'Le problème de la légitimité', p. 17 and p. 29.
19 *Ibid.*, pp. 18–20.
20 *Ibid.*, pp. 24–5 and p. 21. Leiris's ethnological qualification was from the 'religious science' department of the Ecole Pratique des Hautes Etudes.
21 Rivière, 'Préface', in *Sculptures anciennes d'Afrique de d'Amérique, Collection G. de Miré* (Paris: Hôtel Drouot, 16 December 1931), p. 2.

22 Goldwater, *Primitivism in Modern Art* (London: Belknap Press, 1986), p. 11.

23 Coombes, 'Ethnography, Popular Culture, and Institutional Power: Narratives of Benin Culture in the British Museum, 1897–1992', *Studies in the History of Art*, 47 (1996), pp. 143–57, and see also her *Reinventing Africa: Museums, Material Culture and Popular Imagination in Late Victorian and Edwardian England* (London and New Haven, CT: Yale University Press, 1994).

24 Delafosse, 'Statues des rois de Dahomé au Musée ethnographique du Trocadéro', *La Nature*, 1086 (24 March 1894), pp. 262–6, 'Le Trône de Béhanzin et les portes des palais d'Abomé au Musée ethnographique du Trocadéro', *La Nature*, 1090 (21 April 1894), pp. 326–30, 'Une statue dahoméenne en fonte', *La Nature*, 1105 (4 August 1894), pp. 145–7.

25 Besson, *Le Totémisme* (Paris: Rieder, 1929), plate LII, and see Leiris, *Journal* (Paris: Gallimard, 1992), p. 186.

26 See for instance Paulme, *African Sculpture* (London: Elek, 1962), Laude, *Les Arts de l'Afrique noire* (Paris: Librairie Générale Française, 1966), and Leiris and Delange, *Afrique noire: La Création plastique* (Paris: Gallimard, 1967).

27 Apollinaire, 'Sur les musées', p. 123.

28 Fierens, 'L'art du Benin', *Feuilleton du Journal des Débats* (26 July 1932), MH/2 AM 1 B4a.

29 R.[ené] D.[aumal], 'Au Musée d'Ethnographie du Trocadéro', *Nouvelle revue française* (1 December 1933), p. 942, MH/2 AM 1 B5a.

30 G. P., 'L'exposition ethnographique du Trocadéro évoque la création du monde', *Comoedia* (11 July 1931), MH/2 AM 1 B4a.

31 Simmel, *The Philosophy of Money* [1900/1907], ed. David Frisby (London: Routledge, 1991), p. 474.

32 See Patrick Elliott, 'Alberto Giacometti: An Introduction', in *Alberto Giacometti, 1901–1966* (Edinburgh: National Galleries of Scotland, 1996), p. 12.

33 For a summary of these interpretations, see Rosalind Krauss, 'Giacometti' in Rubin, *"Primitivism"*, pp. 504–8 and particularly footnotes 12–14, p. 528, and see also Chapter 5 below.

34 Bois, 'Kahnweiler's Lesson', *Representations*, 18 (spring 1987), pp. 33–68. Kahnweiler's 1948 essay 'Negro Art and Cubism' is reprinted in Flam and Deutch, *Primitivism and Twentieth-Century Art*, pp. 284–91.

35 Casimiro de Crescenzo, *Alberto Giacometti, Early Works in Paris (1922–1930)* (New York: Yoshii Gallery, 1994), p. 47.

36 Leiris, 'Alberto Giacometti', *Documents*, 1:4 (1929), pp. 209–10.

37 See Ades, 'Surrealism: Fetishism's Job' in Shelton (ed.), *Fetishism: Visualising Power and Desire* (London: South Bank, 1995), pp. 67–87 and Mary Drach McInnes, 'Alberto Giacometti, le féticheur', in Aspley *et al.*, *From Rodin to Giacometti: Sculpture and Literature in France 1880–1950* (Amsterdam: Rodopi, 2000), pp. 169–83.

38 Leiris, 'Alberto Giacometti', p. 210.

39 Apollinaire and Guillaume, *Sculptures nègres* [1917] (New York: Hacker, 1972).

40 Guillaume, 'Exposé', *ibid.*, np [p. 6].

41 *Ibid.*, [p. 5].

42 Apollinaire, 'A propos de l'art des noirs', *ibid.*, [p. 3]. A variant of this essay was published as 'Mélanophilie ou Mélanomanie' in *La Vie anecdotique*, 1 April 1917, *Oeuvres en prose complètes*, Vol. 3 (Paris: Gallimard, 1993), pp. 252–5.

43 Apollinaire, *The Cubist Painters* (E. Sussex: Artists Bookworks, 2002), p. 37 and p. 41.

44 Verneau, 'Le fetichisme à travers les âges', *La Nature*, 2221 (22 April 1916), p. 259.

45 *Ibid.*, pp. 258–9.

46 Apollinaire and Guillaume, *Sculptures nègres*, plate IX. By 1926, when this piece was reproduced to accompany an article by Rivière in *Cahiers d'art*, its fibrous part had been removed, presumably having decayed due to the Trocadéro's then poor storage facilities, *Cahiers d'art*, 1:7 (1926), p. 180.

47 Guillaume and Munro, *Primitive Negro Sculpture* (London: Jonathan Cape, 1926), p. 66 and p. 77. This book was published in French with an expanded range of plates from European museums and private collections, but without these close formal analyses, Guillaume and Munro, *La Sculpture nègre primitive* (Paris: G. Crès, 1929).

48 Chauvet, *Les Arts indigènes en Nouvelle-Guinée* (Paris: Société d'Editions Géographiques, Maritimes et Coloniales, 1930), p. 13, notes 1 and 2. The vested interest in Chauvet's disinction between 'high' and 'low' was clear in his inclusion of pieces from his own collection amongst the former, including a decorated stool.

49 See for instance John Mack, 'Kuba art and the birth of ethnography' and Curtis A. Keim, '*Artes Africanae*: The Western Discovery of "Art" in Northeastern Congo', in Schildkrout and Keim, *The Scramble for Art in Central Africa* (Cambridge: Cambridge University Press, 1998), pp. 63–78 and pp. 109–32, and Phillips and Steiner, 'Art, Authenticity and the Baggage of Cultural Encounter', in Phillips and Steiner (eds), *Unpacking Culture: Art and Commodity in Colonial and Postcolonial Worlds* (Berkeley: University of California Press, 1999), pp. 3–19.

50 See Penny, *Objects of Culture*.

51 Frobenius, *Die Masken und Geheimbünde Afrikas* (Halle: Karras, 1898).

52 *Ibid.*, pp. 201–13.

53 *Ibid.*, p. 85.

54 Apollinaire and Guillaume, *Sculptures nègres*, plate IV.

55 Ratton, *Masques africains* (Paris: Librairie des arts décoratifs, 1931), plate 15.

56 Einstein, *Negerplastik* (1915), reprinted in *La Sculpture nègre*, trans. and ed. Liliane Meffre (Paris: L'Harmattan, 1998).

57 See Potts, *The Sculptural Imagination: Figurative, Modernist, Minimalist* (London and New Haven, CT: Yale University Press, 2000), pp. 129–31.

58 Einstein, *Negerplastik*, p. 58 and pp. 61–2.

59 Baacke, 'Rezeptionsgeschichtliche Anmerkungen zur "Negerplastik"', *Carl Einstein, Negerplastik* (Berlin: Fannei und Walz, 1992), pp. 153–60.

60 *Ibid.*, p. 156, and Einstein, *Afrikanische Plastik* (Berlin: Ernst Wasmuth, 1921).

61 Einstein, *La Sculpture africaine* (Paris: G. Crès, 1922).

62 Einstein, *Afrikanische Plastik*, pp. 5–6.

63 *Ibid.*, p. 16.

64 This head-dress later entered Tzara's collection, see Raoul Lehuard, 'La vente Tristan Tzara', *Arts d'Afrique noire*, 68 (winter 1988), p. 14.

65 Lévy-Bruhl, *Les Fonctions mentales dans les sociétés inférieures* (1910) (Paris: Félix Alcan, 1922), pp. 102–10.

66 Its exact price was 29,325 francs. See *Sculptures Anciennes d'Afrique et d'Amérique, Collection G. de Miré*, plate V, cat. no. 46, and the review of the sale by Ratton, 'Les ventes, Collection G. de Miré. Sculptures d'Afrique et d'Amérique', *Cahiers d'art*, 6:9–10 (1931), pp. 453–4. This figure was later acquired by Jacob Epstein.

67 Clouzot and Level, *Sculptures africaines et océaniennes* (Paris: Librairie de France, 1924), p. 14.

68 Faure, *Histoire de l'art*, Vol. 5 (Paris: G. Crès, 1927), p. 395.

69 Focillon, *L'Art bouddhique* (Paris: Henri Laurens, 1921), p. xiv.

70 *Ibid.*, p. xiv.

71 For the role of the hand-held object in reinforcing avant-garde group identity in Britain in the 1910s, see Wood, 'Ornaments, talismans and toys: the hand-held sculptures of Henri Gaudier-Brzeska', in *Blasting the Future, Vorticism in Britain 1910–1920* (London: Estorick Collection, 2004), pp. 41–8.

72 Leiris's source for Lévy-Bruhl's theories was Blondel, *La Mentalité primitive* (Paris: Stock, 1926), see Leiris, *Journal*, p. 188.

73 Leiris, 'Alberto Giacometti', p. 210.

74 Classens, 'La valeur et le sens des sculptures et des peintures des noirs', *L'Art et les artistes*, 25:118 (June 1931), pp. 313–15. Consecutive issues of this periodical were nevertheless intended to 'promote' the Colonial Exhibition.

75 Doré, 'Art Nègre', *La Femme et l'enfant* (1 August 1932), p. 564, MH/2 AM 1 B4a.

76 Apollinaire and Guillaume, *Sculptures nègres*, [p. 2].

77 Durkheim, *Les Formes élémentaires de la vie religieuse* [1912] (Paris: Presses Universitaires de France, 1960).

78 Desplagnes, *Le Plateau central nigérien: Une mission archéologique et ethnographique au Soudan français* (Paris: Emile Larose, 1907).

79 Rattray, *Ashanti* (Oxford: Clarendon Press, 1923), and the edited volume *Religion and Art in Ashanti* (Oxford: Clarendon Press, 1927). The latter contained in particular a chapter by Vernon Blake on 'The Aesthetics of Ashanti' that deliberately set out to broach a topic which had not yet been examined, pp. 344–81.

80 Frobenius, *Das unbekannte Afrika* (Munich: C. H. Becksche, 1923).

81 *Ibid.*, plate 181.

82 Clouzot and Level, *L'Art nègre et l'art océanien* (Paris: Devambez, 1919), p. 46.

83 *Ibid.*, pp. 34–5. On Frobenius's project to rediscover and appraise pre-Islamic African civilisations, to the extent of positing the lost continent of Atlantis as the precursor to Yoruba culture, see Suzanne Marchand, 'Leo Frobenius and the Revolt against the West', *Journal of Contemporary History*, 32:2 (1997), pp. 153–70.

84 The work of Emile Mâle embraced this shift in focus from the Gothic to the Romanesque: Mâle had published his *L'Art religieux du XIIIe siècle en France* (written in 1899) in 1902, and in 1922 brought out his study *L'Art religieux du XIIe siècle en France* (Paris: Armand Colin).

85 Clouzot and Level, *L'Art nègre et l'art océanien*, p. 47.

86 Focillon, *L'Art des sculpteurs romans* [1931] (Paris: Presses Universitaires de France, 1964). Focillon succeeded Mâle as the chair of medieval art history at the University of Paris in 1924.

87 Clouzot and Level, 'Caractéristiques de l'art des noirs', *L'Art vivant*, 1:5 (1 March 1925), p. 11.

88 Loango was thought to be a Congolese empire. These figures would now be commonly identified as Bakongo nail figures.

89 Clouzot and Level, *L'Art nègre et l'art océanien*, p. 41.

90 *Ibid.*, p. 41.

91 Clouzot and Level, 'Afrique équatoriale française, sculptures et objets d'usage', *La Renaissance de l'art français*, 5:4 (1922), p. 223.

92 Clouzot and Level, *Sculptures africaines et océaniennes*, p. 4.

93 Appropriate to his post at the Musée Galliéra, the state costume collection. Clouzot's publications also included *Le Style moderne dans la décoration intérieure* (Paris: Massin, c.1921).

94 Focillon, *L'Art bouddhique*, p. iii.

95 *Ibid.*, p. iii.

96 *Ibid.*, p. iv.

97 Mâle, *Religious Art in France. The Twelfth Century* (Princeton, NJ: Princeton University Press, 1978), p. 4.

98 See the collection of primary source accounts of Bourdelle's work edited by Lavrillier and Dufet, *Bourdelle et la critique de son temps* (Paris: Paris-Musées, 1992), where the association of Bourdelle's work with Romanesque and medieval sculpture is common.

99 See Marchand, 'The Rhetoric of Artifacts and the Decline of Classical Humanism: The Case of Josef Strzygowski', *History and Theory*, 33:4 (1994), p. 109.

100 See Sauerländer, 'En face des barbares et à l'écart des dévots, l'humanisme médiéval d'Henri Focillon', in Kubler *et al.*, *Relire Focillon* (Paris: Musée du Louvre, 1998), pp. 54–74.

101 A defence of the Western, 'Latinate' world view that Romanesque sculpture represented for Focillon became a more urgent cause in the 1930s. On this and the distinction between Focillon's 'Occident' and its right-wing variant, see Walter Cahn, 'Focillon's *Jongleur*', *Art History*, 18:3 (September, 1995), pp. 345–62.

102 Hardy, *L'Art nègre* (Paris: Henri Laurens,1927).

103 Hardy was the prolific author of colonial texts such as *Une conquête morale: l'enseignement en Afrique Occidentale Française* (1917), *Histoire de la colonisation française* (1927), *Géographie et colonisation* (1933) and *Le Problème religieux dans l'empire français* (1940).

104 Hardy, *L'Art nègre*, p. 1.

105 *Ibid.*, p. 10 and pp. 82–3.

106 *Ibid.*, pp. 111–13.

107 *Ibid.*, p. 112 and p. 113.

108 Basler, *La Sculpture moderne en France* (Paris: G. Crès, 1928), p. 5.

109 *Ibid.*, pp. 37–40.

110 *Ibid.*, pp. 51–2.

111 George, *Profits et pertes de l'art contemporain* (Paris: Chroniques du jour, c.1932), in particular pp. 83–9.

112 Basler, *L'Art chez les peuples primitifs* (Paris: Librairie de France, 1929).

113 *Ibid.*, p. 5.

114 *Ibid.*, p. 5.

115 *Ibid.*, p. 6.

116 Green, 'Humanisms: Picasso, Waldemar George and the politics of "man" in the 1930s', *Comparative Criticism*, 23 (2001), pp. 231–54.

117 See Morton, 'National and Colonial: The Musée des Colonies at the Colonial Exposition, Paris, 1931', *Art Bulletin*, 53:2 (June 1998), p. 359.

118 In *Les Fonctions mentales*, Lévy-Bruhl concluded that so-called 'pre-logical' and 'logical' ways of thinking co-existed in Western mentality, pp. 454–5. On this point see also Jean Cazeneuve, *Lucien Lévy-Bruhl*, trans. Peter Rivière (Oxford: Blackwell, 1972), pp. 4–6.

119 Mauss, 'Les arts indigènes', in *Lyon Universitaire* (April–May 1931), p. 1.

120 Griaule, 'Un coup de fusil', *Documents*, 2:1 (1930), p. 46.

121 George, 'Le crépuscule des idoles', *Les Arts à Paris*, 17 (May 1930), p. 7.

122 Lavachery, 'L'exposition d'art africain et d'art océanien du Théâtre Pigalle, à Paris', *Cahiers de Belgique*, 3:4 (April 1930), p. 112.

123 See Cowling, '"L'oeil sauvage": Oceanic Art and the Surrealists', in Greub (ed.), *Art of Northwest New Guinea* (New York: Rizzoli, 1992), p. 181.

124 See Ageron, 'L'exposition coloniale de 1931, mythe républicain ou mythe impérial?' in Nora (ed.), *Les Lieux de mémoire*, Vol. 1 (Paris: Gallimard, 1984), pp. 561–91, and Morton, *Hybrid Modernities: Architecture and Representation at the 1931 Colonial Exposition, Paris* (Cambridge, MA: MIT Press, 2000).

125 See Hodeir and Pierre, *L'Exposition coloniale* (Brussels: Complexe, 1991), pp. 125–34, Blake, 'The Truth about the Colonies, 1931: Art indigène in the Service of the Revolution', *Oxford Art Journal*, 25:1 (2002), pp. 37–58, and Mileaf, 'Body to Politics: Surrealist exhibition of the tribal and the modern at the anti-Imperialist exhibition and the Galerie Charles Ratton', *Res*, 40 (autumn 2001), pp. 239–50.

126 G. P., 'L'exposition ethnographique du Trocadéro évoque la création du monde', *Comoedia* (11 July 1931), anon, 'Paris Exhibits Weird Works of Savage Art', *New York American* (August 1931), and anon, *New York Times* (5 July 1931), MH/2 AM 1 B4a.

127 Lebovics, *True France* (Ithaca, NY: Cornell University Press, 1992), pp. 32–5.

128 Soustelle, 'A propos de l'Exposition Ethnographique des Colonies françaises au Musée d'Ethnographie du Trocadéro', *L'Art vivant* (1 July 1931), p. 358, MH/2 AM 1 B4a.

129 Tanguy, Sadoul, Aragon, Breton *et al.*, 'Premier bilan de l'exposition coloniale' and 'Ne visitez pas l'exposition coloniale' [1931], reprinted in Maurice Nadeau, *Histoire du surréalisme* (Paris: Seuil, 1948), pp. 330–3.

130 *Le Surréalisme au service de la révolution*, 4 (December 1931), p. 40.

131 Hodeir and Pierre, *L'Exposition coloniale*, p. 132.

132 *Ibid.*, p. 132.

133 Gallotti, 'Les arts indigènes à l'exposition coloniale', *Art et Décoration* (September 1931), pp. 74–5.

134 Hodeir and Pierre, *L'Exposition coloniale*, p. 131.

135 Freedman (ed.), *Marx on Economics* (Harmondsworth: Penguin, 1973), p. 51.

136 Marx's 'fetishism' analogy drew upon, as he put it, 'the mist-enveloped regions of the religious world', *ibid.*, p. 51.

137 On this contradiction, see Blake, 'The Truth about the Colonies, 1931', pp. 56–7, and Mileaf, 'Body to Politics', pp. 248–9. On Breton and Eluard's dealing activities for Ratton, see Cowling, '"L'oeil sauvage"', p. 189, note 16.

138 *Sculptures d'Afrique, d'Amérique, d'Océanie, Collection André Breton et Paul Eluard* (Paris: Hôtel Drouot, 1931, and reprinted New York: Hacker, 1972).

139 As listed in *Comoedia* (19 June 1932), MH/2 AM 1 B4a.

2

Classifying: the 'irritating' object
and its disciplines

In his manifesto-like article 'Archéologismes', published in *Cahiers d'art* in 1926, the jazz musician and art consultant Georges Henri Rivière offered an enigmatic model for dealing with a whole range of new and challenging art forms.[1] The dominance of the heritage of Ancient Greece was now over, he argued in this text, his first published piece of art writing, and a call to arms whose significance for modern archaeology is now beginning to be recognised.[2] The museum as a repository of this heritage had been 'overturned' ('bouleversé') by new archaeological discoveries of Precolumbian, Chinese or Minoan artefacts, and archaeology itself, for Rivière, took on the role of a murderous and rebellious child, a 'parricide daughter of humanism'. If this was an upheaval of traditional western artistic canons, it was a violent and irrationally unsettling one.

Rivière was urging his readers to take up his call to find new ways of responding to the material revealed by archaeology, given too the growing availability of accompanying information. His brief for this, however, was ambiguous. Rivière condemned what he saw as 'the disgrace of artistic liberalism' and 'vain eclecticism', demanding greater rigour in treating these objects. At the same time, the kind of approach that he was advocating was by no means dryly scientific. Within the pages of *Cahiers d'art*, he continued, the reader could encounter 'documents drawn from diverse civilisations', while the scientific apparatus pertaining to these would be restricted to, and thus sidelined in, footnotes. Furthermore, any attempt to trace the origins of these works would lead only to confusion, Rivière concluded: 'those who think they are returning to origins will find confusion'.[3] While rejecting the *artistic* treatment of objects and artefacts from other cultures, Rivière was also calling for a move away from the prevailing 'scientific' approach, with what he saw as its empty speculation on origins.

Rivière's allusion to the search for origins can be read as a critique of several prevailing archaeological approaches. It suggests a dismissal of evolutionist archaeology, which had sought to make connections between ancient artefacts and modern 'civilisation' as part of a teleological schema of 'progress'. Our fathers, Rivière said, could use the museum as a place to compare the modern with the ancient, implying that for a new generation a sense of historical progression was no longer valid. It could also be seen as a sideswipe at culture-historical views of the past, which used the investigation of 'origins' as an ideological tool in the promotion of national identity. A prime (and later notorious) example of this was Gustaf Kossinna's *Die Herkunft der Germanen*, published in 1911.[4] Rivière's reference to a range of different, identifiable 'cultures' such as the Precolumbian, the Minoan and so on implied the residue of these kinds of approach. However, he avoided any simplistic elision of archaeological interest with nationalist interest in his example of the contemporary 'investigator', represented by two French writers visiting not Aurignac or Lascaux, but Altamira in Spain. 'We no longer go to the museum like our fathers did', he wrote. 'Louis Aragon and Jean Lurçat, if they took along their top hat and bowler hat to Madrid, would still ignore the Prado, but instead take the path to Altamira'.[5]

In 1926, Rivière had just completed several years at the Ecole du Louvre where he had specialised in classical archaeology.[6] Yet in this article he rejected the text-based classical tradition in favour of the compelling material evidence of other ancient and unfamiliar cultures. This changing perspective may have been inspired in part by his mentor Georges Salles, curator at the Louvre and supporter of non-western art.[7] Rivière also moved in the circle of Joseph Hackin, archaeologist and curator at the Musée Guimet. Rivière's first exhibition of 1928, which led directly to his appointment at the Trocadéro, was the first major presentation of Precolumbian art in Paris. He also worked for two high-profile collectors, David David-Weill and Charles Vignier, producing a catalogue of the latter's archaeological library.[8] Rivière's article embodied the diversity of his activities, as well as reflecting the complex attitudes towards non-western cultures expressed across the literature in the 1920s, with regard to the tensions between 'artistic' and 'scientific' approaches and the need for some other, fresh position. His text suggested a questioning not only of the museum, but also of the discipline of archaeology itself. Its title indicated plurality and also the excitement of avant-garde artistic movements, echoing Jean Arp and El Lissitzky's book *The Isms of Art* of 1925 with his evocation of '-isms' rather than the more scientific '-ologies'. Rivière's only concrete example of a new approach (Aragon and Lurçat at Altamira) conjured up a potent image of modern, urban sensibility (their hats) combined with the immediacy of an encounter with the ancient (the caves). A new category of 'archaeologisms' would rely neither on science nor on artistic borrowings, but would rather consist of direct experiences free from intellectual baggage.

Most telling in Rivière's account with regard to then current archaeological approaches was his emphasis on a range of material artefacts, to be regarded as 'documents'. In the case of Minos, for instance, archaeology might strip away 'its halo of legends' in favour of the evidence of its palaces with their treasures and frescos. The illustrations of African and Oceanic pieces that accompanied his article, although not discussed explicitly, served to back up his appeal for directness and concreteness in dealing with material things. Most of the works shown were from the collections of the Trocadéro, including the Dahomean *Gou* god of metalwork, acquired in 1894,

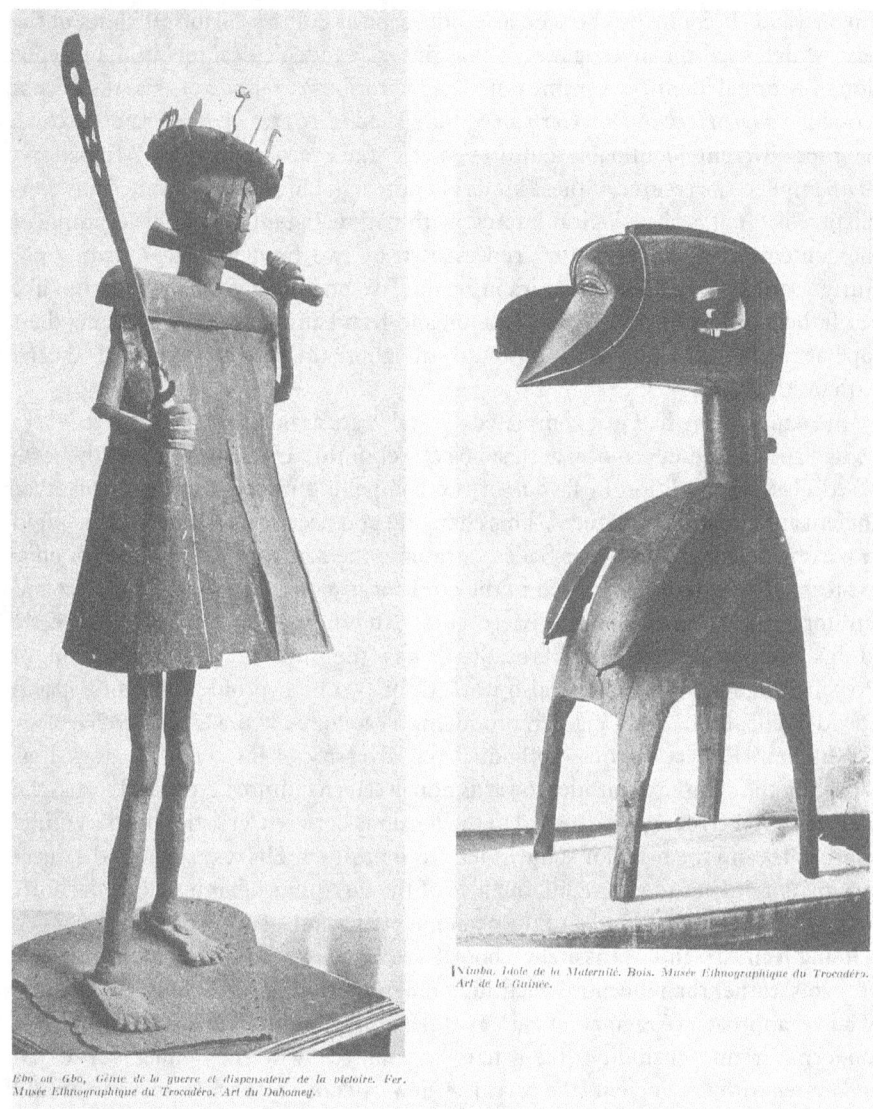

Nimba. Idole de la Maternité. Bois. Musée Ethnographique du Trocadéro.
Art de la Guinée.

Ebo ou Gbo, Génie de la guerre et dispensateur de la victoire. Fer.
Musée Ethnographique du Trocadéro. Art du Dahomey.

6 Akati Ekplékendo, *Sculpture dedicated to Gou, god of metalwork and war*, Dahomey (Togo), before 1858, iron and wood, 165h, and Baga *nimba* shoulder mask, Guinea, wood, Trocadéro Ethnographic Museum, Paris, in *Cahiers d'art*, 1:7 (1926).

and a Baga *nimba* mask from Guinea, acquired in 1902. From the evidence of the photographic reproductions, both of these works had been specially set up to be photographed in isolation against a plain background, in a neutral, but also rather downplayed way (figure 6). The Baga shoulder mask was placed on a rough scrap of cloth to create a blank backdrop, while behind it a corner of decaying wall was visible. These shabby details were a presumably accidental reflection on the sorry state of the

Trocadéro itself, pre-renovation. But they also had a laconic character, as if to sug-
gest the importance of the pieces themselves, specimen-like, over their presentation.
Captions, however, refrained from 'scientific' detail, giving little away. The first two
images that accompanied Rivière's article (an elaborate Bamana headdress, and a
Yoruba equestrian figure from Fénéon's collection) were both described simply as
'African sculpture'. The same equestrian figure, erroneously identified as
Dahomean, had been discussed briefly in an article by Clouzot and Level in *L'Amour
de l'art* in 1924, where the authors had pondered its 'high taste' and connections to
well-known pieces like the *Gou* god of metalwork.[9] What would it mean to strip away
these kinds of received judgements and classifications about non-western objects
circulating in the West, and to start again afresh?

Rivière would play a central role in the extraordinary mix of art writers, ethnographers, ancient historians, art historians and curators who contributed to the periodical *Documents* during its short existence between 1929 and the beginning of
1931, a crucial forum for the presentation of new ethnographic ideas in the period.
Indeed, his combination of personal and professional interests was entirely appropriate to a periodical whose co-existing different approaches were less eclectic than
blatantly irreconcilable, as Leiris later put it.[10] The provocative tone and challenging tensions of Rivière's 1926 text for *Cahiers d'art* were a foretaste of what was
to come in the pages of *Documents*, as a crucial forum for the encounter of ethnography and the art world, in its widest sense. It also brought up themes that were significant points of reference for the journal. The status and role of the disciplines
relative to one another, whose exploration Rivière's article suggested, was a key feature of *Documents*. The tension developed by Rivière between the museum and a
kind of more immediate experience (visiting Altamira), underlay *Documents* too.
Linked through its writers to European museums and collections, the periodical's
closest collaboration was with the Trocadéro, which in turn was juggling the
demands of display and the preparation of ethnographers for field experiences.
Documents would contribute to the build-up to the Dakar–Djibouti expedition, as
the framework for a completely different encounter with objects in situ.

For both Rivière writing in 1926 and for *Documents*, art works and artefacts as
the potential illuminators of great civilisations *outside* the Greco-Roman tradition
were paramount. More significantly, new approaches deriving from ethnography
and archaeology could throw up a range of material which might test and upset
conventions and expectations. According to Leiris, in his 1963 article on the genesis of *Documents*, the journal's publicity material made its attitude clear: 'The
most irritating works of art, yet to be classified, and certain unusual works,
neglected until now, will be the object of studies as rigorous, as scientific, as those
of archaeologists'.[11] *Documents* would deliberately seek out the 'most irritating'
material, which had not yet found a place in systems of classification, or had not
yet been the subject of scientific research. To some degree, the concept of the
'irritating' piece of material as uncharted terrain, attracting attention, with the
ability to annoy and provoke, could be related to the perception of the 'curio' in

the eighteenth and nineteenth centuries, particularly with regard to its moral connotations.[12] In both cases, something that might bother western notions of function, taste and decency, is suggested. The 'curio', of course, ceased to be such
when it became reclassified as 'ethnographic object' or 'non-western art work',
when it came into contact with the disciplines. Indeed, anthropological
approaches in particular sought to divest the 'curio' of its negative connotations
within colonialist and evolutionist schemas.

   Documents has usually been discussed in relation to the role of Georges Bataille
as its dominant writer, a figure whose thought has been seen to revolve centrally
around ideas of heterogeneity, the unclassifiable and the 'formless'. Bataille's
famous mock-dictionary definition of the 'informe' scorned the need of philosoph-
ical systems to give a 'mathematical frock-coat' to things, using the French term
'redingote' to suggest a long coat which wraps amply around the body.[13] The tensions between the preservation of the moment of 'formlessness' and the classificatory 'wrappings' of the disciplines ran throughout *Documents*. Scientific enquiry
and research could make what was an 'irritating' object less so. Ethnography, moreover, would additionally have a moral stake in doing so. This chapter will examine
the competing, and often incompatible, strands in *Documents*, with regard to its
treatment and presentation of objects. Bataille's contributions to the periodical
have been analysed at length elsewhere, particularly in relation to the representation of the visual arts in the journal.[14] The chapter will focus not on the 'fine arts' of
its rubric, but on its presentation of material culture through its diverse collaborators – scholars and university academics, museum curators, dealers and collectors,
pre-historians, archaeologists and ethnologists. This perspective will allow for a
closer scrutiny of both the periodical's accommodations with the antiquarian
market for 'curious' objects and its serious engagement with the academic disciplines in the late 1920s.

Documents drawn from diverse civilisations

As in part a vehicle for the so-called 'dissident' surrealists, *Documents* has been
considered in relation to other surrealist journals such as *La Révolution surréaliste*
or *Le Surréalisme au service de la révolution*.[15] Its more immediate context, however, would have been specialist publications like the numismatics journal
Aréthuse, or Herbert Kühn's *Ipek*.[16] Its penchant for 'curiosities' may also arguably
have owed something to *Beaux-Arts*, with which it shared Wildenstein as a
backer.[17] In terms of the presentation of a wide range of ethnographic and archaeological material, the most direct model for *Documents* was undoubtedly the
journal that had carried Rivière's call for new approaches and encounters, *Cahiers
d'art*. The most prominent art periodical of 1920s and 1930s Paris, *Cahiers d'art*,
had been founded by Christian Zervos in 1926, as vehicle for the promotion of an
eclectic range of art from all periods, but with a particular focus on the art of its
time. One of its trademarks came to be its inclusion of a large number of good-

quality reproductions, in particular in the generous form of one painting or sculpture per page. *Cahiers d'art* embraced especially art works from non-western cultures, initially from Africa and Oceania, in keeping with the interests of its editor: Zervos published a lavishly illustrated article devoted to 'L'art nègre' in 1927.[18] It functioned in this respect as a champion of non-classical cultures, including in the same 1927 issue Salles' justification for the inclusion of African sculpture in the Louvre.[19] The periodical also drew upon professional anthropologists and prehistorians: Frobenius contributed a series of articles on South African rock art in 1929 and 1930, complemented by the work of Henri Breuil, the eminent palaeontologist.[20]

Cahiers d'art's anti-classical tendencies were directly linked, in several of its articles, to the artistic production of its time. The connection between what modern artists were doing and new ways of interpreting the development of art through history was already a well-established art critical trope by the late 1920s. This connection was often expressed rhetorically rather than analysed in detail, as in Marius de Zayas's 1916 book *African Negro Art: Its Influence on Modern Art*. One of its initial formulations was in Worringer's 1910 foreword to the reprint of *Abstraction and Empathy* (1908). Worringer's thesis of artistic volition resulting in abstraction rather than mimetic beauty, which used non-classical art as its basis, was, he felt, vindicated by current artistic developments: 'The most recent movement in art has shown my problem to have gained an immediate topicality, not only for art historians, whose concern is with the evaluation of the past, but also for practising artists striving after new goals of expression.'[21] Within the pages of *Cahiers d'art*, however, this notion of artistic topicality was taken as far as to proclaim the equal participation of artists and scholars in exploring non-classical cultures. Salles, for instance, in his defence of African and Oceanic art, expressed this wish: 'Let's hope that our Trocadéro museum, which will soon wake up to a new life, will be the seat of a happy collaboration between artists and scientists'.[22] The German scholar Hans Mühlestein, a frequent contributor to *Cahiers d'art* in 1929 and 1930, and author of a well-publicised book on Etruscan art, went further to claim that only an artistic mind could fully come to terms with the energy and spontaneity of art forms outside the classical tradition.[23]

Documents certainly shared *Cahiers d'art*'s interest in non-western and archaic cultures, but it took this much further, actively challenging academic conventions. It shared some of the same authors as points of reference, particularly German writers like Frobenius and Eckart von Sydow. Georges Pudelko, for example, wrote a glowing review of Mühlestein's study of Etruscan art for *Documents* in 1930.[24] However, where *Cahiers d'art* saw a future in the input of artists for the development of art historical approaches, *Documents* adopted a much more complex stance. *Cahiers d'art*'s subtitle advertised its breadth of coverage of the arts: 'Painting – sculpture – architecture – music'. The subtitles of *Documents*, however, promised not a breadth of artistic media, but a combination of disciplinary areas: 'Doctrines – Archaeology – Fine Arts – Ethnography', soon amended to Archaeology – Fine

Arts – Ethnography – Miscellanies'.[25] Rather than pointing to a happy expansion of a field of enquiry, the combination of disciplines in *Documents*' subtitle openly risked friction and incompatibility.

A commitment to non-classical cultures was proclaimed in *Documents* from the outset. It was certainly implicit in the plans for the journal drawn up by one of its significant founding collaborators, Carl Einstein, and in his letters to potential contributors, as Conor Joyce has shown.[26] In a letter of January 1929 to Richard Hamann at the University of Marburg, published by Joyce, Einstein suggested the kinds of material the journal was seeking:

> We're going to put together essays from the most diverse research areas, beginning with prehistory, Mediterranean art, the early Middle Ages, up to Asia Minor, Egypt, Arabia, China and Japan; that means things from all countries and all times.[27]

To make such a claim in the late 1920s inevitably implied a shift away from the dominance of the classical canon. Ethnography and archaeology could play a role in bringing into focus material evidence that could challenge the authority of text-based classical history. In Leiris's recollection of *Documents*' desire to examine the 'most irritating works of art', cited above, archaeology provided the model for the kind of rigorous study now needed.[28] *Documents* probably took as one of the examples of this approach the journal *Aréthuse*, whose articles were often premised on obscure and recent archaeological findings, and to which Bataille contributed several articles and reviews. Excavations frequently provided the rationale for *Documents*' contents: a Viking tomb found in Norway in 1904, Greco-Celtic vases found in the Lorraine in 1928, bronze objects found north of Baghdad (figure 7).[29] The prehistoric discoveries that Rivière had alluded to in his 'Archéologismes' also played a role in *Documents* in the presentation of new rock art: Henri Martin described new finds in the Roc valley in 1927 and 1928.[30]

Documents' first issue opened with an article on Sumerian sculpture by Georges Contenau, a curator at the Louvre who had previously published studies of Phoenician and ancient Asian culture.[31] Sumeria was still a hot topic from an archaeological point of view in the late 1920s, the object of numerous international excavations after the initial finds of the French consular agent Ernest de Sarzec in the late 1870s. Sumerian sculpture was also just beginning to be taken up by European artists like Giacometti (using the Louvre's collection) and Henry Moore in Britain, as a new formal and intellectual source of inspiration.[32] A series of authors whose other published work treated more obviously classical and canonical material also contributed studies to *Documents* of pre-classical or non-western works of art. These included classical historians like Valentin Mueller, Charles Theodore Seltman, and Paul Jacobsthal, writing respectively on archaic Greek statuary, Cycladic art, and the prehistoric sculptures of the village of Roquepertuse, in Southern France.[33] Jacobsthal wrote of the recently discovered archaic heads of Roquepertuse: 'that mortuary gravity, that lethargic immobility

which recalls rather the primitive Roman style, is far from any classical art of what-
ever period'.[34] René Grousset, assistant curator at the Musée Guimet and author of
broad-based studies of Asian culture, like his four-volume *Les Civilisations de
l'Orient* and widely read *Sur les traces du Bouddh*a, both of 1929, contributed an
article on just one of the regions in which he specialised: Kafiristan in
Afghanistan.[35] The Kafir statuary he discussed also happened to be obscure in
origin and iconography, as one of the less familiar areas of his scholarly interest, still

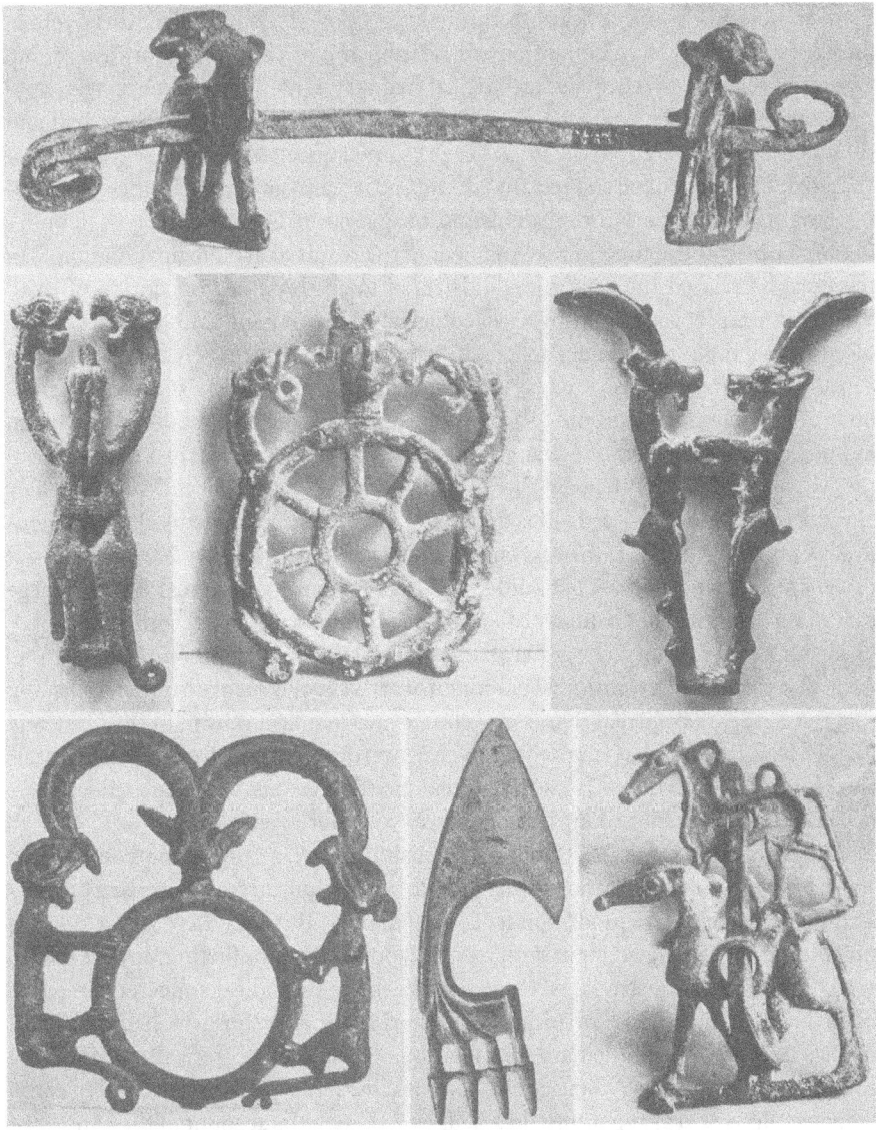

7 Bronze objects from Louristan (Iraq), collections David-Weill, Nazareaga, Pierre, in *Documents*, 2:6 (1930).

under research through the expeditions of his colleague Joseph Hackin, an acquaintance of Rivière since 1923. Hackin's finds in Afghanistan had also served as the basis for one of Bataille's articles for *Aréthuse* on Sassanian numismatics.[36] Significantly, Hackin, Grousset and Contenau, along with Salles, Rivière's mentor, all taught courses at the Ecole du Louvre in the mid- to late 1920s and early 1930s, which might be seen as one of *Documents'* institutional affiliations in its antagonism towards the Sorbonne.[37]

Archaeological and ethnographic information was drawn upon in articles by these writers in diverging ways to throw light upon the unfamiliar works repro- duced, especially with reference to their relationship to a classical figurative canon. Contenau referred to recent archaeological evidence to identify a Sumerian figure in the Louvre as female, comparing the position of its cloak, with the right arm and shoulder left uncovered, to the dress of a presumed queen found in an excavation of 1927–28.[38] He went on to suggest that the figurative conventions of Sumerian sculp- ture might have their origins in a deliberate exaggeration of the 'ethnic type' familiar to the sculptor at the time, rather than being the result of artistic imagination.[39] In this way, he related the sculptures illustrated to an imputed conception of 'real' Sumerian people, supported by archaeological finds. In contrast, Grousset, in his discussion of the extraordinary articulations of the human form in Kafir wood sculp- tures, linked these to previous artistic conventions, such as the stylised physiog- nomies on ancient Iranian coins.[40] One of the most striking of these, a seated woman in wood captioned in *Documents* as an 'ancestral statue', had in fact just been given to the Musée Guimet in 1929 by the Afghan King Amânoullâh, and so was a new 'arrival' to Paris and the West. This figure's head droops down over its chest and pen- dulous breasts, while face, hands, knees and feet are decorated with frontal incised designs. Lacking a neck, its shoulders sit higher than its face, just below a large carved turban, in what Grousset called a 'very curious anatomical conformation'.[41] Grousset's conclusions, echoing Worringer's famous conclusions in *Abstraction and Empathy*, turned the evolutionist paradigm of art's development on its head, arguing that these works implied a 'regressive' shift away from naturalism, in the same way that African art could be regarded as an (abstract) development from (more natural- istic) Egyptian precedents. It was no coincidence that Grousset also related Kafir art to Oceanic art, with its striking lack of naturalistic references.

To some degree, these differences in position were a familiar outcome of the study of non-western material in this period, whose figurative unfamiliarity gener- ated new interpretative models in its commentators. But they were also a key fea- ture of *Documents'* engagement with new, and potentially conflicting, approaches to art works, objects and artefacts. Contributors to the periodical appeared almost to be attuned to the desire to pick out 'irritating' objects for which disciplinary models provided no immediate illumination. Louis Clarke from the Cambridge Ethnographic Museum focused on pieces from the Solomon Islands whose ethnography was still apparently in a fledgling state.[42] His account of the context of these works rather sensationally stressed the extreme 'otherness' of the Solomon

Islands: 'They are inhabited by one of the most primitive races yet encountered. Not long ago, this race was still in the stone age and did not know any kinds of metal. Cannibalism is still practised there, except in places where a local police force is taking steps to prevent it.'[43] Eckart von Sydow, the eminent German specialist on West African art, in an article on the Janus masks of the Crossriver region on the Cameroon/Nigeria borders, also appeared to have deliberately singled out works whose historical evolution and meanings were unclear.[44] What ethnographic information did exist was limited, according to the author. For example, von Sydow drew upon documentary materials in Berlin's Ethnographic Museum to suggest that these double-faced masks represented a male–female opposition, reflected in a contrast between dark and light-coloured surfaces.[45] However, he was quick to point out the difficulties in applying this theory to all Janus masks. He also reproduced in his illustrations striking examples from German museums that directly eluded any available explanation. A mask from the Hamburg Museum für Völkerkunde, showing a male horned head surmounted by a bare-breasted female figure was included precisely because of its unusual appearance. This exceptional piece was clearly of more significance to the author than any *typical* piece, as he made clear: 'This mask deserves a particular interest as much because of its size as because of its construction ... Through the freedom of its conception, this work is classed among the most curious of African art objects.'[46]

Precious discoveries and private collections

Notions of uniqueness and 'curiosity' had a long history of association in the reception of non-western objects with discourses of novelty and commerce. *Documents* has been seen as operating in opposition to systems of 'exchange-value', in Denis Hollier's preface to the Jean-Michel Place re-edition of 1991, 'The Use-Value of the Impossible'.[47] However, the periodical was not at all immune to the forces of the art market: indeed, these were one source of its energising tensions. Connotations of preciousness and financial value were implicit in some of the 'discoveries' *Documents* presented: 'A Macedonian Eldorado 500 years B.C.', 'The treasure of Nagy-Szent-Miklosz'.[48] The diverse range of works from ancient and non-western cultures shown and discussed in *Documents* came both from European museums and from private collections. For museums this was surely a chance to air certain pieces (often recently accessioned), while for writers it was an opportunity to pick out and reinterpret works subsumed into much larger collections, such as the Bibliothèque Nationale manuscripts discussed by Bataille and Leiris. In the case of private collections, the reproduction of newly acquired pieces by periodicals like *Cahiers d'art* or *Documents* could have a direct impact upon market value, and indeed often preceded the sale of those pieces. In some cases, private collections could provide more interesting material for scholarly debate than the corresponding museums, and this was reflected in some of the articles for *Documents*. The prolific and eminent Paul Pelliot, who had led an expedition to Central Asia in the 1910s, used David David-Weill's collection of pre-Han North Chinese bronze open-work reliefs to set out the arguments around the relative influence of Siberian on ancient Chinese art.[49] These objects lent themselves so perfectly to his discussion because of their unusual appearance and as yet mysterious functions, making them unlike other North Chinese works in museum collections (in this case, the Hermitage).[50]

Non-western material in Paris was especially likely to be found in private collections, given the state of museum collections (primarily the Trocadéro) in the 1920s. An exhibition of 1930 at the Galerie Pigalle brought together several pieces from Africa and Oceania in Parisian private collections, and was used by Einstein in *Documents* that year as the basis for a discussion of the iconography and functions of African art.[51] This exhibition became in fact an important focus for debates about the status of non-western material and its institutional representation in Paris in the period. An announcement for it in *Cahiers d'art* took the opportunity to make a sideswipe at the Trocadéro, claiming that its poor collection and inability to contribute fully to such a show was due to the museum's misplaced administrative concerns.[52] A review by Albert Sautier for the journal *Formes* emphasised the success of the exhibition in bringing out the 'artistic' value of its exhibits.[53] One of the pieces that Sautier singled out for special notice was the Trocadéro's Solomon Islands shield ('a curious buckler decorated in red, black and ochre').[54] The same object had been used in a different way by Rivière in *Documents* to accompany his article on the museum's ongoing renovation, where he explicitly looked to distance the Trocadéro's aims from the 'purely aesthetic' rationale of other Parisian museums.[55]

The interplay between *Documents* and *Cahiers d'art* and the dynamics of the art market in 1930 came to the fore in their coverage of this show. The Galerie Pigalle exhibition of African and Oceanic objects underwent a strikingly aestheticised treatment in *Cahiers d'art*, in an article by Stéphen Chauvet on objects made from bronze, gold and ivory.[56] The journal's editors conceived this article as a kind of supplementary 'guide' to some of the less familiar and less documented pieces in the Galerie Pigalle show.[57] While Chauvet's text provided information about the uses and motifs of gold weights and ivory masks, its illustrations comprised a sequence of spreads of small, intricately worked objects, laid out in ordered rows across the page, creating a jewel-box effect (figure 8). These carefully composed reproductions, combined with Chauvet's discussion of the qualities of different colours and depths of patination, served to load this article with an implicit statement of the high financial value of these particular pieces. The private collectors to whom they belonged were being construed as *pioneers*, seeing in these small bronze ornaments and ivory figurines what others could not see, but also as smart *investors*, amassing the rare and the precious. Naturally some of the works reproduced belonged to the article's author himself. A red ivory Warega mask from the Belgian Congo, owned by Georges de Miré, would raise 17,300 francs in the 1931 sale of his collection of African and Precolumbian sculptures, its second most valuable object.[58]

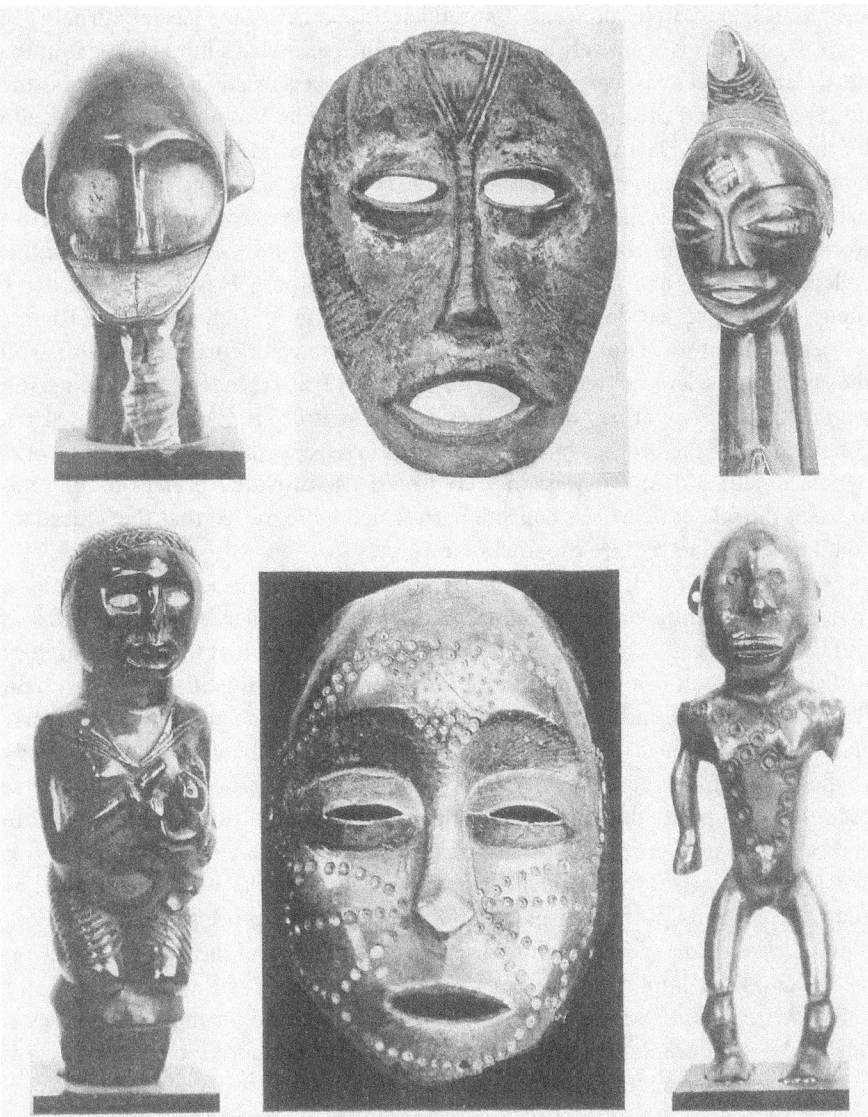

8 Masks and figurines, Tanganyika, Belgian Congo and Angola, patinated ivory and patinated red ivory, collections of Heim, Stora, de Miré, in *Cahiers d'art*, 5:1 (1930).

The plates to Einstein's article for *Documents* included three works from de Miré's collection, one of which, a Dogon hermaphrodite sculpture, went on to sell for 14,000 francs in 1931.[59] Clearly the reproduction and discussion of such works could bolster their market value, and *Documents* was no exception to this. The tension between the promotion of financial worth and disinterested analysis was unresolved in its pages, which included advertisements for dealers in antiquities, such as Edgar Worch, alongside its publicity for other avant-garde journals. To some degree this was entirely expected, given the periodical's initial instigator, the dealer and collector Georges Wildenstein, who specialised in old masters, the most valuable and prestigious end of the market.[60] The Viscount de Noailles and David and Pierre David-Weill, supporters of the art of their time, played important roles in the background of *Documents*, as well as being the most significant private backers of the Trocadéro museum.[61] Leiris first encountered Giacometti's work at the home of the de Noailles, and reproduced the *Gazing Head* from his collection in his 1929 *Documents* article on the sculptor. Privately in his diary, though, he expressed doubts about his association with such a milieu.[62] Rivière was a significant mediator between the world of the wealthy private collectors and the scholarly, 'scientific' realms of *Documents* and the Trocadéro, and the person who more than any other would represent this tension. Rivière orchestrated the commission by the brother of his former employer, Pierre David-Weill, of works by Giacometti and André Masson.[63] He would also provide a preface to the catalogue of the sale of de Miré's collection, in which he regretted that the Trocadéro could not afford to acquire the works for sale.[64]

Within this context, Einstein's article based on the Galerie Pigalle exhibition took up a deliberate stance. Although illustrated with visually powerful African and Oceanic pieces, his article avoided any direct discussion of them. He was keen to distance himself from any consideration of their artistic qualities: 'we must treat this art historically, and no longer only consider it from the point of view of taste and aesthetics'.[65] Instead, Einstein recommended the study of African mythology as the key to understanding African objects, putting together a series of diverse examples to support this, in which sculptures, masks and furniture all served to embody primarily attitudes towards sex and death. The contrast between this article for *Documents* and Einstein's 1915 study *Negerplastik* was considerable: by 1930, the question of the formal qualities of African sculpture seemed irrelevant. Nevertheless his article still maintained a link to the realm of the 'star' Parisian collectors and their implicit antiquarian values, figures such as Ratton, Pierre Loeb and de Miré, as did *Documents* as a whole. To move beyond the non-western 'jewel box' to the ethnographic 'box of tricks' would require yet more extreme readings of material culture in all its forms.[66]

Marcel Mauss, one of the tutelary spirits of *Documents*, and minor contributor to its special issue devoted to Picasso's work, had provided a discussion of the significance of 'precious' circulating objects in his 1923–24 *Essai sur le don* (*The Gift*).[67] In the Trobriand *kula* and Northwest Coast American *potlatch*, a distinction was made, in Mauss's analysis, between more ordinary objects of consumption and 'precious things belonging to the family' that possessed 'productive power' as part of ceremonies of exchange.[68] The importance of these special things was attributable to their investment with *mana*, a sacred transferable force that required also that they were used with reverence. Mauss noted this among the Kwakiutl thus:

The dishes and spoons used solemnly for eating, and decorated, carved, and emblazoned with the clan's totem or the totem of rank, are animate things … things are mixed up with spirits, their originators, and eating instruments with food.[69]

'Preciousness' was determined by wider systems of social interaction, Mauss's 'total social phenomena'. But while his study of gift exchange focused on specific non-western artefacts – Haïda and Tlingit emblazoned copper objects and Trobriand shell bracelets and necklaces – the implications of Mauss's discussion of the forces embodied by these pointed beyond discrete individual things. In his lectures at the Ethnological Institute in the late 1920s, attended by Griaule and Bataille, he was already stressing the importance of the study of bodily techniques and technology as the determining context for the social life of objects.[70] Much more 'humble' artefacts would find as central a significance here as the most 'precious' collectable or exchangeable things. Ethnographic thinking in *Documents* would reflect Mauss's thinking, as well as finding reinforcement in a more unexpected art historical source.

Ethnography, technology and the 'invisible object'

Documents' presentation of collectable *things* – such as Neolithic Japanese figurines, Greco-Celtic vases, Peruvian pottery, Macedonian coins and German evangelaries – was undermined in fact in its very first issue. Josef Strzygowski, professor in art history at the University of Vienna, condemned the close links between art-historical research and museum collections, as well as those between private collectors and periodicals.[71] Of course these were precisely the connections that on some level the journal cultivated, due to the personal networks described above. Strzygowski's antagonism was the result of a distinction that he made between art history and what he termed 'research into the plastic arts'. The former had been and continued to be excessively concerned with extant monuments and objects, while new approaches of the latter could look to impermanent and now lost works of art from less familiar parts of the world. Examples of such neglected materials included nomadic art, architecture in unfired brick and wood, or wooden ornamentation, things which had not necessarily been conserved for posterity to enter the loaded realms of the museum or art market.[72] Strzygowski argued for the decline of scholarly methods obsessed with dates and with juxtaposing cycles of artistic development, to be replaced with independent research into *types* of work rather than isolated monuments.[73]

Strzygowski's position came out of his training as a medievalist: in part he related his distaste for 'art history' to the nineteenth-century destruction of Romanesque churches and monuments in line with then prevailing aesthetic values.[74] It also had a distinct agenda, in challenging the centrality of Rome and Byzantium within accounts of art's development in Europe, an argument that Strzygowski had first established in his major 1901 study *Orient oder Rom?*. The book that he published in Britain in 1928, *Early Church Art in Northern Europe, with special reference to timber construction and decoration*, had proposed a revision of accepted versions of the origins of medieval European art based on his analysis of wooden architecture in Eastern Europe, Scandinavia and England.[75] This ran directly counter to the theories of Focillon concerning the 'Occidental' origins of Romanesque art, and indeed Strzygowski made a dig at the 'Sorbonnard opinions' he perceived as dominating art history in his article for *Documents*.[76] The periodical held a deliberate bias against 'Occidental' values, perhaps resonant with Leiris's notorious outburst at the Saint Pol-Roux banquet, 'Vive l'Allemagne!'. Heinrich Ehl's article 'L'heure de naissance de l'art européen occidental' deliberately raised the conflicting theories of European art's 'Latin' or 'Germanic' origins, which, he argued, could only be seen as mutually interactive.[77] However, his reproduced examples, manuscripts from collections in Munich, Cologne, and including the eleventh-century Prum lectionary from the Rylands Library in Manchester, clearly asserted the neglected significance of these Franco-Saxon and 'Germanic' sources in the development of Christian art. He cited Flaubert as having conceded that 'the best of the French spirit had always been "Germanic"'.[78] *Documents* also carried an account of an Essen gold-working workshop of the tenth century, and a presentation by the Dutch scholar F. Adama van Scheltema of the royal treasure found at Oseberg in Norway in 1904.[79]

Strzygowski's participation in *Documents* was significant. His subsequent support for the National Socialist regime meant a negative posthumous reputation (he died in 1941); nevertheless, Strzygowski's legacy can still be felt in current art-historical approaches, as both Suzanne Marchand and Jas Elsner have pointed out.[80] Against the dominance of the text in classical history, Strzygowski opposed the concrete evidence of the material artefact. Related to his interest in previously little-known or supposedly 'primitive' cultures, and his own vast specialised knowledge of artefacts, Strzygowski's emphasis on objects for which no textual explanation existed could challenge traditional historiography. The art historian, he contended, should adopt methods corresponding to the particular needs of the objects under study, and as the visual arts, for him, predated forms of writing, the art historian could delve much further back into cultural history.[81] In *Documents*, then, he argued stridently for the importance of once-extant artefacts, available now neither through texts nor through extensive material remains, but recoverable by archaeological and ethnographic methods.

Strzygowski, in his concern with object-types, did find a methodological ally in Paul Rivet's advocacy of comparative ethnography in issue three of *Documents*. Rivet's article 'The study of material civilisations: ethnography, archaeology, prehistory', proposed a unification of these three disciplinary areas.[82] The Trocadéro's director argued for an ethnographic method that would treat civilisations as interrelated wholes, an implicitly functionalist approach deriving broadly from the work of Durkheim (Rivet mentioned sociology as a potential model).[83] His methodology, however, was mixed, attempting to reconcile evolutionism and the

Kulturkreisen of ethnologists like Frobenius, while praising the diffusionism of Nordenskiöld.[84] Within this melting pot of methods, perhaps symptomatic of *Documents*' overall confrontation of approaches, several key points emerged. Rivet posited the significance of the typical and the average as better indicators of a civilisation's make-up than the exceptional and the rare. He praised the 'exhaustive digs' of prehistorians and criticised the tendencies of previous archaeologists and ethnographers: 'It only takes a quick look at museums to confirm that their collections are too often made up of choice objects, remarkable either for their rarity, or for their artistic or careful workmanship.'[85] Rivet contended, in an unintentionally comical example, that a map of distribution of the nose flute that included Paris because a blind busker happened to be playing one in the street there would be inexact ethnographically.[86] By implication, the unusual, the unexpected and the 'curiosity' were to be excluded from 'serious' analysis. The qualities precisely that might attract an artist or collector to a piece of ethnographic material, and that additionally motivated the selection of certain objects for reproduction in *Documents*, were firmly rejected.

The ethnographic principles proposed by Rivet were not only at odds with the intriguing and 'irritating' objects with their clear market value, but also with the interests of Bataille in the 'monstrous'. For Hollier, this tension corresponded to a fault-line within the journal that is most prominent in relation to the concept of 'use'.[87] 'Use-value' in his terms relates to 'documents' which are only consumable 'on the spot', without the possibility of being collected, and his key example of this is Bataille's shoe-fetishist: 'I defy any lover of painting to love a canvas as much as a fetishist loves a shoe'.[88] The shoe-fetishist contradicted the ethnographic concept of use, as the shoe was being diverted from its 'normal', 'everyday' use, i.e. walking. In relation to Marx's analysis of the commodity, 'use-value' has been defined as 'an intrinsic property of a thing desired or discovered by society at different stages in its historical evolution'.[89] Following Hollier's logic, in Bataille's challenge to commodification within *Documents*, 'value' was removed by 'use', as this moment of desire or discovery could happen only once. Where Bataille did discuss artefacts centrally implicated in both 'use' and 'exchange', like the Gallic coins in his article 'The Academic Horse', he focused not on their social function, as he had done in similar studies for *Aréthuse*, but on the 'irrational' qualities of their figurative markings.[90] The appeal to him of the 'phantasms' of 'savages' was not without ambivalence within the 'humanist' framework of the discipline of ethnography: Bataille's position at times echoed the rhetoric of writers like Basler who also liked to stress the 'monstrous' and 'grotesque' aspects of non-western cultures.[91]

Bataille's position in relation to the ethnographic approaches presented by *Documents* was certainly complex, particularly as it is tempting to interpret his writings there in the light of his later 'anthropological' theories of general economy. Bataille would read the system of gift exchange analysed by Mauss in the mid-1920s, for example, as 'a deliriously formed ritual poker'.[92] Bataille certainly had a strong interest in ethnology in the 1920s, largely through his friendship with

Alfred Métraux, even if his uses of it were often deliberately perverse.[93] His *Documents* review of G.-H. Luquet's 1930 study *L'Art primitif* re-interpreted Luquet's concept of 'intellectual realism' as a kind of destructive and debasing scribbling.[94] Bataille did note, though, the fact that Luquet had not attempted to apply his theory to three-dimensional forms, arguing that 'alteration' might also be a feature of sculpted Aurignacian figures such as the Lespugue Venus (a significant focus for competing archaeological theories in this period), or children's toys.[95] One of the studies that Luquet himself had drawn upon, Henry Balfour's *Evolution of Decorative Art*, had devoted a section to the discussion of the emergence of sculpture, where its author, like Luquet, had argued for the role of accident in the rise of figurative forms and marks.[96] Balfour's examples of objects whose accidental resemblance to animals or human figures had led them to be selected, venerated and further transformed, included stone charms, mandrake roots, Eskimo arrow-straighteners and knobbed clubs. The three-dimensional object, for Balfour, was more primal, closer to the roots of all art-making than the more 'advanced' graphic image could be, and the basic implement or tool preceded the art work, as a more fundamental need.[97] Bataille, notably, did not include such functional objects in his interpretation of prehistoric art.[98]

The ethnographic presentation of objects and their functions in *Documents* was, however, not as straightforward as Bataille's apparent aversion to them suggested. In an article on musical instruments from the Trocadéro's ethnographic collections, the musicologist André Schaeffner drew the reader's attention to their variety and range.[99] While a guitar or violin would easily fall within recognised western categories, the ethnographer, argued Schaeffner, must also study the most humble wooden box used to produce sound. He did, however, draw particular attention to a few objects whose status as collectibles was already assured and whose meanings were enigmatic, including a Mangbetu anthropomorphic harp. Recent work on these objects has pointed out that they were in fact never integral to the Mangbetu musical repertoire and were produced primarily for the tourist market, which may have accounted for their ethnographic 'impenetrability' in the late 1920s.[100] Mangbetu harps were well known to artists and collectors in the 1910s and 1920s: Georges Braque had one in his studio, and Schaffner referred in a footnote to a famous example owned by Jos Hessel and reproduced in *Cahiers d'art* in 1927.[101] Schaeffner admitted the *exceptional*, rather than typical, nature of these harps, which often had anatomically detailed sexual organs and soundboards, covered in 'human' skin, attributing to the mysterious origin and function of these instruments a certain 'troubled psychology'.[102] At the same time as dealing with increasingly prized objects like this, Schaeffner was also concerned with the least conservable of musical instruments: an Abyssinian 'earth drum' consisting of two holes in the ground of differing heights. This instrument could only be captured photographically, and indeed was virtually illegible in the dark photograph by Griaule published alongside the article, where only the position of the player's hands and arms gave any indication of its existence.[103]

The dissolution of the clearly delimited ethnographic or archaeological artefact which Strzygowski's polemic had pointed to found an alternative formulation in *Documents* in discussions of technology and bodily techniques. Schaeffner's 'earth drum' was constituted as much through a technique of the body (and the context of a performance) as through the physical configuration of the ground. The ethnographer Erland Nordenskiöld, a specialist of South America, in his article on scales and balancing poles used to weigh different loads, provided a similar example: 'A primitive "scales" that we all make use of is formed by our hands when we compare the weight of two objects by placing one in the left hand and the other in the right hand.'[104] Nordenskiöld claimed that his wife had seen 'Indian' children weigh out sugar in this way on several occasions.[105] The elaborate deco-rated Peruvian scales he reproduced, from the collection of the Gothenburg museum, had their intangible counterpart in a practice that could only be observed at the moment of its execution. They were accompanied by a drawing of a much more 'humble' balance made of a wooden stick (figure 9). The collection and preservation of artefacts could lead to a neglect of their crucial contingent qualities, as Griaule argued in a dictionary definition of 'Pottery':

9 Peruvian pan scales, Gothenburg Museum, Seri Indian balancing pole and 'Indian' carrying a balancing pole, in *Documents*, 1: 4 (1929).

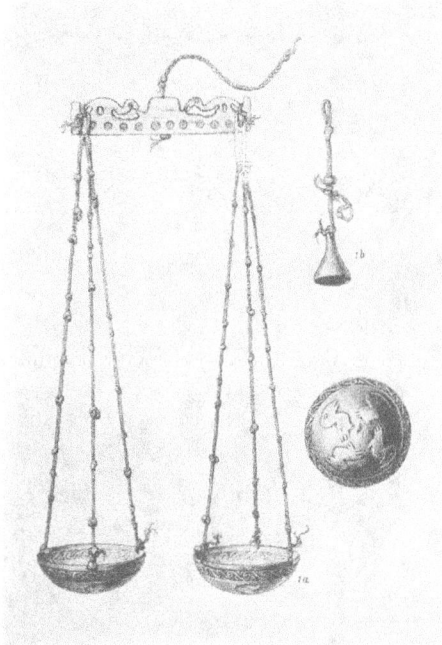

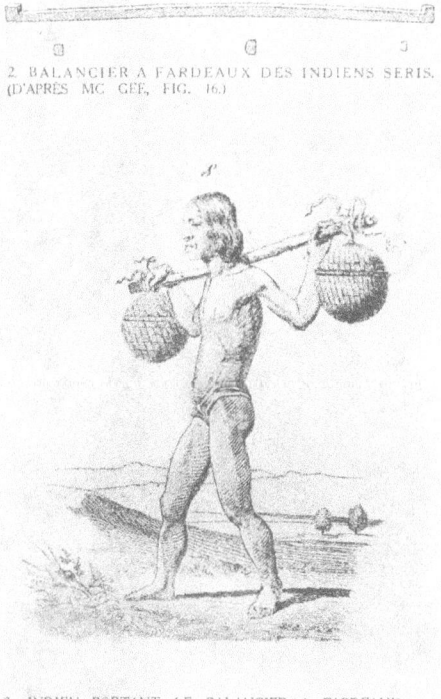

2. BALANCIER A FARDEAUX DES INDIENS SERIS. (D'APRÈS MC GEE, FIG. 16.)

1. BALANCE A PLATEAUX TROUVÉE SUR LA COTE DU PÉROU. MUSÉE DE GÖTEBORG. 25-11-8.

3. INDIEN PORTANT LE BALANCIER A FARDEAUX. (D'APRÈS OVIEDO, T. I. LAM. 2. FIG. 8.)

The archaeologists and aesthetes are interested in the container and not in the contents, in the rural scenes and the animals on the surround, and not in the milk pouring directly from the udder; in the colour of the clay and not in the smell that it could give to this milk ... We will admire the form of a handle, but be wary of studying the position of the man who drinks[106]

Griaule's short article pointed to the clay pot as simply the residue of something else, something more compelling with which it was intimately linked in a ritual of function. The apparently humble object could be impregnated with smell, touch and sound, the direct experience of which the ethnographer would hunt down.

The classification of such technological manifestations as the 'earth drum' or the 'hand scales' clearly relied to some extent on the ethnographer's perspective, as the observer and recorder of a moment of 'authentic' experience. In one of the most radical ethnographic articles for *Documents*, Griaule hinted at the problems of the

10 Detail of Baoule drum, Ivory Coast, wood, 198h x 48d, Trocadéro Ethnographic Museum, Paris, in *Documents*, 2: 1 (1930).

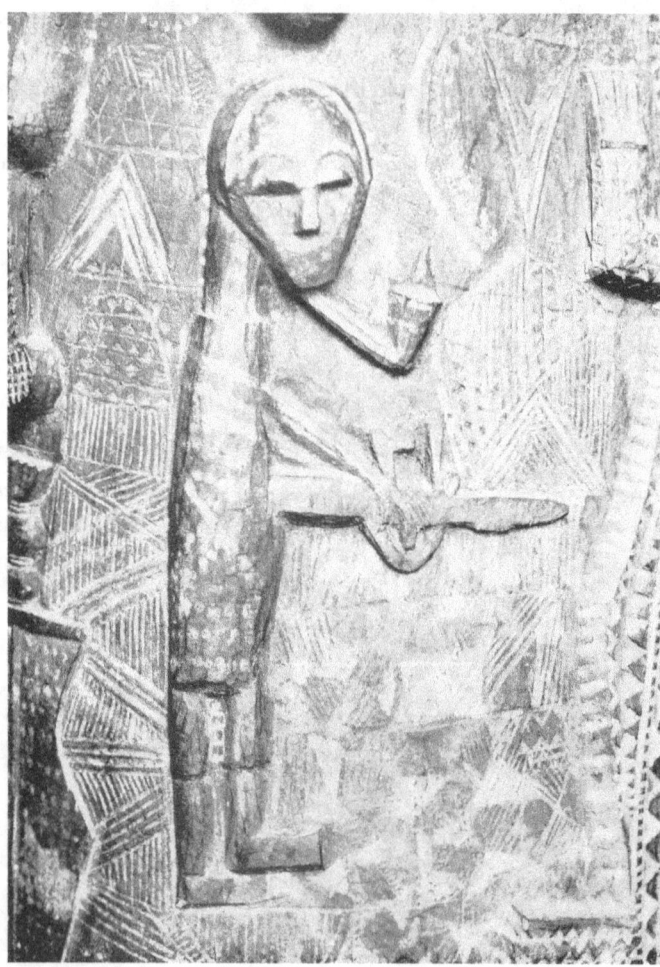

ethnographer's vision, and tackled explicitly the notion of the cultural 'purity' of the objects of scientific enquiry.[107] In an analysis of a Baoule drum from the Ivory Coast, a prime piece in the Trocadéro's collection, Griaule picked out a detail of a man holding a rifle, which he claimed had been seen to devalue the drum (figure 10). He scathingly mocked the viewpoint of those who, he argued, did not realise that the 'primitive' public was interested in sixteen-litre petrol cans, cheap alcohol and good-quality weapons. Griaule gave examples of the transformation of western industrial products in Africa: spears sold on Djibouti market made from stolen sleepers from the Franco-Ethiopian railway, and roof finials decorated with fragments of Chianti bottles thrown from passing trains. Griaule's article deliberately challenged the myth of a 'pure' non-western 'art' free from the messy concerns of colonial contact, particularly those involving trade transactions. His examples were chosen to critique the values of antiquarianism, to which ethnography could be opposed, but they could also be interpreted in two different ways: as instances of the absurdity of revering the everyday and the throwaway as 'art', or as ingenious re-uses and trans-formations of insignificant things. This ambivalence was a central difficulty in ethnography's approach to 'rubbish' and the 'humble' object, as we will see in Chapter 3.

While Griaule's agenda was to expose the hypocrisies of western aesthetic atti-tudes, his article did also suggest the lability of the ethnographic discipline, as an approach whose methods might embrace contradictory positions, in taking up both the 'typical' and the extraordinary. Ethnography could go, Griaule claimed, 'as far as to think that the abuse of oak in the rooms of the Sorbonne is the sign of special conceptions of the aesthetic of wood'.[108] His example was obviously barbed, and tallied with *Documents*' general hostility towards the Sorbonne, but nevertheless suggested the fascination of culturally-loaded objects, whose interest might lie in the fact that they were commonplace and hitherto overlooked. In fact, Griaule's example might evoke the surrealist 'discovery' of the apparently banal, where something without obvious aesthetic qualities could become highly significant through its selection by the writer or artist. Ethnography, Griaule argued, was not only suspicious of the beautiful, as something rare and 'monstrous' within a civili-sation, but it was also suspicious of itself as a 'white science', 'tainted with preju-dices'. His own approach might undermine itself, in Griaule's warning gunshot across the bows of his own discipline.

Documents' approach to material artefacts provided some models for the Dakar–Djibouti expedition that would set off in May 1931, a few months after the periodical's last issue appeared. The treatment of individual pieces of material as evidence, as 'documents', was a clear fundamental message, as was the emphasis on humble and overlooked objects and their ritual and technological contexts. But the subsequent interpretation of these was left open to question. *Documents* encour-aged new and provocative readings, but it also produced maverick readings. Ethnographic and archaeological principles were brought to bear on ideas in for-mation, rather than fully established theories: indeed one of the exciting aspects of the periodical was precisely this sense of openness and experimentation. Writing in the 1960s, Leiris would comment that the 'impossible' mix of *Documents* had in part been due to its 'diversity of disciplines – and of indisciplines'.[109] This unruly side to the periodical came in part from the fact that many of its contributors published articles unlike their usual scholarly work, on more obscure subjects, or using more daring arguments. The combination of respected 'experts', curators from major national museums, and establishment figures with young ethnographers and art writers posed a challenge to any clear-cut 'professional' standing. Strzygowski, who himself has been described as a 'Grub Street' academic, pointed to this in the journal's first issue, when he claimed: 'an independent organ is indispensable so that those who belong to no school can express themselves'.[110]

The flouting of professional expertise was a feature too of the Dakar–Djibouti expedition, appointing Leiris as its secretary despite his lack of ethnographic training. The author of an autobiographical novel, *Aurora*, of dream accounts and a punning 'glossary' in *La Révolution surréaliste*, Leiris brought to *Documents* and the Dakar–Djibouti expedition a sense of reflexivity and a profound self-consciousness with regard to 'scientific' purpose.[111] The inspirational examples that Leiris referred to in the journal's pages in the build-up to the expedition were hardly models of new functionalist ethnographic practices, consisting amongst other things of Raymond Roussel's *Impressions d'Afrique* (itself generated by word play) and the explorer and voodoo initiate William Seabrook.[112] In his 1930 article 'The Eye of the Ethnographer', Leiris set out his apparently irreconcilable motivations for taking part, split between the 'public' good and his own 'private' needs. Such an expedition could serve to correct the 'deforming glasses' and 'white mentality' of the average European:

> A study trip undertaken according to ethnological disciplines … should contribute to the dissipation of a good few of these errors, and, therefore, to the collapse of many of their consequences, among others racial prejudice, an iniquity against which one can never protest too much. That is enough to give to the enterprise, as well as its scientific interest, great human import.[113]

At the same time, however, Leiris continued to view the expedition in the light of his own early obsessions with the exotic, like Roussel's play: 'As for me, who sees above all in the trip – besides the best method of acquiring a real knowledge, that is to say living knowledge – the fulfilment of certain childhood dreams'.[114]

Leiris's ambivalent presentation of the ethnographer's 'vision' already hinted, like Griaule's discussion of the Baoule drum, at the problems of ethnographic subjectivity and at the inability of escaping one's western mentality. For Leiris writing in *Documents* prior to the Dakar–Djibouti expedition, the anthropological project ought to inspire a radical questioning of the self, by emulating the hero of a Songhay parable cited in his article, who awoke to find his identity had been 'stolen' by a companion and could only cry in despair.[115] Any 'scientific' persona was inseparable from its less controlled and disciplined human counterpart, prey to impulses of fantasy, desire or anxiety. The ethnographic approach that the Dakar–Djibouti expedition would adopt towards materials collected, which had already begun to find formulation in *Documents*, would not only reflect the original contexts of their 'discovery', in their ritual and everyday uses. It would also begin to make manifest the inescapable role of the ethnographers themselves in bringing meanings to the things they selected, analysed, reproduced and displayed. Leiris's account of fieldwork experience, itself a product of his own 'impossible mix' of ethnographic 'discipline' and poetic 'indiscipline', would anticipate later processes of anthropological self-critique by creating a model for encountering objects in which the ethnographer–collector was both physically and subjectively implicated.

Notes

1 Rivière, 'Archéologismes', *Cahiers d'art*, 1:7 (1926), p. 177.

2 See the special issue of *Modernism/Modernity*, 'Archaeologies of the Modern' (ed. Jeffrey Schnapp, Michael Shanks and Matthew Tiews), 11:1 (2004), pp. 7–8. A translation of Rivière's essay is included in this volume, p. 179.

3 *Ibid.*, p. 177.

4 For an overview of culture-historical archaeology, see Bruce Trigger, *A History of Archaeological Thought* [1989] (Cambridge: Cambridge University Press, 2000), pp. 148–206.

5 Rivière, 'Archéologismes', p. 177.

6 See Gorgus, *Der Zauberer der Vitrinen*, p. 32.

7 Rivière had first met Salles, who encouraged him to take up courses at the Ecole du Louvre, at the Sunday salon of his artist uncle Henri Rivière, *ibid.*, p. 9, p. 32. In 1927, Salles published his 'Réflexions sur l'art nègre' in *Cahiers d'art*, 2:7–8 (1927), pp. 247–58.

8 Vignier had been one of the first wave of collectors of African material in Paris, and several of his pieces were used as plates for Einstein's 1915 *Negerplastik*.

9 Clouzot and Level, 'L'Art indigène des colonies françaises et du Congo belge au Pavillon de Marsan en 1923', *L'Amour de l'art*, 5:1 (1924), p. 21.

10 'abruptement carpe et lapin bien plutôt qu'éclectique', Leiris, 'De Bataille l'impossible', p. 37.

11 *Ibid.*, p. 28.

12 See Thomas, 'Licensed Curiosity: Cook's Pacific Voyages', in Elsner and Cardinal (eds), *The Cultures of Collecting* (London: Reaktion, 1994), pp. 116–36, and in particular pp. 122–3.

13 Bataille, 'Informe', *Documents*, 1:7 (1929), p. 382.

14 See Didi-Huberman, *La Ressemblance informe* (Paris: Macula, 1995), McInnes, *Taboo and Transgression: The Subversive Aesthetics of Georges Bataille and* Documents (Ann Arbor: University of Michigan Press, 1994), and Teixera, *Georges Bataille: La Part de l'art* (Paris: L'Harmattan, 1997).

15 *Documents* was famously situated for the first time centrally within a surrealist context in Ades (ed.), *Dada and Surrealism Reviewed* (London: Arts Council, 1978).

16 *Aréthuse*, a 'three-monthly review of art and archaeology', was published by Jean Babelon and Pierre d'Espezel (one of the backers of *Documents* and an acquaintance of

Rivière), and its remit included 'Coins and Medals. Plaques. Seals. Engraved gem-stones. Archaeology. Minor Arts. Criticism.' *Ipek* was an 'Annual Review of Prehistorical and Ethnographical Art' whose collaborators included the Abbé Breuil, the Swedish ethnologist Erland Nordenskiöld (a contributor to *Documents*) and Paul Rivet.

17 *Beaux-Arts*, which had begun as a supplement to the *Gazette des beaux-arts* (also produced by Wildenstein between 1929 and 1939) called itself a 'chronicle of the arts and of curiosity' in 1929. Leiris was editing manager of both of these journals as well as *Documents* in 1930.

18 Zervos, 'L'art nègre', *Cahiers d'art*, 2:7–8 (1927), pp. 229–46.

19 Salles, 'Réflexions sur l'art nègre'.

20 Frobenius, 'L'art de la silhouette', *Cahiers d'art*, 4:8–9 (1929), pp. 397–400, 'Bêtes, hommes ou dieux?', *Cahiers d'art*, 4:10 (1929), pp. 443–4, and 'L'art africain', *Cahiers d'art*, 5:8–9 (1930), pp. 395–430. Henri Breuil, 'L'art oriental d'Espagne', *Cahiers d'art*, 5:3 (1930), pp. 136–8.

21 Worringer, *Abstraction and Empathy*, p. xiv.

22 Salles, 'Réflexions sur l'art nègre', p. 249.

23 Mühlestein, 'Histoire et esprit contemporain', *Cahiers d'art*, 4:8–9 (1929), pp. 377–81.

24 Pudelko, 'L'art étrusque', *Documents*, 2:4 (1930), p. 223. Pudelko referred erroneously to 'Mühlenstein'.

25 The revised subtitle came into force in issue 4 in September 1929. The inclusion of 'miscellanies' ('variétés') may have echoed *Cahiers d'art*'s own 'Feuilles volantes' section.

26 Joyce, *Carl Einstein* in Documents, see in particular appendix I, correspondence with Dr G. F. Reber, pp. 222–7.

27 *Ibid.*, p. 244.

28 Leiris, 'De Bataille l'impossible', p. 28.

29 Scheltema, 'La trouvaille d'Oseberg', *Documents*, 1:3 (1929), pp. 121–9, Babelon, 'Les vases de Bouzonville', *Documents*, 1:6 (1929), pp. 337–40, Bataille, 'Les Trouvailles de Louristan', *Documents*, 2:6 (1930), pp. 372–3.

30 Martin, 'L'art solutréen dans la vallée du Roc (Charente)', *Documents*, 1:6 (1929), pp. 303–9.

31 Contenau, 'L'art sumérien, les conventions de la statuaire', *Documents*, 1:1 (1929), pp. 1–8, *La Civilisation phenicienne* (Paris: Payot, 1926), and *L'Art de l'Asie occidentale ancienne* (Paris: G. van Ouest, 1928).

32 See Wood, 'Gods, graves and sculptors: Gudea, Sumerian sculpture and the avant-garde c.1930–1935', *Sculpture Journal*, 10 (2003), pp. 67–82.

33 Mueller, 'La sculpture grecque de l'Asie Mineure au Ve siècle avant J.-C.', *Documents*, 2:6 (1930), pp. 347–51. Mueller had previously published on Greek and Syrian art, and a recent book *Frühe Plastik in Griechenland und Vorderasien* (Augsburg, 1929). Seltman had published his study of Athens with Cambridge University Press in 1924, before his article 'Sculptures archaïques des Cyclades', *Documents*, 1:4 (1929), pp. 188–90. Jacobsthal, author of 'Les Têtes de Roquepertuse' for *Documents*, 2:2 (1930), pp. 92–4, had published on the motif of lightning in Greek art, and on Greek and German vase ornament.

34 *Ibid.*, p. 94.

35 Grousset, 'Un cas de régression vers les arts "barbares", la statuaire du Kafiristan', *Documents*, 2:2 (1930), pp. 73–8. Grousset's extensive publications also included *Histoire de la philosophie orientale* (1923), *Le Reveil de l'Asie* (1924), and the two-volume *Histoire de l'Extrême-Orient* (1929).

36 Bataille, 'Notes sur la numismatique des Koushans et des Koushan-shahs sassanides', *Aréthuse*, 5:1 (1928), pp. 19–35, and reprinted in *Oeuvres complètes*, Vol. 1 (Paris: Gallimard, 1970), pp. 122–43. The article responded to a gift of Sassanian material by Hackin to the Cabinet des Médailles.

37 See Therrien (ed.), *L'Histoire de l'art en France* (Paris: C.T.H.S., 1998), p. 488 and pp. 491–2 for lists of courses offered at the Ecole du Louvre by these figures, which included Salles on 'Les bronzes et les métaux: art chinois, art barbare, art musulman', Contenau on 'L'art archaïque de l'Elam et de Sumer' and Hackin and Grousset on 'L'art indien ancien'.

38 Contenau, 'L'art sumérien', p. 2.

39 *Ibid.*, p. 8.

40 Such as Bataille had discussed, see note 29, above.

41 Grousset, 'Un cas de régression', p. 74.

42 Clarke, 'L'art des Iles Salomon', *Documents*, 2:5 (1930), pp. 277–81.

43 *Ibid.*, p. 277.

44 Sydow, 'Masques-Janus du Cross-River (Cameroun)', *Documents*, 2:6 (1930), pp. 321–8.

45 *Ibid.*, p. 328.

46 *Ibid.*, p. 326.

47 Hollier, 'La valeur d'usage de l'impossible', *Documents* (1929–30) (Paris: Jean-Michel Place, 1991), pp. vii–xxxiv.

48 Babelon, 'Un Eldorado macédonien cinq cents ans avant Jésus-Christ', *Documents*, 1:2 (1929), pp. 65–74, and anon, 'Le trésor de Nagy-Szent-Miklosz', *Documents*, 1:6 (1929), pp. 320–3. The gold vases and cup excavated in Bulgaria and held in the collection of the Kunsthistorisches Museum in Vienna, also served *Documents'* anti-classical agenda, as the anonymous author claimed of their decorative motifs 'The subsisting Hellenistic elements are dominated, moreover, by the Asiatic elements', p. 320.

49 Pelliot, 'Quelques réflexions sur l'art sibérien et l'art chinois, à propos de bronzes de la collection David-Weill', *Documents*, 1:1 (1929), pp. 9–21. The results of Pelliot's expedition were published between 1914 and 1923, following on from his study *Les Grottes de Touen-Houang. Peintures et sculptures bouddhiques des époques des Wei, des T'ang et des Song* (Paris, 1914). In 1924 and 1925 he also published two books on Chinese antiquities based around the collection of C. T. Loo.

50 Pelliot, 'Quelques réflexions sur l'art sibérien', p. 18. Pieces from David-Weill's collection also accompanied Bataille's short review 'Les trouvailles de Louristan', p. 373.

51 Einstein, 'A propos de l'Exposition de la Galerie Pigalle', *Documents*, 2:2 (1930), pp. 104–10.

52 Anon, 'Afrique-Océanie (Galerie Pigalle)', *Cahiers d'art*, 5:1 (1930), p. 52.

53 Sautier, 'Exhibition of African and Oceanic Art at the Pigalle Gallery', *Formes*, 3 (March 1930), pp. 12–13.

54 *Ibid.*, p. 13.

55 Rivière, 'Le Musée d'ethnographie du Trocadéro', *Documents*, 1:1 (1929), pp. 54–8.

56 Chauvet, 'Objets d'or, de bronze, et d'ivoire dans l'art nègre', *Cahiers d'art*, 5:1 (1930), pp. 33–4.
57 *Ibid.*, p. 33.
58 *Ibid.*, p. 40. This mask was reproduced in the catalogue for the de Miré sale, Sculptures anciennes d'Afrique et Amérique, no. 86, plate X. For the prices paid for works in this sale, see Ratton, 'Les ventes: Collection G. de Miré', p. 454.
59 Einstein, 'A propos de l'Exposition de la Galerie Pigalle', p. 112.
60 The only living artist that Wildenstein dealt in was Picasso, representing him in partnership with Paul Rosenberg between 1919 and 1932.
61 De Noailles ran the Société des amis du musée d'ethnographie du Trocadéro (SAMET). In 1929, David David-Weill was supporting the museum's staff with 9,600 francs per year, while his brother Pierre gave 40,000 francs to support its library. In 1932, de Noailles contributed 10,000 francs, David-Weill 17,000 francs and Wildenstein 7,000 francs for the museum's bulletin. Rivière himself gave 60,000 francs. These figures are from the memos of the Trocadéro Ethnographic Museum, MH/ 2 AM 1 G2c and e.
62 Leiris, *Journal*, p. 194. Leiris claimed to be ashamed of his own snobbery during an evening at the de Noailles.
63 Masson's murals for Pierre David-Weill were reproduced to accompany Georges Limbour's article 'André Masson: le dépeceur universel', *Documents*, 2:5 (1930), pp. 286–9.
64 Rivière, 'Préface', in *Sculptures anciennes d'Afrique et Amérique, Collection G. de Miré*, pp. I–III.
65 Einstein, 'A propos de l'Exposition de la Galerie Pigalle', p. 104.
66 Bataille used the term 'boîte à malices' in his article 'Joan Miró: Peintures récentes', *Documents*, 2:7 (1930), p. 399.
67 Mauss, *The Gift* (1923–24), trans. W. D. Hall (London: Routledge, 1993). Mauss's few lines in homage of Picasso were published in *Documents*, 2:3 (1930), p. 177.
68 Mauss, *The Gift*, pp. 43–4.
69 *Ibid.*, p. 44.
70 These lectures were 'reconstructed' after Mauss's death, see *Manuel d'ethnographie* (1947) (Paris: Payot, 1967). Mauss also published a lecture given in 1934 on 'Techniques of the Body' in 1936, in *Sociologie et anthropologie* (Paris: Presses Universitaires de France, 1950), pp. 363–86.
71 Strzygowski, '"Recherches sur les arts plastiques" et "histoire de l'art"', *Documents*, 1:1 (1929), pp. 22–6.
72 *Ibid.*, p. 22.
73 *Ibid.*, p. 23.
74 *Ibid.*, p. 23.
75 Strzygowski, *Early Church Art in Northern Europe, with special reference to timber construction and decoration* [1928] (New York: Hacker, 1980).
76 Strzygowski, 'Recherches sur les arts plastiques', p. 23.
77 *Documents*, 2:8 (1930), pp. 1–9.
78 *Ibid.*, p. 9.
79 'La trouvaille d'Oseberg', *Documents*, 1:3 (1929), pp. 121–9.
80 Marchand, 'The Rhetoric of Artifacts', and Elsner, 'The Birth of Late Antiquity: Riegl and Strzygowski in 1901', *Art History*, 25:3 (June 2002), pp. 358–79.

81 See Marchand, 'The Rhetoric of Artifacts', p. 123.

82 Rivet, 'L'étude des civilisations matérielles', *Documents*, 1:3 (1929), pp. 130–4.

83 See Trigger, *A History of Archaeological Thought*, pp. 245–7 on the close relationship between functionalist archaeology and social anthropology, and its derivation from Durkheim.

84 Rivet, 'L'étude des civilisations matérielles', p. 134 and p. 132. On the 'cultural circles' of Frobenius, see Marchand, 'Leo Frobenius and the Revolt against the West', p. 158. Nordenskiöld's diffusionist charts have been described as 'a thorn in functionalist eyes', Lowie, *The History of Ethnological Theory*, p. 252.

85 Rivet, 'L'étude des civilisations matérielles', p. 133.

86 *Ibid.*, p. 131.

87 Hollier, 'La valeur d'usage de l'impossible', p. xiv.

88 *Ibid.*, p. xiv, p. xvii and pp. xxii–iii. Bataille's comment is from his article 'L'esprit moderne et le jeu des transpositions', *Documents*, 2:8 (1930), pp. 490–1.

89 Gregory, *Gifts and Commodities*, p. 10.

90 Bataille, 'Le cheval académique', *Documents*, 1:1 (1929), pp. 27–31 and 'Les monnaies des Grands Mogols au Cabinet des Médailles', *Aréthuse*, 4 (October 1926), pp. 133–42. On the tensions between these articles, see Dominique Lecoq, 'L'oeil de l'ethnologue sous la dent de l'écrivain', in Lecoq and Lory (eds), *Ecrits d'ailleurs*, pp. 110–11.

91 Bataille, 'Le cheval académique', p. 29, and see Basler, *L'Art chez les peuples primitifs*, p. 5 and p. 7.

92 Bataille, 'The Notion of Expenditure' (*La Critique sociale*, 1933), in Botting and Wilson (eds), *The Bataille Reader* (Oxford: Blackwell, 1997), p. 174.

93 See Francis Marmande, 'Georges Bataille: le motif aztèque', in Lecoq and Lory (eds), *Ecrits d'ailleurs*, pp. 19–29.

94 Bataille, 'L'art primitif', *Documents*, 2:7 (1930), pp. 389–97.

95 *Ibid.*, p. 392 and p. 396. Luquet had admitted the impossibility of distinguishing between 'intellectual realism' and the 'visual realism' of the ('civilised') adult in the case of three-dimensional forms, Luquet, *L'Art primitif* (Paris: G. Doin, 1930), p. 67. On the role of the Lespugue Venus, see Charles Miller, '"Mad memorials": Picasso's 1927 Apollinaire Monument Designs and the Politics of Commemoration', *Immediations* 1:1 (spring 2004), pp. 48–9.

96 Balfour, *The Evolution of Decorative Art* (London: Percival, 1893), pp. 77–95.

97 *Ibid.*, pp. 78–9.

98 He would, however, engage more closely with archaeological theory in his 1955 study of Lascaux. See Noland, 'Bataille Looking', *Modernism/Modernity*, 11:1 (2004), pp. 125–60.

99 Schaeffner, 'Des instruments de musique dans un musée d'ethnographie', *Documents*, 1:5 (1929), pp. 248–54.

100 Schildkrout and Keim, *African Reflections: Art from Northeastern Zaire* (Seattle: University of Washington Press, 1990), p. 233–8 and p. 247.

101 Schaeffner, 'Des instruments de musique', p. 254.

102 *Ibid.*, p. 250.

103 The 'earth drum' is reproduced in ibid., p. 253.

104 Nordenskiöld, 'Le balancier à fardeaux et la balance en Amérique', *Documents*, 1:4 (1929), pp. 178–9.

105 *Ibid.*, p. 180 and p. 179, note 1.
106 Griaule, 'Poterie', *Documents*, 2:4 (1930), p. 236.
107 Griaule, 'Un coup de fusil', *Documents*, 2:1 (1930), p. 46.
108 Griaule, 'Un coup de fusil', p. 46.
109 Leiris, 'De Bataille l'impossible', p. 27.
110 Strzygowski, '"Recherches sur les arts plastiques"', p. 23, and see Marchand, 'The Rhetoric of Artifacts', p. 107.
111 Leiris, *Aurora* (Paris: Gallimard, 1946), written in 1927–28 (an extract was published in the *Cahiers du sud* in July 1929). Leiris's dream accounts were later collected in *Nuits sans nuit et quelques jours sans jour* (Paris: Gallimard, 1961) and his poetic definitions in *Glossaire j'y serre mes gloses* (Paris: Galerie Simon, 1939). For a detailed discussion of the transition in his work from the surrealist to the ethnographic context, see Hand, *Michel Leiris*, pp. 45–60.
112 Leiris, 'L'oeil de l'ethnographe', *Documents*, 2:7 (1930), pp. 405–14, 'L'île magique', *Documents*, 1:6 (1929), p. 334 and 'Le "caput mortuum" ou la femme de l'alchimiste', *Documents*, 2:8 (1930) [1931], pp. 461–6.
113 Leiris, 'L'oeil de l'ethnographe', p. 413.
114 *Ibid.*, p. 413.
115 *Ibid.*, p. 414. Songhay was a fifteenth- and sixteenth-century Sudanese empire.

3

Collecting: fieldwork and its discontents

In his 1920 essay 'L'art nègre', André Salmon lamented the lowly status that had for so long been accorded to African and Oceanic pieces.[1] Large quantities of 'stuff' had arrived in Europe: 'shields, clubs, bludgeons, spears, arrows, and assagais pell-mell in curiosity shops'.[2] Those who had ventured into unexplored areas had brought back crates of things while taking little interest in them. '"Toys" for the explorers, lecturers, and professors of anthropology and geography', noted Salmon, huffily.[3] 'I buy 3 curios', noted the seminal fieldworker Malinowski laconically in his private diary in 1917.[4] While avant-garde artists and writers in the 1920s wanted to re-evaluate the influx of artefacts as 'art', some strands of anthropology kept their distance. A proliferation of material had been used in the late nineteenth century to shore up evolutionist theories, in the work of the British natural historians-cum-anthropologists Balfour and Haddon, for instance. In his 1893 *Evolution of Decorative Art*, Balfour used close observation of the subtle differences between Peruvian pots to set out a progression from figurative features to decorative designs.[5] The famous displays of the Pitt-Rivers museum, of which Balfour was curator from 1891 until his death in 1939, similarly used large amounts of artefacts to make comparative visual arguments. For 'progressive' ethnology in the twentieth century, it was as if such accumulated artefacts were implicitly tainted with evolutionism.

Certain key developments in ethnology served to marginalise artefacts and objects, sometimes unintentionally. The emphasis in the work of Durkheim on the study of cultural wholes as they were available to the anthropologist in the present was highly influential. In his analysis of the phenomenon of Australian Aboriginal totemism, for example, the only specific category of artefacts discussed were churingas, seen in relation to systems of ritual and belief.[6] Further, the major revolution in early twentieth-century anthropology, the rise of participant-observation fieldwork represented most influentially by Malinowski, favoured textual accounts, where earlier approaches had used photography and drawing more centrally. This is not to say that ethnography with a strong focus on material artefacts was not taking place. In the USA, the work of Frank Cushing amongst the Zuñi in the 1880s (an early example of participant-observation, given Cushing's initiation as a Zuñi priest), and the work of Franz Boas from the 1890s onwards provided examples of this.[7] The dominant emerging ethnographic paradigm, nonetheless, appeared to regard the accumulation and analysis of artefacts as retrograde.

The French state ethnographic expedition crossing Africa from Dakar to Djibouti between 1931 and 1933 had an uneasy and intriguing status within anthropology's development in this respect. Devoted mainly to the acquisition of material for the Trocadéro Ethnographic Museum, the expedition, led by Griaule, has been dismissed by one anthropological commentator as a brutish enterprise to 'bring back the goods'.[8] This was undeniably one of its motives, as I will discuss, but this neglects the important theoretical underpinnings of the expedition, which was prefaced by a mission statement entitled 'Summary Instructions for Collectors of Ethnographic Objects'.[9] This text was one of the few explicit extended considerations in the first half of the twentieth century either in Europe or the USA of the concerns of what we might now term 'material culture'.[10] The Dakar–Djibouti expedition consciously did not set out to examine 'primitive art', which by the late 1920s had acquired some ethnographic authority through Boas's work.[11] But it did take up artefacts and manufactured objects as a particular category of thing, whose collection and classification might play a central role in the ethnographic construction of the cultures in question.

Within early twentieth-century French ethnological and ethnographic accounts, such artefacts were not a prime concern. The colonial anthropologist Delafosse paid little attention to objects in themselves, subsuming them within a broader analysis of religious practices and even consciously rejecting terms suggesting the specific use of material artefacts, such as 'fetishism'.[12] The persistence of Western aesthetic categories in some anthropological accounts meant that only material perceived as especially 'precious' could attract separate comment and analysis. The work of Desplagnes, whose collecting forays gave the Trocadéro's African holdings what was perceived to be a much-needed boost, was a good example of this. From his 1903–06 expedition in the Sudan, Desplagnes brought back for the Trocadéro unique pieces sufficient to fill two large vitrines in the museum, as its then director Ernest Théodore Hamy pointed out in the preface to the expedition's account.[13] Desplagnes's team were one of the first to study in detail the Dogon (known at the time as the 'Habbé' or 'pagans'), a population whom the Dakar–Djibouti expedition would make their own. His account was illustrated with numerous photographs, from a collection of over 500 taken in Africa, some of which featured significant artefacts such as Dogon granary doors. His commentaries, however, privileged 'precious' things, such as 'astounding jewels cast in lost wax or filigreed' made by 'expert and delicate workers'.[14] It was clear that Desplagnes's assessment was based on western criteria of beauty and artisanal skill, and the analysis of the Sudan's archaeological past in his account suggested a colonial agenda: to 'return' what were seen as now 'primitive' peoples to an acceptable level of civilisation. Wooden figurative house posts, carved door locks, masks and other Dogon ritual objects like the *bazou*, despite being photographed in situ, were passed over as they did not serve this end (figure 11).

The Dakar–Djibouti expedition of the early 1930s would take up a very different approach to objects. It would consciously work against western notions of

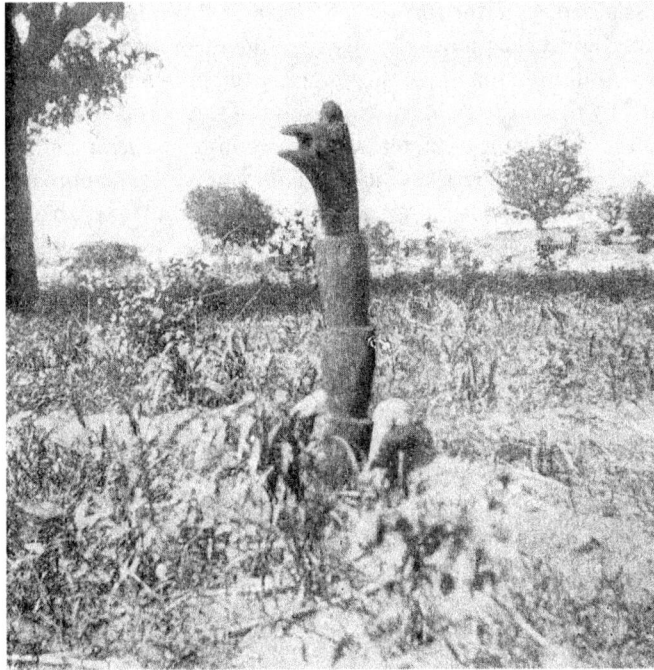

11 *Bazou*, Dogon, Tiogou, wood, in Desplagnes, *Le Plateau central nigérien* (1907), plate LXXVIII, fig. 152.

'art', even if assumptions of artistic merit inevitably crept into play. It deliberately sought out lowly, everyday things that would be the opposite of the precious, the delicate and the finely wrought. It took an interest in masks and figures in wood, especially when these had been apparently discarded and left to decay. Most importantly, it set out to collect objects that were an integral part of ritual practices, particularly obscure and unfamiliar rituals. Desplagnes had described Dogon funeral rites and cosmogony, but without connecting these in any detail to particular artefacts. The Dakar–Djibouti expedition, on the other hand, wanted to use objects as the means to illuminate ceremonies of circumcision, sacrifice and ritual possession. Where Desplagnes's narrative adopted a tone of confident authority in keeping with a controlling, colonial perspective, the Dakar–Djibouti expedition's findings attempted to reveal secret and mysterious practices which might be only partially (and tantalisingly) uncovered. Its ethnographic collectors would also develop an important degree of self-consciousness about their own interrelationships with the objects they acquired.

To have and to hold: instructions for collecting

There was one strand of French ethnological theory in the early twentieth century that did feed directly into the approach of the 'collectors of ethnographic objects' of the Dakar–Djibouti expedition. The work of Mauss was an explicit source for the 'Summary Instructions', as the text that Griaule conceived, and Leiris wrote up, was based on Mauss's lectures at the Institut d'Ethnologie.[15] While his mentor and uncle Durkheim was concerned more directly with the theoretical problems of social beliefs, Mauss would pursue much more closely the problems posed by the objects encountered by the anthropologist. Some hint of this was given in the extraordinary attention to the details of material processes in his *General Theory of Magic*, co-written with Henri Hubert, and in *The Gift*. But Mauss's approach was most clearly evident in the *Manuel d'ethnographie* published in 1947, based on his lecture notes for courses at the Institut d'Ethnologie between 1926 and 1939. This little-known text, which has yet to be translated into English, had its source in the Ethnological Institute's project to produce 'Descriptive ethnographic guidelines for the use of travellers, administrators and missionaries': a set of practical fieldwork guidelines on the model of the Royal Anthropological Institute's *Notes and Queries* series. Lacking the theoretical coherence of some of Mauss's other published works, the *Manuel d'ethnographie* consists of a series of classificatory fields and the kinds of reflection they might impose upon the anthropologist. Mauss maintained in this work a compromise position between the pre-existing theories of the ethnographer and the impact of his or her findings (he himself, of course, had never taken part in fieldwork). In his opening remarks, he stated, for example: 'The young ethnographer who sets off into the field must be aware of what he already knows, in order to bring to the surface what is as yet unknown'.[16] The theoretical justification of the Dakar–Djibouti expedition would place a greater emphasis still on ethnographic 'discovery', in the form of objects and artefacts.

The work of the Paris Institut d'Ethnologie had an inescapable colonial framework, hence the fieldwork 'instructions' intended for use not just by academic ethnographers, but also by colonial administrators and even missionary explorers. The Dakar–Djibouti expedition too had an explicitly colonialist function, despite its left-wing credentials. The ethnologists backing the new early 1930s expedition – such as Rivet, Mauss and Lévy-Bruhl, the co-founders of the Institut d'Ethnologie – operated in opposition to the more dominant (and right-wing) establishment anthropology of Louis Marin and his followers.[17] These figures are now considered to have been at the forefront of the development of the discipline in France, as a symbolic and legitimising triumvirate uniting the Durkheimians (Mauss), the Sorbonne (Lévy-Bruhl) and the Ecole anthropologique (Rivet).[18] The expedition's leader, Marcel Griaule, was a protégé of the Institut, the first student to have been trained there. Ironically, however, the expedition's rationale was in part unavoidably backward-looking, as it was intended to enable the French state to make up ground on other international museums in the matter of colonial holdings. Relative to other institutions in Europe and the USA, the Trocadéro's collection was perceived not to reflect adequately enough France's colonial position. Previous ethnographic expeditions had not capitalised sufficiently on their opportunity to bring back specimens for display at home. One of the legal cases made for the state funding of the expedition cited the Terveuren Museum of the

Belgian Congo, the Colonial Institute in Amsterdam, and the Smithsonian Institution in Washington as direct models of museum collections built in close association with colonial expeditions.[19] The French government initially promised 700,000 francs for the expedition out of a total projected budget of about 1,000,000 francs, indicating its investment in the accumulation of colonial goods. Before French ethnology could progress, presumably, some catching up was needed at the level of material acquisition.

The status of the 'Summary Instructions for Collectors of Ethnographic Objects' then was ambivalent. On the one hand it served a retrograde purpose, providing an intellectual justification for filling in gaps in museum holdings in order to better 'compete' on an international colonial stage. On the other hand, it was drawn up and inspired by figures regarded now as seminal ethnological and ethnographic thinkers, like Mauss and Griaule. It was attempting to provide a new framework for the study of material artefacts within ethnology that could liberate them from the ideological bias of evolutionist comparisons. Unlike other more populist French expeditions of the 1920s, like the so-called 'Croisière noire', the Dakar–Djibouti expedition set out to apply this new ethnographic thinking rigorously. Georges-Marie Haardt and Louis Audouin-Dubreuil's mid-1920s Citroën expedition, for example, had entrusted its 'ethnographical studies' to the artist Alexandre Iacovleff, and its emphases lay with the technical feat of crossing Africa and the pioneering spirit of its team.[20] By contrast, the Dakar–Djibouti expedition was attuned to collecting not just objects as 'booty', like the big game bagged and proudly displayed by Haardt and Audouin-Dubreuil, but as crucial cultural testimonies that needed careful documentation.[21]

One instance of this new ethnographic rigour in the Dakar–Djibouti expedition's preparatory 'Summary Instructions' concerned the status of things collected. The objects to be collected should never, the authors insisted, be chosen according to the values of 'purity' or 'rarity'.[22] A 'pile of rubbish' could yield a more interesting find than seeking out so-called 'precious' objects.[23] Rivet had made a similar point in his *Documents* article, where it had clear political overtones: 'what is important to know are all aspects, or at least the average aspects of a civilisation and not the exceptional aspects it assumes in the privileged classes … the houses of the poor are as precious, if not more precious, to study than the palaces of the rich.'[24] The evaluation of objects normally seen as aesthetically significant was deliberately rejected in the expedition's rationales. One of the lists of the 'material aims' of the expedition drawn up by Griaule in 1930 ran as follows:

> Mechanical instruments, basketry, pottery, ropes, sparterie, dyed objects, weapons for war, for hunting and for ceremonies, transportation equipment (navigation, portage, etc.), clothing and adornments, domestic utensils, agricultural instruments, religious objects, musical instruments, aesthetic and juridical objects, etc.[25]

The placing of 'aesthetic objects' here, almost as an afterthought, functioned as a very deliberate statement of inverted artistic snobbery.

The place of the 'aesthetic' was, however, more complex than these examples might suggest for the anthropologists involved in conceiving the expedition. The ethnographer ought to explore unlikely places in order to find interesting arte-facts, but this did not mean that these things were un-aesthetic. In Mauss's *Manuel d'ethnographie*, aesthetic meaning could be more potent in apparently unprepossessing objects, in an arbitrary and colourful selection typical of his writings:

> One begins the study of the plastic arts by collecting all art objects, including the most humble: paper dolls, lanterns made of bladders, etc. A tree can be sculpted on all sides; in this case, the worker has had the feeling for volumes and relationships; a cannibal fork handle is sculpture; a nice example of an American whistle is sculpture.[26]

Mauss further drew attention to the designation of an object as 'art' by reference to its perception as such by its cultural environment:

> One will study carefully all the circumstances which surround each object, each artistic event: where, who, when, as what, for whom, for what. An art object, by defi-nition, is an object recognised as such by a group. One needs therefore to analyse the sensations of the individual who makes use of that object.[27]

The 'Summary Instructions' for the Dakar–Djibouti expedition provided similar, if rather enigmatic, guidelines with an emphasis on the user:

> Gather all possible objects, everyday or not. All objects are aesthetic to some degree. There is no real difference between the potter when he is making something and the potter when he is decorating something. The plate that I am using, I have *chosen*.[28]

The involvement of the former surrealist Leiris in the production of these 'instructions' tempts a comparison with the surrealist interest in the 'found object', the random find uncovered in the least likely place. The significance of these objects would be guaranteed by the finder's response to them, the fact that he or she had chosen them. For the surrealists as well as the ethnographer, discarded 'rub-bish' was certain to throw up more interesting things than other sources, and the flea market was crucial because it contained objects that had been rejected by someone else. If the ethnographers of the expedition deliberately rejected conven-tional 'value', preferring the 'hovel' to the 'palace', the surrealist interest in the found object can be seen as an attempt to short-circuit the system of commodity exchange. The realm of the second-hand provided a repertory of things outside, or to one side of, modern consumerism (the flea market on the 'margins' of the city). The kinds of objects attracting André Breton in *Nadja* of 1928 were unique oddi-ties, whose precise meaning he was not at pains to discover, indeed the more obscure, or 'perverse' as he termed it, the better. Breton's description of a three-dimensional demographic model that he found at the Saint-Ouen flea market pro-vides an example of his approach:

that kind of irregular white half-cylinder, varnished, showing reliefs and depressions with no meaning for me, with horizontal and vertical red and green stripes, preciously enclosed within a case, beneath an inscription in Italian, that I took home with me and through examining which at length I came to admit that it could only correspond to the statistics, rendered in three dimensions, of the population of a town in such-a-such year, which for me does not make it more legible.[29]

However, Breton's evocation of this 'lucky find' also points to some of the complexities of the ethnographic find. His text provided a detailed description of the graph, despite it having 'no meaning' for the narrator, while also being examined by him 'at length' as a material thing, like a connoisseur poring over a prize possession. While his example suggested that the found object's meaning should remain wilfully mysterious, its maker's or original user's intentions erased, Breton's text did note from the evidence of the special case that this object must have been 'precious' to someone else. To seek out and acquire second-hand things may be less of a 'critical' practice than initially imagined, serving to validate refinements of taste and judicious 'selection'.[30] The ethnographic collector might want to diverge from the surrealist in the emphasis laid in the 'Summary Instructions' on a deep, systematic analysis of each object, giving each one 'legibility'. The lack of interest shown by Breton to find out exactly what his demographic model might demonstrate would be unacceptable, for example, in the terms of the Dakar–Djibouti expedition, as were its 'special' qualities, marking it out from all the other flea-market objects. The authors of the 'Summary Instructions' advocated the assembly of specimens of stages in the manufacture of a particular object, worn and broken objects, and multiples (for use in museum classificatory displays or as tokens of exchange with other museums).[31] However, the wish to avoid singularity and uniqueness was inevitably problematised by the process of ethnographic collecting itself, as Barbara Kirschenblatt-Gimblett has claimed: 'Though once multiple, in becoming ethnographic many objects become singular ... collecting induces rarity by creating scarcity ... collectors create categories that from the outset ... are marked by the challenges they pose to acquisition'.[32] The choices made by the collectors of the Dakar–Djibouti expedition might be closer to the surrealist hunt for the 'oddity' than they would want to admit. In 1933, on its return, René Daumal reported Leiris's ambivalent thoughts on object selection:

We forced ourselves to put aside the aesthetic prejudices that ordinarily guide the ethnographer's choice; the result is in general an arbitrary collection of objects representative of the particular taste or the personal theories of the scientist. We tried to keep everything that ... bore evidence of the cultures of these peoples ... But that won't last as there isn't enough space; sadly, we will have to choose.[33]

The aggressively acquisitive principles of the 'Summary Instructions' were not, and arguably could not be, actually carried out fully by the expedition. The processes of acquiring objects turned out to be much less straightforward, involving complicated human transactions and a large degree of cunning. The ethnographer's 'choice' of the object was also much more problematic than the expedition's guidelines implied. The role of the 'discarded' object, for example, was in practice less simple than merely sifting through piles of rubbish. To collect what had been thrown away had obvious practical advantages, as it would not require payment and could not normally offend its original owners. It also had a distinct colonial agenda of recuperation, a key trope in early twentieth-century ethnographic collecting. The Dakar–Djibouti expedition was no exception to this, citing the disappearance of African material culture as one of the rationales of the undertaking, in order to secure state funding. The expedition would pick up objects that had been thrown away and left to disintegrate, above all amongst the Dogon. A photograph of a 'used' and discarded Dogon dance mask was included in the special issue of *Minotaure* published on the expedition's return (figure 12).[34] But this mask could also demonstrate one of the problems of the expedition's stated collecting aims. There could be rubbish and rubbish. To collect and bring back something that had once had meaning for its originating culture, but had now been thrown away, was quite unlike gathering debris wholesale. The act of choosing would always be loaded.

The 'Summary Instructions' for the Dakar–Djibouti expedition in fact contained a central tension with regard to the object's material status. Could an object stand on its own as evidence, or did it need accompanying documentation? The authors made clear that collecting objects had its own special and separate

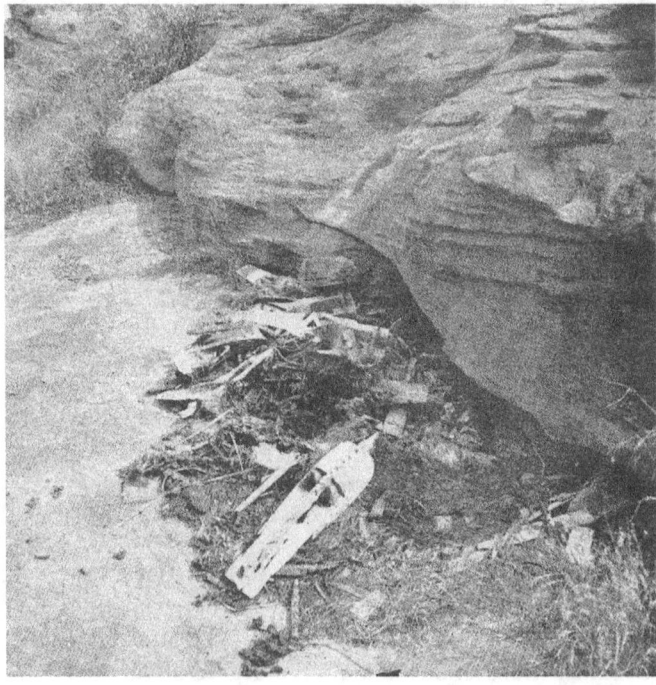

12 'Used masks, abandoned under a rock', *Minotaure*, 1:2 (1933).

significance, in the creation of archives that were more concrete than written ones, in line with the broader 'historiographic revolution' in the humanities promoted by writers like Strzygowski.[35] It was a question for them of 'authentic and autonomous objects, which cannot have been made for the needs of the case and which characterise better than anything types of civilisation'.[36] The case being made here for the special power of material artefacts over and above textual records anticipated debates in the anthropological sub-discipline of 'material culture' today. The different categories of object in the Dakar–Djibouti expedition's collecting 'manifesto' reinforced this attitude, appearing to provide a comprehensive inventory of things to look out for. The model for these detailed guidelines for the ethnographer–collector was undoubtedly the British Association for the Advancement of Science's *Notes and Queries on Anthropology*, a handbook for fieldworkers whose fifth edition came out in 1929.[37] The *Notes and Queries*, however, provided a collection of key questions to guide the ethnographer, whereas the 'Summary Instructions' listed only the types of artefact to be gathered. These artefacts were often not comparable as categories of things, as an example from the section for the 'Aesthetic of objects' shows:

(See 'Technology' and 'Monuments of social activity')
Skins, antlers, pottery, brasses, iron, baskets, tools, weapons, musical instruments, etc…
Functional objects and ceremonial objects (monstrance axes).
Zoomorphic, phylomorphic, skeuomorphic, anthropomorphic designs.
Architecture. (See 'Technomorphology' and 'Habitation')[38]

A clay pot, a skeuomorphic design, and 'architecture' were clearly not directly comparable as elements of a list, anticipating the famous 'Chinese encyclopaedia' of Borges, which for Michel Foucault represented taxonomic 'impossibility'.[39] Beneath the apparently 'neutral' inventory of things which might interest the ethnographer also lay a network of prior interpretation, as the cross-referencing in the quotation above indicates.

The ethnographic object for the 'Summary Instructions' appeared to be at once a brute fact, a thing to be accumulated and listed and an archival record *in itself*, and at the same time a complex cipher accompanied by extensive documentation. In order that once transplanted to the museum in France the artefact should not become a 'dead object', it was necessary to surround it with a mass of information: precise labels, descriptive fiches made in duplicate, inventories and collectors' diaries. The authors stressed that all information, even indirectly related to the object, might later be of use.[40] Such information, of course, brought the ethnographer–collector, and his or her subjectivity, into a relationship with the object, which was treated as 'alive': 'A collection of ethnographic objects is above all a collection of living things. In this way it can be distinguished from other kinds of collection.'[41] This conception of the object recalled theories of animism, an ethnological leitmotif since Charles de Brosses's 1760 study of 'fetish gods'.[42] The British ethnologist Edward Tylor, in his influential *Primitive Culture* of 1871, provided an example of an indigenous 'collector', a Guinean man 'sitting amid twenty thousand fetishes in his own private fetish-museum', visited by the anthropologist Römer:

> The visitor took up a stone about as big as a hen's egg, and its owner told its history. He was once going out on important business, but crossing the threshold he trod on this stone and hurt himself. Ha ha! thought he, art thou here? So he took the stone, and it helped him through his undertaking for days.[43]

The approach of the collectors of the Dakar–Djibouti expedition also suggested the animistic object, to be studied in detail *'from its birth to its destruction'*.[44] While the object as a 'living thing' might be akin to the zoological specimen that the expedition also 'collected' to bring back to France, its rationale went further than this.[45] For the Dakar–Djibouti expedition, the object took on the function of an emphatically italicised *'witness'*.[46] The object as *witness* was not only a passive subject – studied, inventoried, photographed and collected – it could also *look back* at the ethnographer–collector. By implication, it had its own volition and needed to be carefully cultivated by the ethnographer just as a native informant would be. It was as if the fieldwork dynamics of seminal ethnographers like Malinowski, with its emphasis on the discrepancies between what informants said and what they did, was being transposed onto collected materials.[47] Certainly, these dynamics would play a crucial role in Leiris's perception of the expedition, where his sense of 'being watched' in a kind of ethnographic 'performance' came to the fore.[48]

The shadow of adventure

It would be impossible in a sense for the expedition itself to live up to the high-minded aims of the 'Summary Instructions'. The team that Marcel Griaule took to Africa in May 1931 was relatively small and its members mainly young, and included a few 'amateurs' with little or no ethnographic training, like Leiris, or the painter Gaston Louis-Roux, who joined the team in Ethiopia.[49] Other team members included the musicologist André Schaeffner, the naturalist Marcel Larget, technician Eric Lutten, and linguists Jean Mouchet and Deborah Lifchitz. The eminent pre-historian Henri Breuil had been included in the initial plans for the expedition but did not take part. In order to supplement the state support for the expedition, Rivière, as the Trocadéro's assistant director, engaged in an extensive campaign of fund-raising. In addition to organising the famous boxing gala featuring the American Al Brown, which raised 101,350 francs, and whose extraordinary role as an exotic spectacle has been analysed by Jean Jamin in detail, Rivière rigorously pursued a number of private sponsors, including most successfully the Rockefeller foundation.[50] The archives of the Musée de l'Homme contain evidence of Rivière's lively correspondence with potential donors and commercial collaborators before and during the expedition, such as Paramount films (whom Rivière tried to persuade to provide technical assistance and equipment), Ford motors and a range of French companies. Private donors included the Trocadéro's main sponsors in this period, Charles de Noailles and David David-Weill, as well as Raymond Roussel, who gave 10,000 francs despite his reduced financial circumstances at the time.

The Dakar–Djibouti expedition's departure was preceded by a display in the Trocadéro's galleries of its equipment, lasting only a few days between 30 April and 3 May 1931 (figure 13). In part this was an opportunity for sponsors to advertise their support of the expedition, such as Menier chocolate, Huntley and Palmer biscuits and the trucks provided by Ford. Its opening was a high-profile affair, attracting visitors including Dr Charcot, Mauss, Valéry, Man Ray, Laurens, Miró, Marcoussis, Jouhandeau, Roland-Manuel, Bataille and Al Brown.[51] Press reports mentioned with enthusiasm the mock-up of a field camp shown to the Parisian public, including different kinds of tent for sleeping, writing, washing, storing weapons, sound recording and photographic development. In front of the Trocadéro were parked two trucks and a touring car, while inside was displayed the collapsible metal boat to be used by the expedition. One press commentator felt that the display of equipment was so realised for the spectator as to 'wake up the greatest desires and dreams in their imagination', while another described the

13 Exhibition of the equipment of the Dakar–Djibouti expedition, Trocadéro, Paris, May 1931.

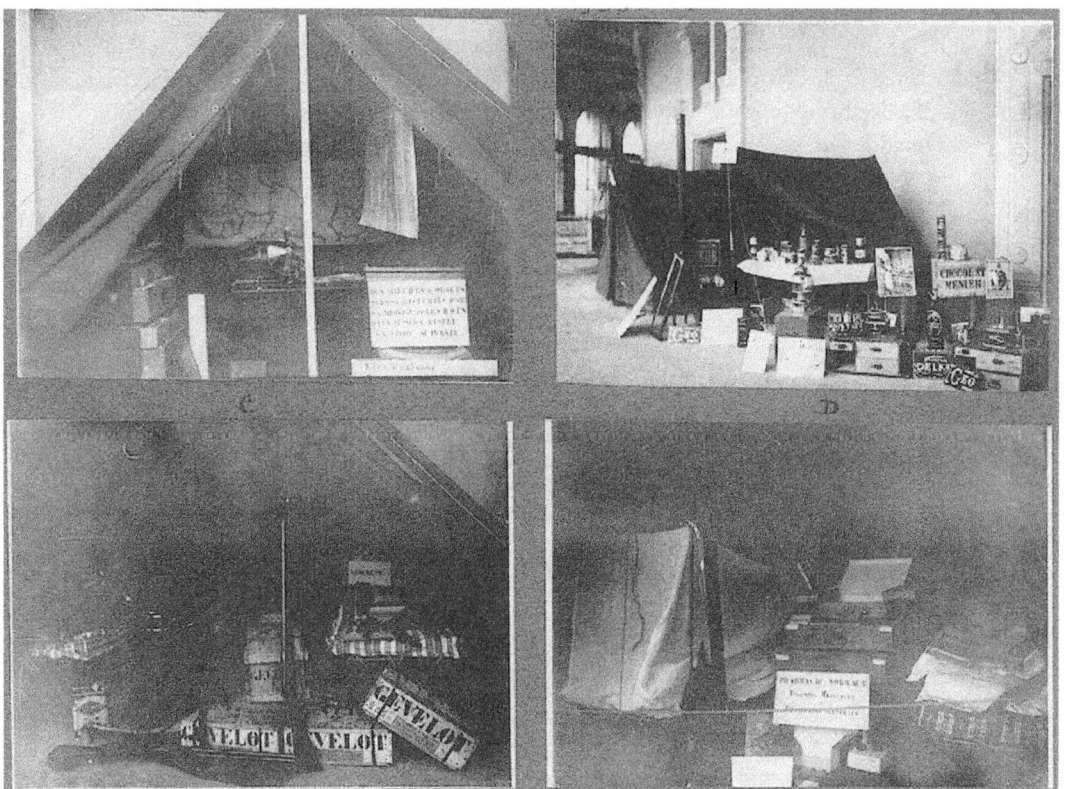

effect as producing 'an irresistible invitation to travel'.[52] The former also noted the presence of large numbers of children at the opening.

The appeal of 'adventure' that the display of the expedition's equipment implied had already been a feature of Leiris's article 'The Eye of the Ethnographer', in which he described the impact of Roussel's imaginary 'Africa' of extravagant contraptions and cruel rituals: 'I was dreaming of far-off countries and tortuous discoveries'.[53] Connotations of boyhood adventure also attached themselves to Griaule, the expedition's leader. Griaule had recently led an expedition to Ethiopia in 1928–29, and two of his photographs were used in *Documents* in 1930 to illustrate Leiris's article. From this fieldwork he produced a book of Abyssinian 'recipes' for spells, one of which, concerning the 'evil eye', involved the consumption of the victim's flesh and blood.[54] A review of this book in *Comoedia* speculated that the ethnographer himself might be 'something of a magician'.[55] Another review in the same newspaper in the build-up to the expedition's departure commented on the appropriateness of Roussel's donation of 10,000 francs to its fund. It pointed out a poetic connection 'between a writer [Roussel] enamoured of strangeness and exoticism and a young scholar [Griaule] whose brave undertaking has in it a whiff of adventure'.[56] One of Griaule's models of ethnographic endeavour was Frank Cushing, as he explained in an article published on the expedition's return, because of Cushing's immersion in Zuñi culture.[57] Leiris looked to a similarly 'committed' figure in Seabrook, whose *Magic Island* gave an account of his initiation, culminating in the possession of the daughter of the voodoo priestess by the spirit of a sacrificial goat. Seabrook's text emphasised the 'horrific' aspects of this ritual, its participants 'blood-maddened, sex-maddened, god-maddened', while setting out his own ambivalent reaction:

> Thus also my unspying eyes beheld this scene in actuality, but I did not experience the revulsion which literary tradition prescribes. It was savage and abandoned, but it seemed to me magnificent and not devoid of a certain beauty. Something inside myself awoke and responded to it … I believe that that the thing itself – their thing, I mean – is rationally defensible.[58]

Seabrook's participation in the voodoo rites he described clearly appealed to Leiris prior to his African journey. Tellingly, however, Leiris reacted unfavourably to *Jungle Ways*, Seabrook's account of the Dogon, describing his book as 'pure rubbish', exemplifying, for him, the 'American "bohemian aesthete" spirit in the basest way' through its lack of colonial awareness.[59]

The team of young 'adventurers' had to be at the same time serious 'collectors of ethnographic objects'. Their day-to-day activities in Africa were recorded by Leiris as the expedition archivist, and consequently are available to us historically mainly from the perspective of Leiris's own concerns. His field diary, consisting of frank and frequently disconnected reflections as well as accounts of the expedition's experiences, was published in 1934 virtually unchanged as *L'Afrique fantôme*, 'Phantom Africa'.[60] The book's title evoked the disillusionment felt by its author, having hoped that his travels would give rise to personal revelation and transformation. Leiris's field account functioned as a kind of anti-ethnography, as well as an 'anti-adventure', premised not on a process of learning about other cultures, but on a process of self-exploration which seemed destined to fail. In this respect, it foreshadowed the explicit self-critical tone and the implicit diversionary strategies of his 1939 autobiographical novel *L'Age de l'homme*, whose presumed purpose in presenting a 'true' picture of its author was constantly subtly mediated and undermined through a series of self-conscious literary set pieces.[61] Like other ethnographic travel writing of the period, *L'Afrique fantôme* drew upon fictional accounts, particularly the work of Joseph Conrad.[62] Unlike them, however, it played up the banality of the ethnographic expedition. Mary Louise Pratt has analysed the openings of ethnographic accounts in the early twentieth century in relation to mythic tropes of first contact or scientific tropes of detached authority, both deriving from a tradition of travel writing.[63] The first few pages of Leiris's *L'Afrique fantôme* presented neither, including a series of laconic and darkly humorous impressions: prostitutes in a harbour, a goat (the ship's mascot) getting an erection, Rimsky-Korsakov's *Sheherazade* being played on the expedition's record player (a gift from the Viscount de Noailles), Leiris himself reading an article by Griaule on 'Labour in Abyssinia'.[64]

The opening of *L'Afrique fantôme* inaugurated its apparently banal, 'scientific' tone, but also subtly pointed to its fictional and literary status. Leiris's reference to his own reading matter recalled the frequent allusions in André Gide's 1927 *Voyage au Congo* to books and articles consumed by the narrator during his trip, a kind of parallel 'journey'.[65] To evoke the storyteller of the Arabian Nights also signalled the other, hidden function of the 'diary' as beguiling and potentially misleading narrative. Leiris later claimed that one of his early inspirations had been Robert James Fletcher's *Isles of Illusion*, a bitter epistolary account of life in the South Seas published anonymously in 1923.[66] Apparently autobiographical, this book played with the reader's trust in its quasi-ethnographical 'truths', its 'editor' exposing the narrator as unreliable by his own admission: 'I always have been, and always shall be, a liar … I do often get hopelessly mixed up between what happens to my "waking" and what to my "subconscious" self.'[67] The trope of 'confession' would also play a central role in Leiris's account of the Dakar–Djibouti expedition, particularly in relation to its collecting activities, but both its ethnographic detachment and its shocking 'exposés' were arguably tempered by its need to tell tales.

The accounts that Leiris gave of the actual processes of acquiring objects in *L'Afrique fantôme* were much more prosaic and awkward that the fervent tone of the 'Summary Instructions' had suggested. He was drawn to the difficult human dimensions of the transactions that the expedition instigated. For instance, during the first part of their stay in the French Sudan (western Mali), the expedition became aware of the key role played in the acquisition of some Toucouleur dolls by the interpreter assigned to them, Mamadou Vad. Leiris's description of his collecting activities was telling and worth quoting at length:

The *tardjouman* [interpreter] has shown all of his ingenuity in gathering interesting objects (yesterday a kind of rattle made of two calabashes joined with string and whose seeds make a noise when you shake them in your hand after having thrown one in such a way as to strike the other, nestled in the hollow of your hand; some dolls; a 'devil', a simple piece of calabash which makes a humming sound when you spin it quickly around the axis of the string that runs through it). Today he is bringing a fish that is taboo for the *tyouballo* caste of fishermen; some more dolls; a child's bow. Because of this, Griaule decided that we would take him with us. Since this morning, he's sporting a fez, walking about proudly, and running all over the country to get objects for us.[68]

Leiris's description makes clear the expedition's reliance on native contacts as a means of acquiring 'interesting' objects. Having already noted Mamadou Vad's extensive knowledge of local magical practices, it seems clear that for Leiris his value was as an interpreter not just of language but of culture, who could pre-select things for the team's collection.[69] The 'recruitment' of informants from one area who would then travel with the team and help them in other regions, taking on themselves an ethnographic function as observers of local differences, had also been a technique used by Frobenius.[70] The 'objective' and exhaustive collection implied by the 'Summary Instructions' for the Dakar–Djibouti expedition was compromised by such inter-subjective interventions. Interpreters and informants, in Leiris's account, emerged as strong and significant characters, and the strategic moves of Griaule to flatter various contacts were highlighted. Throughout *L'Afrique fantôme*, it is clear that the expedition had considerable difficulties in matching up their field research with the collection of appropriate objects. A dance helmet sold to them in Kita (Mali) was striking and was the work of a named artist, Baouré, a blacksmith from Birgo; however, it came to them with no accompanying explanation of its possible meaning.[71] Conversely, while engaged in an in-depth study of circumcision rituals amongst the Wolof, the expedition found it hard to gather pieces from the boys and girls with whom they were working, so Mamadou Vad gave to them his own circumcision bonnet.[72] The intention to assemble 'typical' things was certainly complicated by acquisitions like this.

If the object was construed as a 'witness', the expedition team to some degree bore themselves as judicial interrogators or police detectives. Griaule suggested as much in his 'Methodological Introduction' to the special issue of *Minotaure* published on the expedition's return.[73] In a newspaper article in 1933, Griaule described the strategies of his team as 'police ethnography'. He referred to his impression that the Dogon in particular were trying to mislead, and withhold information from, the expedition. He felt that his teamwork methods involving simultaneous interviews with prominent figures so that they could not confer, and a bluffing approach intended to fool the Dogon into believing that the French team knew more than in fact they did, had been successful examples of this 'detective work'.[74] Jamin has analysed the role of suspicion as a methodological spur, pointing to Griaule's favouring of legal-judicial metaphors such as 'deposition', 'expert assessment', 'letters rogatory' and 'summons'.[75] The negotiations involved to obtain objects, as reported by Leiris, often partook of a certain amount of deception on both sides. The ways in which he described the behaviour of African contacts suggested their own awareness of the problems of dealing with a European expedition, and thus their own potential to conceal things from their interlocutors. The acquisition of dance masks from two contacts from Ireli, a Dogon village, led to a complex game of subterfuge intended to conceal any commercial exchange. The sellers asked that it be known the masks had been 'requisitioned' rather than willingly sold, and they accepted money as a gift amongst friends.[76] Descriptions of this kind, and the judicial terminology used by Griaule, picked up an anthropological tendency to read informants' accounts against the grain, most notable in the work of Malinowski, whose reputation Leiris at least hoped to emulate.[77]

Leiris's L'Afrique fantôme, however, made this construction of the ethnographer–informant relationship more complex by emphasising the duplicity on both sides. An afternoon and evening spent meeting Dogon elders inspired an angry outburst on the mutual falseness of not only their behaviour, aimed expressly at the 'tourist' observer as he saw it, but also of his own 'sweetness and light' attitude.[78] Leiris's account is notable for its frank questioning of his own behaviour, particularly with regard to his failure to maintain an 'objective', 'scientific' position. Early on in the narrative, he made it clear that the actual work processing collected objects was beginning very quickly to bore him. In letters to his wife, Zette, he complained about the emphasis placed on collection: 'I'm still regretting only talking to Negros [sic] about objects and not being able to take on more human topics ... it seems to me that it is an insipid activity to go and see blacks ... in order to systematically buy from them work tools'.[79] In a letter of 4 July 1931 he lamented: 'We have a job that is increasingly overwhelming. We spend all day collecting objects, labelling them, recording them and wrapping them. I have the impression much more of being an accountant than an adventurer'.[80] One of the titles that Leiris considered for his field diary registered this sense of disappointment explicitly: 'L'Ombre de l'aventure' – 'the shadow of adventure'.[81]

Blood on their hands: implicated objects

The 'adventure' that Leiris was looking for in the expedition's collecting activities was not long in taking shape, however. In some of the most notorious and striking parts of L'Afrique fantôme, Leiris described incidents where objects were deliberately stolen. This in itself was nothing new for ethnographers, as an almost 'conventional' aspect of ethnographic practice. Griaule's 'hero' Cushing, for instance, had 'collected' large quantities of ceremonial objects from Zuñi shrines without the knowledge of most Zuñi.[82] What was different in Leiris's record of the Dakar–Djibouti expedition was the self-conscious unease that permeated it. Ethnography had presumably 'advanced' since the 1880s, when fieldworkers like Cushing were not always completely aware of their wrongdoings.[83] The way that

Leiris's *L'Afrique fantôme* almost revelled in 'telling tales' about the expedition, partially in accordance with literary tropes of 'adventure', brought to the fore both the untidy complications of collecting and the fraught accommodations of 'fiction' and 'objectivity' in the ethnographic account itself.

The first theft described by Leiris took place in Kemeni in the then French Sudan (now Mali) in September 1931. After having visited a Senufo sacred hut and being allowed to view its fetish, Leiris and Griaule came across a Bambara (Bamana) altar containing a *kono* 'fetish', which they were allowed to see after two sacrifices had taken place, one for each inquisitive ethnographer. As the arrangements for these began to become more and more delayed, the two men lost their patience and entered the compound anyway, where Griaule took photographs and slid a couple of flutes into his boots. As the arrangements were still continuing with much complication, Griaule told the head of the village that he must sell them the *kono* (which turned out to be a mask) for ten francs to avoid trouble from the local colonial administration. 'Terrible blackmail', commented Leiris.[84] The very next day another fetish was acquired in Dyabougou. This time Leiris and Lutten were sent out expressly to steal the *kono* that had been spotted by Griaule during a sneaky visit to its shrine. Leiris described the escapade in his field diary:

> My heart is beating very loudly, as, after yesterday's scandal, I am aware in a more acute way of the enormity of what we are committing. With his hunting knife, Lutten cuts the mask from the costume decorated with feathers to which it is attached, passes it to me, so that I can wrap it up in the canvas we have brought, and also gives me, at my request – because it is one of those bizarre forms that yesterday intrigued us so very much – a sort of piglet, again of brown nougat (that is to say, coagulated blood) which weighs at least 15 kilos and which I wrap up with the mask. The lot is quickly taken out of the village and we return to the cars through the fields. As we leave, the head villager wants to give back to Lutten the 20F that we had given to him. Lutten leaves them for him, naturally. But that doesn't make it less ugly.[85]

This object, now known as a *boli* altar figure, became a star piece in the Musée de l'Homme's collection, and was included in the Royal Academy's *Africa, The Art of a Continent* exhibition in 1995–96 (figure 14).[86]

The desire of the Dakar–Djibouti expedition to gain access to secret places and to acquire 'forbidden' artefacts apparently led them to abandon the high-minded ethical principles implicit in their 'Summary Instructions'. Leiris's accounts of these activities have a frankness that might suggest a moralistic condemnation of them, and their narrator as a kind of hero blowing the whistle on the arrogance of the colonial expedition. Certainly it might be tempting to read them in this way in the light of the fact that Leiris was later one of the first French intellectuals to take up an explicitly anti-colonial position.[87] But this would be a misreading. After these thefts, Griaule expressed regret that there were no more sacred pieces of this kind in the area to be collected. Leiris noted that he felt regret too, but not for the loss of

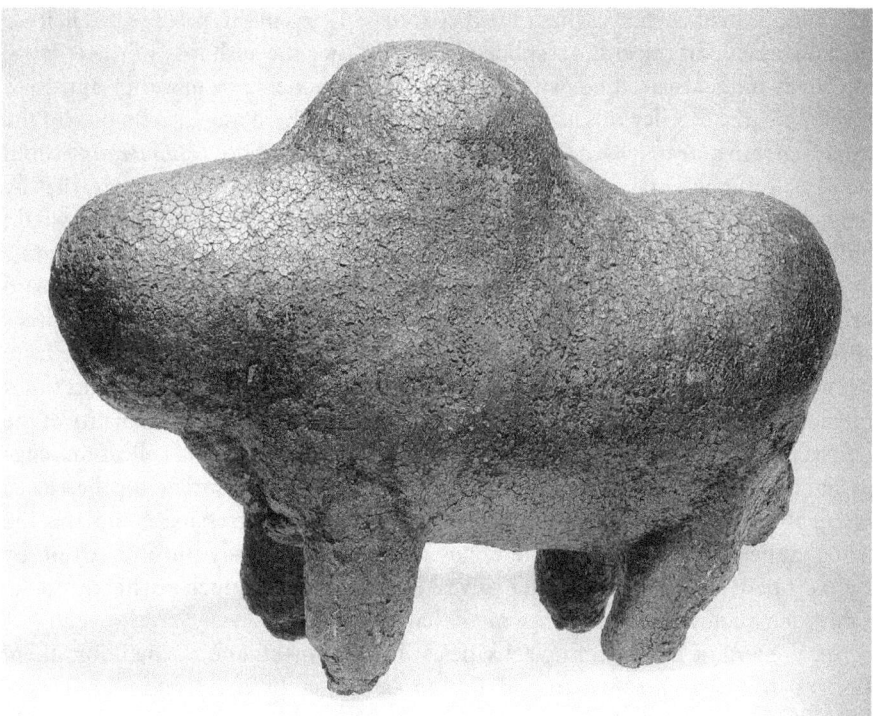

14 Altar figure (*boli*), Bamana, Mali, wood and encrustation, Musée du quai Branly, Paris (formerly Musée de l'Homme).

any potential 'scientific' gain; rather, he had acquired a taste for profanation.[88] The expedition's activities in Dogon country arguably provided Leiris with the 'adventure' he was seeking, at least as his diary recounted them. Leiris was undoubtedly conscious of the narrative model of boys' adventure stories in these accounts, which included many descriptions of exploratory forays across difficult terrain and into hidden, inaccessible caves.[89] Leiris's perception of himself as a marauding 'pirate' reached a climax shortly before leaving Sanga, the main Dogon village, in November 1931. The expedition had been refused some sacred statues and a special figure with raised arms, and the Dogon had impressed upon the visitors the great significance of these pieces to them. This had not, however, prevented Leiris from taking his own action:

> saying goodbye this morning to the old people who were overjoyed that we had spared them, we are looking at the huge green umbrella, usually opened to give us shade, but today carefully tied up. Swollen with a strange tumour that makes it look like a pelican's beak, it now contains the famous statuette with raised arms which I stole myself … First I hid it under my shirt, with a small ladder which is the means by which God descends. Then I put it in the umbrella … pretending to piss to divert attention.[90]

The collection of objects in the context evoked by Leiris in this passage had neither the 'objectivity' of the ethnographer-as-scientist, nor the authority of the ethnographer-as-judge. Instead he painted himself to his readers as a maverick anti-hero revelling in the sacrilegious acts he was committing. There was an echo here of the ironic narrative strategies of Gide, a line from the end of whose *L'Immoraliste* could stand as a coincidental commentary on Leiris's own ploys: 'We felt, alas, that by telling his story, Michel had made his action more legitimate'.[91] Indeed, he would build the apparently 'confessional' impulse into his subsequent work, for example in his deprecating self-portrait in *L'Age de l'homme* as a physically repellent and prurient obsessive.[92] Beyond the indulgence of boyhood fantasy implicit in Leiris's attitude in *L'Afrique fantôme*, there was a more serious point, made in a private letter to his wife: 'there are sublime objects which it would be a thousand times more ignoble to buy than to steal'.[93] Leiris's general disgust with the banality of the transactions the expedition had to undertake in order to build its collections suggested that only a daring and transgressive act could be appropriate for the sacred pieces it coveted. The Maussian principle that 'the transgression completes the taboo' appeared to be at work here, possibly self-consciously put into action by Leiris. Theft, like the gift, served to invest the object with a much greater symbolic value than a commercial exchange might have.[94]

As a record of the collecting activities of the Dakar–Djibouti expedition, then, Leiris's *L'Afrique fantôme* turned out to be a highly compromised account. Johannes Fabian has recently shown that the factors that might mitigate the supposed objectivity of ethnographic writing could be more common than we assume. The influence of drink and drugs, erotic obsession and forms of mental instability can be seen to permeate fieldwork accounts of the early twentieth century, although usually carefully concealed from the reader.[95] Leiris made no attempt to hide such tendencies in one of the major ethnographic studies he undertook during the Dakar–Djibouti expedition, amongst adepts of the *zar* cult in Ethiopia, where he became infatuated with the daughter of the cult's leader, Emayawish. While Leiris was producing his frank and deliberately subjective African diary, he was also filling a series of small notebooks with inventories of objects collected. These dry lists, where each find is numbered, dated, located and briefly described, were anonymous expedition records, attributable to Leiris on the basis of his handwriting.[96] In a reversal of the 'revelation' of Malinowski's intimate diaries in relation to his public ethnographic work, the flip side to Leiris's charged narrative of colonial gain, with all its ruses to attract and repel the reader, was the impartial (and 'dull') record of material 'evidence'.[97] How to talk about things collected remained for the expedition a paradoxical task: one requiring neutral objectivity but inevitably entailing subjective involvement.

The special character of Leiris's accounts of the Dakar–Djibouti expedition anticipated the self-reflexivity that began to feature strongly in 1980s ethnographic theory, in what Marcus and Fischer have called 'cultural critique'.[98] Leiris was a crucial point of reference for the work of James Clifford, and exemplified a new kind of reading of ethnographic texts in which the anthropologist was construed 'as author', in the words of Clifford Geertz.[99] In *L'Afrique fantôme* the ethnographic 'authority' of participant-observation was exposed, as for Leiris, as Marc Blanchard has claimed, 'the best ethnographer is both an ironist and an accomplice'.[100] Leiris certainly did not shy away from seasoning his fieldwork accounts with personal speculation, including the texts and diary extracts published in *Minotaure* in 1933 as part of the presentation of the expedition's findings, aimed at a wider, less specialised audience. In Leiris's article 'Dogon funerary dances', recalling a night spent with a group of very drunken dancers, he transformed his informant, Ambara Dolo, into a Nervalian night-creature: 'I am the only spectator. Ambara … flits about in front of me, the skirts of his fitted coat fluttering like the wings of a sylph'.[101] The next day, he described the bowing movement of a tall Dogon *sirigue* mask during a funeral rite as being like 'a penis getting hard again after having gone limp'.[102] And in the article 'Fragments sur le Dahomey' in the special issue of *Minotaure* dedicated to the Dakar–Djibouti expedition, Leiris compared the appearance of a male sanctuary figure with a pince-nez in Ouidah to his own father.[103]

Griaule, on the other hand, in this important forum for presenting the expedition, was keen to stress the efficacy of the expedition's intensive and extensive fieldwork methods as a means of uncovering reluctantly withheld details from informants and contacts. To this end he pointed up the benefits of: 'a disciplined and large team, each member of which, while having a heightened sense of their own responsibility, knows that without the others he is nothing but an immovable cog.'[104] This evocation of teamwork eschewing individual personalities could be read as a veiled barb at the subjective indulgences of Leiris's diary. Crucially, at this point, the approaches of Leiris and Griaule, the two most prominent members of the expedition team, began to diverge.[105] Griaule's major account for *Minotaure*'s special issue concerned the funeral rites of a Dogon hunter, in which he aimed to present 'the document arising from the direct observation of a ceremony in an almost bare way'.[106] Leiris, presenting not a complete ritual, but a series of artefacts, stressed not the thorough and 'efficient' *penetration* of secret and sacred power, but its *preservation*. In the introduction to his discussion of Dogon objects, he claimed:

> Dogon country is too magically full of sanctuaries, ritual objects, sacred places of all kinds, the minds of the people who inhabit it crossed by a too dense network of myths and beliefs, their lives too continually linked to a web of rites for this account to be a panoramic one, still less an enumeration verging on the exhaustive.[107]

If, in Griaule's method, the object as 'witness' needed a stiff and intensive interrogation, for Leiris, its guarding of secrets might be an integral part of its identity. Leiris's interest in this regard was later reflected in the title of the dissertation he produced in 1938 at the Ecole des Hautes Etudes but only published a decade later, *La Langue secrète des Dogons de Sanga*.[108]

The *impenetrable* in Leiris's presentation of Dogon ritual objects collected by the expedition appeared to thwart the principles it had set out with: to gather, catalogue and describe meticulously. But Leiris's approach more broadly also offered a way out of the methodological impasse that the 'Summary Instructions' embodied. Jamin has pointed to the tautological outcome of the expedition's urge to describe and authenticate the ethnographic object:

> In each definition, on each label and each index card was expressed – through that redundancy that was meant to bring them forth – the doubt or mistrust, if not the suspicion, in which the ethnographic object was held, as if they wanted to efface the fact that for a long time it had only been an object of curiosity.[109]

The significance of the object as 'witness' with regard to the presentation of the expedition's findings in *Minotaure* and elsewhere was to imply not the 'veracity' of its 'testimonial', but its implication within a dynamic web of interrelationships. In Leiris's accounts of thefts and mutual ruses in *L'Afrique fantôme*, the object was cast as the observer and victim of duplicitous acts, unceremoniously 'kidnapped', stuffed up a shirt or into a bag. The objects collected by the Dakar–Djibouti expedition could introduce the European public to new and unfamiliar rituals in which they had been used, serving to further anthropological understanding. But in their new 'lives' in the glossy pages of the art magazine *Minotaure*, and in the stores and displays of the Trocadéro museum, they also had the potential to expose the faultlines of such 'holistic' models of comprehension. Ethnography's contingency and *creativity* could be glimpsed in and between the complex human negotiations that the ethnographic object, wrenched from its original context, imposed.

Notes

1 Salmon, 'L'art nègre' [1920], in *Propos d'atelier* (Paris: G. Crès, 1922), pp. 115–33.
2 *Ibid.*, pp. 116–17.
3 *Ibid.*, p. 116.
4 Malinowski, *A Diary in the Strict Sense of the Term* (1967) (Stanford: Stanford University Press, 1989), p. 141.
5 Balfour, *The Evolution of Decorative Art*, p. 41.
6 Durkheim, *Les Formes élémentaires*, pp. 167–80. The fact that Durkheim's work did not focus on available African material from France's colonies may have been due to the rift between theory and practice in the French social sciences, see Karady, 'Le problème de la légitimité', p. 30 and p. 33.
7 See Parezo, 'Cushing as Part of the Team: The Collecting Activities of the Smithsonian Institution', *American Ethnologist*, 12:4 (1985), pp. 763–74, and Jacknis, 'The Ethnographic Object and the Object of Ethnology in the Early Career of Franz Boas', in Stocking (ed.), *Volksgeist as Method and Ethic: Essays on Boasian Ethnography and the German Anthropological Tradition* (Madison: University of Wisconsin Press, 1996), pp. 185–214.
8 van Maanen, *Tales of the Field* (Chicago: University of Chicago Press, 1988), p. 37.

 9 Griaule and Leiris, *Instructions sommaires pour les collecteurs d'objets ethnographiques*
     (Paris: Musée d'Ethnographie, 1931).

10 See Miller, *Material Culture and Mass Consumption* [1987] (Oxford: Blackwell, 1994),
     pp. 109–12.

11 Boas, *Primitive Art* [1927] (New York: Dover, 1955).

12 Delafosse, *Haut-Sénégal-Niger* (1912) (Paris: Maisonneuve and Larose, 1972),
     pp. 161–2.

13 Desplagnes, *Le Plateau central nigérien*, p. 2.

14 *Ibid.*, pp. 367–8.

15 Jamin, 'Aux origines du musée de l'homme: La mission ethnographique et linguis-
     tique Dakar-Djibouti', *Cahiers ethnologiques*, 5 (1984), p. 10.

16 Mauss, *Manuel d'ethnographie*, p. 8.

17 See Lebovics, *True France*, pp. 28–35.

18 Karady, 'Le problème de la légitimité', p. 33.

19 Annexe to the minutes of the sitting of 24 March 1931, Chambre des députés, p. 2,
     MH/2 AM 1 M2.

20 Haardt and Audouin-Dubreuil, *The Black Journey: Across Central Africa with the
     Citroën Expedition* (London: Geoffrey Bles, 1928), p. 13.

21 See the photograph in *ibid.*, facing p. 134, 'The result of a morning's hunting'.

22 Griaule and Leiris, *Instructions sommaires*, p. 8.

23 *Ibid.*, p. 9.

24 Rivet, 'L'étude des civilisations matérielles', p. 133.

25 Griaule, 'Projet de la Mission ethnographique et linguistique Dakar-Djibouti'
     (21 September 1930), p. 5, MH/2 AM 1 M2g.

26 Mauss, *Manuel d'ethnographie*, pp. 95–6.

27 *Ibid.*, p. 89.

28 Griaule and Leiris, Instructions sommaires, p. 18.

29 Breton, *Nadja* (1928) (Paris: Gallimard, 1964), p. 59.

30 See Gregson and Crewe, *Second-Hand Cultures* (Oxford: Berg, 2003), p. 11.

31 Griaule and Leiris, *Instructions sommaires*, p. 9.

32 Kirschenblatt-Gimblett, 'Objects of Ethnography', in Karp and Levine
     (eds), *Exhibiting Cultures* (Washington, DC: Smithsonian Institution Press, 1991),
     p. 391.

33 R.[ené] D.[aumal], 'Au Musée d'Ethnographie du Trocadéro', p. 942, MH/2 AM 1
     B5a.

34 *Minotaure*, 1:2 (1933), p. 51.

35 See Marchand, 'The Rhetoric of Artifacts', pp. 108–11.

36 Griaule and Leiris, *Instructions sommaires*, p. 7.

37 *Notes and Queries on Anthropology*, 5th ed. (London: Royal Anthropological Institute,
     1929).

38 Griaule and Leiris, *Instructions sommaires*, p. 19.

39 Michel Foucault, *The Order of Things* [1966] (New York: Vintage, 1973), p. xv.

40 Griaule and Leiris, *Instructions sommaires*, p. 10 and pp. 23–5.

41 *Ibid.*, p. 10.

42 de Brosses, *Du Culte des dieux fétiches* [1760] (Paris: Fayard, 1988).

43 Tylor, *Primitive Culture*, p. 145.

44 Griaule and Leiris, *Instructions sommaires*, p. 9.

45 The expedition had an official colonial 'license for scientific capture' reproduced by Jamin in Leiris, *Miroir de l'Afrique* (Paris: Gallimard, 1996), p. 17.

46 Griaule and Leiris, *Instructions sommaires*, p. 8.

47 See Kuper, *Anthropologists and Anthropology: The British School 1922–72* (Harmondsworth: Penguin, 1978), p. 30.

48 On the 'theatrical' impulse in Leiris's ethnographic work, see Lotringer, 'Leiris et son double', *Gradhiva*, 13 (1993), pp. 43–50.

49 Leiris had attended some of Mauss's lectures at the Institut d'Ethnologie, but by all accounts had little specific ethnographic knowledge. See Jamin, 'Présentation' in Leiris, *Miroir de l'Afrique*, p. 68.

50 Jamin, 'Objets trouvés des paradis perdus. A propos de la Mission Dakar-Djibouti', in Hainard and Kaehr (eds), *Collections passion* (Neuchâtel: Musée d'ethnographie, 1982), pp. 69–100, and 'Aux origines du Musée de l'Homme', pp. 8–19.

51 According to an anonymous typescript dated 30 April 1931, 'Exposition de la Mission Dakar-Djibouti', MH/2AM 1 B9 d.

52 Omer, 'Le campement de l'expédition Dakar-Djibouti est installé au musée du Trocadéro', *Paris Midi* (1 May 1931), and M.-L. S., 'Au Palais du Trocadéro, la Mission Dakar-Djibouti', *Annales Coloniales* (2 May 1931), MH/2 AM 1 B9 d.

53 Leiris, 'L'oeil de l'ethnographe', p. 407.

54 Griaule, *Le Livre de recettes d'un dabtara abyssin* (Paris: L'Institut d'Ethnologie, 1930).

55 Georges Mouly, 'Avant le départ de la Mission Dakar-Djibouti', *Comoedia* (28 December 1930), MH/2 AM 1 B9 a.

56 Anon, *Comoedia* (14 February 1931), MH/2 AM 1 B9 a.

57 Griaule, 'Introduction méthodologique', *Minotaure*, 1:2 (1933), p. 8.

58 Seabrook, *The Magic Island* (London: Harrap, 1929), pp. 47–8.

59 Leiris, *Miroir de l'Afrique*, p. 362.

60 Leiris, *L'Afrique fantôme* (Paris: Gallimard, 1934), reprinted in full in *Miroir de l'Afrique*, pp. 61–869.

61 Leiris, *L'Age de l'homme* (Paris: Gallimard, 1939, reprinted with a new foreword in 1946). On the complex textual strategies of this novel, see Hand, *Michel Leiris*, pp. 72–84.

62 See Thornton, 'Narrative Ethnography in Africa, 1850–1920: The Creation and Capture of an Appropriate Domain for Anthropology', *Man*, 18:3 (September 1983), pp. 502–20.

63 Pratt, 'Fieldwork in Common Places', in Clifford and Marcus (eds), *Writing Culture* (Berkeley: University of California Press, 1986), pp. 27–50.

64 Leiris, *Miroir de l'Afrique*, pp. 101–2.

65 Gide, *Voyage au Congo, Carnets de route* (Paris: Gallimard, 1927). Gide's account was dedicated to Conrad.

66 Price and Jamin, 'Entretien avec Michel Leiris', p. 46.

67 'Asterisk' (Robert James Fletcher), *Isles of Illusion, Letters from the South Seas*, ed. Bohun Lynch (London: Constable, 1923), p. xiv.

68 Leiris, *Miroir de l'Afrique*, p. 140.

69 *Ibid.*, p. 136.

70 See Marchand, 'Leo Frobenius and the Revolt against the West', p. 160, note 26.

71 Leiris, *Miroir de l'Afrique*, p. 163.

72 *Ibid.*, p. 181.
73 Griaule, 'Introduction méthodologique', pp. 7–12.
74 Griaule, 'Comment nous avons étudié les Dogons, peuplade du Sangha', *Lyon-Républicain* (16 July 1933), MH/2 AM 1 B4 f.
75 Jamin, 'Aux origines du Musée de l'Homme', pp. 38–9.
76 Leiris, *Miroir de l'Afrique*, p. 255.
77 Malinowski's method had been apparent in one of his earliest essays, 'Baloma, the Spirits of the Dead in the Trobriand Islands' (1916), reprinted in *Magic, Science and Religion* (New York: Doubleday, 1954), pp. 149–274, and see in particular pp. 162–5. In one of his letters to his wife, Zette, Leiris hoped that the work of the expedition would be 'as interesting as that of Malinowski', cited by Jamin in Leiris, *Miroir de l'Afrique*, p. 68.
78 *Ibid.*, p. 225.
79 *Ibid.*, p. 119 and p. 131.
80 *Ibid.*, p. 138.
81 *Ibid.*, p. 396.
82 Parezo, 'Cushing as Part of the Team', p. 767.
83 Cushing in fact became more reluctant to steal objects as his knowledge of the Zuñi and Hopi increased, *ibid.*, pp. 771–2.
84 Leiris, *Miroir de l'Afrique*, p. 191 and p. 194.
85 *Ibid.*, p. 195.
86 Phillips (ed.), *Africa, The Art of a Continent* (London: Royal Academy, 1995), cat. no. 6.7, p. 498.
87 See Leiris' famous article 'L'ethnographe devant le colonialisme', *Les Temps modernes*, 6:58 (August 1950), pp. 357–74.
88 Leiris, *Miroir de l'Afrique*, p. 196.
89 My thanks to Jean-Michel Massing for pointing to the strong presence of adventure story tropes in L'Afrique fantôme during a seminar in Cambridge in 2001.
90 Leiris, *Miroir de l'Afrique*, pp. 266–7.
91 Gide, *The Immoralist* [1902] (Harmondsworth: Penguin, 1986), p. 157.
92 Leiris, *L'Age de l'homme*, pp. 25–8.
93 Leiris, *Miroir de l'Afrique*, letter of 13 November 1931, p. 266.
94 See Appadurai, 'Introduction: Commodities and the Politics of Value' in *The Social Life of Things*, p. 24.
95 Fabian, *Out of our Minds: Reason and Madness in the Exploration of Central Africa* (Berkeley: University of California Press, 2000).
96 These notebooks are in the archives of the Musée de l'Homme. Books V and VI are in another hand, with Leiris adding the very last entry, MH/2 AM 1 M2 B.
97 Malinowski, *A Diary in the Strict Sense of the Term*, and see Clifford Geertz on this text as anthropology's 'Double Helix', *Works and Lives*, p. 75.
98 Marcus and Fischer, *Anthropology as Cultural Critique.*
99 See Clifford, 'The Tropological Realism of Michel Leiris', *Sulfur*, 15 (1986), pp. 4–18, and Geertz, *Works and Lives*, where Leiris's encounter with Emayawish is used as the basis for the last chapter, pp. 129–49.
100 Blanchard, 'Visions of the Archipelago: Michel Leiris, Autobiography and Ethnographic Memory', *Cultural Anthropology*, 5:3 (1990), p. 271.
101 Leiris, 'Danses funéraires Dogon', *Minotaure*, 1:1 (1933), p. 74.

102 *Ibid.*, p. 75.

103 Leiris, 'Fragments sur le Dahomey', *Minotaure*, 1:2 (1933), p. 61.

104 Griaule, 'Introduction méthodologique', p. 12.

105 On the subsequent rift between them, exacerbated by Leiris's reluctance to let Griaule see drafts of his fieldwork diary before going to press, see Price and Jamin, 'Entretien avec Michel Leiris', p. 51.

106 Griaule, 'Le chasseur du 20 octobre', *Minotaure*, 1:2 (1933), p. 31.

107 Leiris, 'Objets rituels Dogon', *Minotaure*, 1:2 (1933), p. 26.

108 Leiris, *La Langue secrète des Dogons de Sanga* (Paris: Institut d'Ethnologie, 1948).

109 Jamin, 'Aux origines du Musée de l'Homme', p. 44.

4

Mediating: ethnography through a lens and behind glass

In the insert that he wrote for his account of the Dakar–Djibouti expedition, Leiris teased and tantalised his readers. *L'Afrique fantôme*, as its title suggested, delivered a 'phantom', illusory 'Africa', producing in its explorer–ethnographer only 'a greater and greater emotional emptiness'.[1] Referring to himself in the third person, Leiris claimed that: 'His attempt at escape has been only a failure, and he also no longer believes in the value of escape'.[2] However, in a playful twist to this lament of ethnographic non-fulfilment, the insert went on to reveal that:

> Such was the general plan for the work the author *would perhaps have written had he not been anxious above all to produce as objective and sincere a document as possible*, pre-ferring to confine himself to his logbook and simply publish that.[3]

What was and is the reader to make of this? The insert claims that subjectivity has been erased from what we are about to read, although of course we suspect already from the very beginning of the diary its central role. Is the text mediated by the emotions and prior experiences of the author and shaped accordingly as a narrative, or is it 'simply' day-to-day jottings? The 1951 edition of the anthropological hand-book *Notes and Queries* gave wonderfully laconic guidelines for the production of a daily ethnographic journal:

Weather.
Self.
Local activities and occupations.
Food.
Special events.[4]

How could an ethnographic account consist simply of a 'document' of this kind, transferring directly to paper 'found events'? How might the reader evaluate or measure the 'truthfulness' of these events?

The tensions that Leiris's fieldwork diary raises are crucial to the concept of ethnographic 'evidence'. A diary itself is already suspicious. As Michel Beaujour put it in an article comparing Breton's *Nadja* to Leiris's *L'Afrique fantôme*, the journal is 'a hypnotic love potion and induces scepticism as soon as we notice that it draws upon the novel's pharmacopoeia'.[5] Even the most banal notes, in keeping with the *Notes and Queries* instructions above, can be subject to poetic embellishment. How to provide proof that the writer really was *there* and saw *that* underlies the ethnographic account. The ethnographer's 'indispensable adjunct' in this respect, as a way to 'document a descriptive account', was photography.[6] Photography could serve to heighten and enhance the effect of 'truth' and authority that ethnography sought. However, as this chapter will examine, by the 1930s the role of photography in ethnography was already a contested one, and its function could only be ambivalent. Photography was central to the presentation of the findings of the Dakar–Djibouti expedition, both in the display mounted by the Trocadéro museum on its return, and in the special issue of the periodical *Minotaure* which served as a kind of exhibition catalogue. In both, photography itself, the interplay of photograph and text, and the juxtaposition of photograph and object set up interrelationships which variously framed, animated or silenced the 'object as witness'.

As Jamin has pointed out, the use of a 'luxury' art periodical to publicise the findings of an ethnographic expedition was not without its tensions.[7] This was particularly the case given that a forum for such material already existed in the form of the *Bulletin du Musée d'Ethnographie du Trocadéro*, which Jamin has described as a 'disciplined' continuation of *Documents* (it shared the same backer, Wildenstein).[8] Unsurprisingly, Leiris, with his art-world connections, largely facilitated the 'collaboration' with *Minotaure*. Using colour and high-quality reproductions, it might be assumed that *Minotaure* was comparatively expensive. Each issue, in fact, sold for fifteen francs, the same price per issue as the 'dryer' *Documents*. Special issues such as that devoted to the Dakar–Djibouti expedition cost 25 francs, but a year's subscription was only 75 francs, as opposed to 120 francs for *Documents*. So cost was not necessarily at stake. Also, *Minotaure* had a much less obvious connection than *Documents* to the trade in precious goods of the antiquarian market, a potential source of compromise, as we saw in Chapter 2. *Minotaure* was arguably, however, more populist in its outlook, and it was this engagement with a broader public realm that had the potential to trouble the ethnographic project.

The tensions that *Minotaure*'s self-positioning could create for ethnography can be brought into focus by two of the advertisements carried by the periodical. One was for 'La Compagnie Neptos', offering tours of Greece and its islands and special cruises for artists (reflecting the Greek connections of Tériade, collaborator and friend of the periodical's editor Albert Skira).[9] The offer of Greek cruises belonged to the realms of travel as leisure, travel writing and travel photography, realms from which ethnography was fighting hard to distance itself. The second advertisement was for the company 'Nord et Alpes', makers of specialist glass and metal vitrines, who had fitted out the Trocadéro during its overhaul in the early 1930s.[10] This piece of publicity signalled the transformation of the museum, from forgotten and unattractive to visitors, to prominent and fashionable. Rivière's work to raise the Trocadéro's profile entailed the staging of exhibitions and displays which would appeal to a broader and a more luxury-conscious audience, and which again would not sit easily with the institution's avowed ethnographic principles.

The shifts between the special issue of *Minotaure* and the Trocadéro displays that this chapter will trace also point to the moment when this meeting of the discipline of ethnography and the art world began to come undone. The bold attempt by the young ethnographers Griaule and Leiris in using an art magazine to constitute their discipline as what Jamin has called an 'epistemological avant-garde', engaging with all aspects of culture, also appeared to mark the limits of such an undertaking.[11] Having flirted with the art world, the Trocadéro Ethnographic Museum became notably more sober after 1933, more strictly treating its objects of display as the metonymic bearers of coherent cultural wholes. By the end of the decade, the new Musée de l'Homme and Rivière's Musée des Arts et Traditions Populaires dedicated to French 'folklore', would both epitomise this humanist vision. 1933 marked a high point, but also the breaking point, of the encounter between ethnography as it saw itself at that time and the avant-garde. This chapter will trace the complex questions raised by documentation and display that led to this theoretical and methodological impasse.

'Concrete trophies': ethnography and photographic evidence

Photography's interrelationship with the emerging discipline of anthropology in the nineteenth century has been extensively analysed.[12] In the twentieth century, however, its role as an ethnographic tool was much more complex and as such it is relatively under-examined. The impact and significance of participant observation served to downplay the importance of the photographic record. In the nineteenth century, anthropology and photography had both shared a discourse of epistemological illumination, the penetration of darkness through light, and of the fixing of temporal distance. In the twentieth, though, the growing stress in anthropological theory on social structures underlying visible phenomena made photography less appropriate as a means of conveying ethnographic findings.[13] The ethnographer's experience of a society's complexity, for instance the contradictions between what people said and what they actually did, seemed best suited to a textual account, such as Malinowski's seminal study of the Trobriand *baloma* spirits.[14] In terms of visual imagery in early twentieth-century ethnography, film, or at the very least photographic series recording the successive moments of an event witnessed, were preferable to the fixity of the still image.[15] Christopher Pinney has argued that the equation of anthropological photography with western knowledge, power and control, based on an assumption of photography's indexicality and denotative function, is undermined as soon as we accept the indeterminacy of a photograph's meaning and the uncertainty of its 'authority'.[16] This perspective allows for more subtle readings of the power dynamics of the photograph as a means of capturing the 'other'. But it also points to the problem of photography for ethnography in the twentieth century: once the medium is no longer seen to be 'authoritative', a piece of 'evidence' or a 'document', its function cannot remain the same.

Surrealist photography and the use of photography in surrealism have marked themselves out as a terrain precisely of the indeterminate and the uncertain, where the indexical nature of the medium is constantly problematised. More pertinent to the ethnographic perspective, recent work by Ian Walker has focused on the surrealists' interest in so-called 'straight' photography: photographic documents and found images inserted into surrealist periodicals, or the apparently banal city snaps of Jacques-André Boiffard for Breton's *Nadja* (1928) and for *Documents*.[17] In *Nadja*, for instance, the inclusion of photographs of places in Paris mentioned in the text can be seen at first as a form of 'proof' of the events recounted. However, the narrative itself is constantly undermining this proof, through its temporal distance to the experiences described and, more importantly, their 'fantastic' nature. Breton had enigmatically examined the concepts of proof and evidence in his 1924 article 'Introduction to the Discourse on the Paucity of Reality', where they emerged as a function of travel accounts.[18] In this text, originally a lecture, Breton made a comparison between a quasi-ethnographic and a poetic proof:

> Let's not forget that only our belief in a certain practical necessity keeps us from according poetic speech a value equal to the one we accord, for example, the speech of an explorer. Human fetishism, which needs to try on the white helmet, to caress the fur bonnet, listens to the tale of our expeditions with an entirely different ear. It must absolutely believe that *this has happened*.[19]

In response to this, Breton proposed the creation of objects seen in dreams: 'to respond to this desire for perpetual verification'.[20] His example of such an object was a strange book whose spine consisted of a wooden gnome with a white beard 'styled in Assyrian fashion', which in his dream he acquired at an open-air market, and which he was sad not to find by his side upon awakening.[21] For Breton, in this striking passage, the reconstitution of such dream-objects was a way of helping to 'ruin those concrete and hateful trophies', presumably those things brought back by the explorer.[22] While questioning the status of this ethnographic 'proof', Breton instead posited objects as a kind of false evidence, the tangible and concrete as testimony of the imaginary. No wonder that these objects, whose creation Breton was encouraging, in what has rightly been seen as one of the first crucial articulations of the surrealist object, would be 'eminently problematic and disturbing'.[23]

Photography within surrealism could play a vital role in the simultaneous materialisation and dematerialisation of objects as false evidence. A good photograph could render the details and textures of an object like the cylindrical graph found at the flea market in *Nadja* (figure 15). But it could also, through its flattening and isolating qualities, especially as the graph is starkly shown against a solid black background, turn the three-dimensional object into an image (like the 'signs' evoked in *Nadja*). In the 1964 edition of *Nadja*, the graph is shown on a page facing a photograph of the Saint-Ouen flea market, its purported origin. However, if the strange cylindrical object is provided here with its originating context, there is no evidence to actually connect them (a photograph of the graph, for instance, *at* the flea market). Both photographs are also curiously disembodied in relation to the main narrative, manifesting no concrete link to either 'Breton', the narrator, or to Nadja. A similar tactic is evident in *L'Amour fou*, where the slipper-spoon and the metal visor found by Breton are again photographed in isolation, of unknown scale, free-floating in an indeterminate space and time, in contrast with the specific connotations the narrative weaves around them.[24] In *Nadja*, of course, this dislocation of the object is partly due to the fact that it refers to events in the past, which the narrative is now attempting to piece together. Photographic 'evidence' thus relates to the period of the creation of the book (summer and autumn 1927), rather than to the time the narrative deals with (primarily the autumn of 1926). The cylindrical graph itself, with its processes of measurement, a bit like the thermometer-cum-eye-chart in the de Chirico painting *The Dream of Tobias* (1917) that hung in the surrealist 'bureau of research', evoked spatio-temporal displacement and disturbance.

Margaret Iversen has argued that both the surrealist 'found object' (in distinction to the 'ready made') and the photograph share a special relationship to the Lacanian 'traumatic real', mediated through Barthes' concept of the photographic 'punctum'.[25] In this sense, these objects double or repeat the function of the

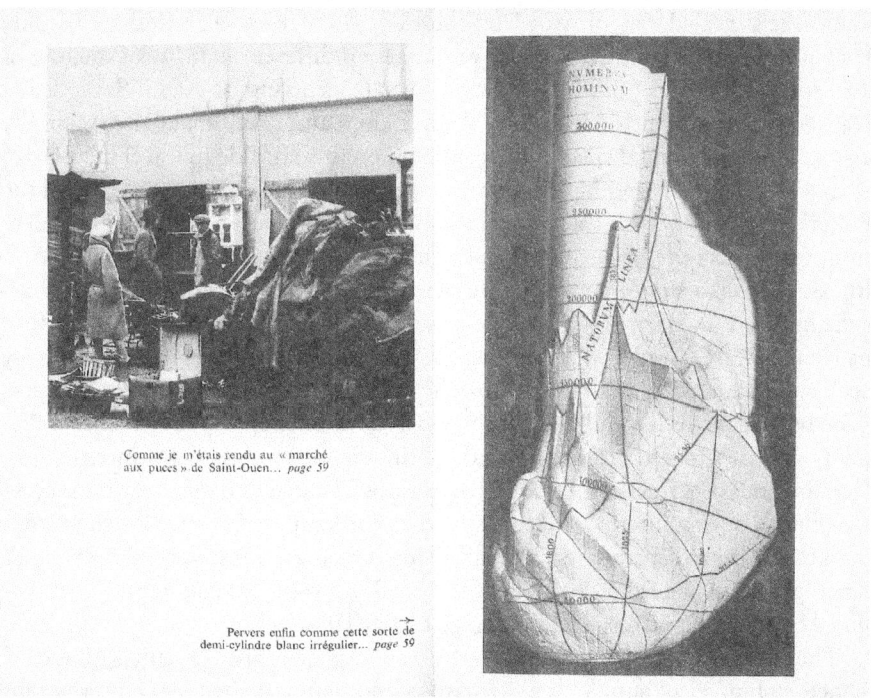

Comme je m'étais rendu au « marché
aux puces » de Saint-Ouen... *page 59*

Pervers enfin comme cette sorte de
demi-cylindre blanc irrégulier... *page 59*

15 Cylindrical object (population curve), plaster, 34.5 x 17 x 9, private collection and Saint-Ouen fleamarket (photographed by Jacques-André Boiffard), in André Breton, *Nadja* (1928/1964).

photographs of them. If the photograph, as Iversen puts it with reference to Barthes, attests to 'a reality in a past state, an ectoplasm, a reality one can no longer touch', then the surrealist found object similarly partakes of this ambivalence, being 'both lost and found'.[26] For the object to have this traumatic effect, as something strange and un-locatable, requires an image of it out of context. Indeed, when one sees the cylindrical graph or the slipper-spoon in the flesh, it is hard to associate them with their dramatically lit photographic images. Clearly, a sense of *loss* is also crucial to the ethnographic object, as a fragment of a lost whole, and as a material thing at threat from cultural change or (literally) from the environment. The 'blankness' of the ethnographic object, as something whose original meaning is lost and which now serves as a space onto which its 'finder' now projects new meanings, also has parallels with the surrealist found object as a bearer of complex narratives. In both cases, the photograph *of* the object can prove its brute existence, but with its slippery surface can also make explicit its constructed nature.

It is via these paradoxes, then, that surrealist found objects might avoid becoming those 'despicable, concrete trophies' decried by Breton. As 'little unimaginable objects', they could make physical the phantasmatic and provide a highly ambivalent kind of 'evidence'.[27] If Breton had imagined a comparison between the poet and the explorer in his early theorisation of the object, in keeping with the role of travel in the surrealist imagination, a striking model for the ambiguities he revealed was provided by the example of Roussel.[28] Roussel became known as an extensive traveller who was largely indifferent to many of the tourist attractions and sights he visited, taking refuge in his luxury caravan.[29] Several surrealists, including Leiris, Desnos and Vitrac, knew and wrote about Roussel in the 1920s, and Leiris would specifically comment on this attitude to travel in his 1935 essay 'The Traveller and his Shadow', written after Roussel's death.[30] One of the writer's concerns was to track down the purported graves of fictional characters from the works of fellow explorer and writer Pierre Loti (Julien Viaud) in Tahiti. Roussel put up a wooden cross beside the grave of the son of one Rarahu, a character in Loti's *Le Mariage de Loti* who in fact was an amalgam of Maori women Loti had encountered, rather than an actual, specific person. Roussel also eagerly acquired a photograph claiming to be of Rarahu from a lawyer in Paris.[31] His enterprise both as a novelist and playwright and as a traveller appeared to make no distinction between fact and fiction, indeed the distinction itself was meaningless. Certain kinds of 'evidence' accumulated by Roussel also found their way into surrealist circles during the 1930s. Jacques Hérold was supposed to have found at a flea market in Paris a display case with a dried rose bearing the inscription in Roussel's hand 'picked by me from the tomb of Aziyadé' (Aziyadé was another of Loti's fictional heroines, based on a real woman he met in Turkey).[32]

The most famous of Roussel's objects was the star-shaped biscuit with a label signed by him, also found at the flea market and photographed by Dora Maar for *Cahiers d'art* in 1936 (figure 16).[33] According to its label, locked into a small five-pointed box with a glass lid was 'a star from a lunch that I had on Sunday 29 July

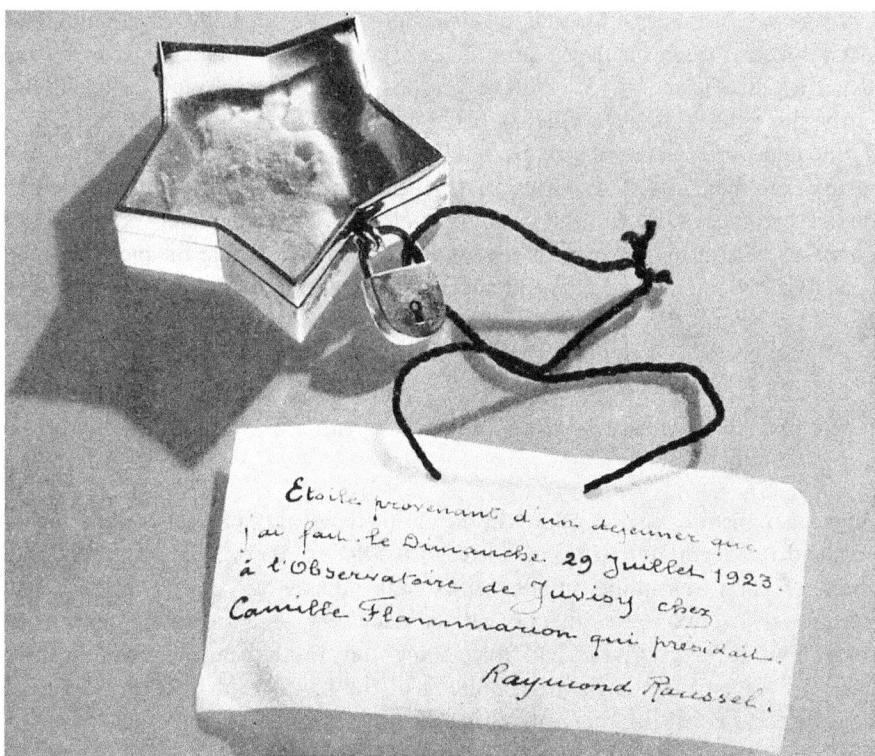

16 Roussel's star-shaped biscuit, photographed by Dora Maar, *Cahiers d'art*, 1–2 (1936).

1923 at the observatory of Juvisy at the home of Camille Flammarion, who presided'. Did this object serve as proof merely of Roussel having attended this prestigious event? For Bataille, who had this object in his desk drawer for several months and could not speak about it 'without being perturbed', the star-biscuit was most significant because of its edible nature, able to be absorbed in the most thorough way.[34] 'The strange object for me', Bataille wrote in an essay on Masson, 'meant that Roussel had achieved in his way the dream that he must have had of "eating a star in the sky"'.[35] Bataille's reading suggested ethnological interpretations of sympathetic and contagious magic, working on principles of similarity (eating a biscuit *like* a star) and actual physical contact (consuming the biscuit). In this way, Roussel's biscuit was *both* a 'concrete trophy' and a dream-object.

While apparently originating at the flea market, domain of the dispossessed object, Roussel's star was not 'illegible' and ownerless: a label like those attached to ethnographic objects set out its identity and provenance. Its label pointed to its additional significance as, presumably, a *gift* from Flammarion. Although acquired as a dislocated commodity, this object can be interpreted as representing an alternative gift economy, an inalienable thing embodying a network of social dependencies. Hence the need to seal away its inherent charge (its 'mana' in Mauss's terms) in a special case, and for Bataille to keep it *inside a drawer*. Following the logic of Bataille's 1933 essay on the 'Notion of Expenditure', this modest biscuit represented a kind of excessive loss, a gift that could now no longer be reciprocated ('lost' in the flea market, its owner dead).[36] The photograph of it published in *Cahiers d'art* could 'verify' its existence, particularly by reproducing, almost more prominently than the encased biscuit itself, its 'authenticating' label. It could also point up the real object's absence, the lack of possible physical 'contagion', and indeed its possible 'fabrication' as a bogus piece of evidence (protesting its specimen-like objectivity too much). In Maar's photograph of Roussel's biscuit, it was doubly distant, held behind the glass lid of its container with a miniature padlock, like the ethnographic object sealed in a vitrine or fixed photographically.

The spectacular and the banal: ethnography and photography in *Minotaure*

Surrealism manipulated expertly the 'scientific' languages of photography for its own ends, undermining its claims to authority. For ethnographers too at the forefront of their discipline, photography was already an outmoded practice. Malinowski later conceded that he had not made very good use of photography in his own work, feeling that he had 'put photography on the same level as collecting curios'.[37] Beyond the intriguing doubling of the photograph and the surrealist object ('curio') that this suggests, it is clear that by the time the special issue of *Minotaure* devoted to the Dakar–Djibouti expedition appeared in 1933, the use of photography for anthropological means was contested and problematic. As Poignant has pointed out, photography's immediacy in fact could lead it to be discredited, as it did not tally with the 'objectifying intentions' of the anthropological monograph: 'The publication of photographs of informants and places exposed the anthropologist's privileged field of view'.[38] As we have seen in Chapter 3, it was precisely the ambiguities of the 'privileged' point of view of the ethnographer that Leiris exploited to great effect in *L'Afrique fantôme*.

Alternative visual means for 'documenting' ethnographic experiences were available in the 1920s and 1930s. Published ethnographic accounts in the early twentieth century still tended to rely quite heavily on drawings as illustrations, as well as using photographs. In Frobenius's account of the 1910–12 German Inner Africa Exploration Expedition, illustrations 'after' watercolours and oil paintings as well as line drawings sat happily alongside photographs providing evidence of significant new archaeological finds.[39] 'Colonial artists', like Iacovleff of the 'Croisière noire', would often accompany expeditions in order to provide a 'recording' service. The work of the artist G. Geo-Fourier, who had travelled in the Middle Congo region collecting objects and making sketches and photographs, was shown at the Trocadéro in spring 1933, a couple of months before the Dakar–Djibouti expedition findings.[40] Where photographs were used, these were not always of good quality and easy to decipher. The only photograph showing

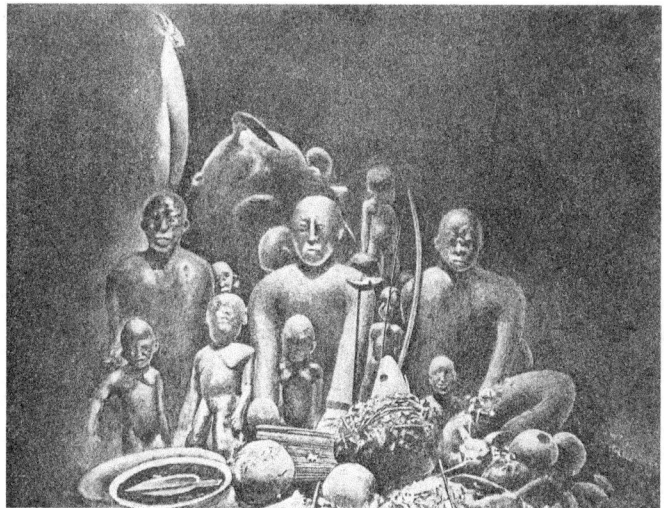

17 Statues and objects in a Birifo funerary chapel, Donko, Gaoua, in Delafosse, *Haut-Sénégal-Niger* (1912), plate XLI, fig. 80.

ritual artefacts in Delafosse's major study of French West Africa, *Haut-Sénégal-Niger* of 1912, had been taken in a poorly illuminated cave, without the knowledge or permission of its guardians, and appeared to have been touched up (figure 17).[41] An image like this blurred the distinction between photographic 'evidence' and artist's (or ethnographer's) impression.

The virtues of photography for physical anthropology were brought into focus by the negative critical responses to an exhibition of ethnographic 'types' by Malvina Hoffmann at the Trocadéro in November–December 1933. Her bronze and patinated plaster sculptures reproducing men and women of 'human races' in minute detail and in exact proportion (although reduced in scale), were considered by one reviewer as redundant in the face of comparable photographic records.[42] However, the ethnographic principles behind the Dakar–Djibouti expedition were intended to go beyond the concerns of anthropometry or 'racial types' that had so dominated late-nineteenth-century anthropology. These discourses lingered in Delafosse's account of French colonies, as we might expect, but also in the Dakar–Djibouti expedition's own presentation in *Minotaure* of 'Some types of North Cameroon'.[43] In the context of Griaule's desire to carry out 'police ethnography' during the Dakar–Djibouti expedition, such photographs could perform a function of surveillance (bearing in mind Griaule's background in the airforce and his penchant for aerial photographs). Some of the fieldwork photographs the expedition produced apparently aimed to convey the speed and confusing bustle of a large event, such as the large-scale ceremonies of the funeral of a Dogon hunter and the sacrifice of an Ethiopian bull. Indifferently lit and composed, seemingly taken quickly and in large numbers, these at times illegible images created a discourse not of the meticulous and detailed 'capture' of their subjects, but of documentary 'authenticity', the on-the-spot snaps of the journalist–detective.

The production of photographic series also pointed to the expedition's (limited) use of film.[44]

The publication of the findings of the Dakar–Djibouti expedition in a special issue of *Minotaure*, however, brought this anthropological material (the recording of bodies) into a confrontation with prevailing conventions for the presentation of art works (the recording of objects). This tension was set out in the second issue's preamble:

> You will notice that, as well as setting aside much space for photographs of objects, we have reproduced a large number of photographs of types, sites, scenes and documents of different kinds. Believing that it is more necessary than ever not to separate science from life, we have forced ourselves to give to the reader all the elements that will allow him to situate the published documents in their true atmosphere[45]

This statement seemed to let slip the admission of those putting together the ethnographic issue, such as Leiris, that 'photographs of objects' could be at odds with 'documents' in their context. Certainly *Minotaure*, like *Documents* before it, drew liberally upon photographs of single objects, a ubiquitous visual language in 1920s and 1930s art magazines. To isolate ethnographic objects, and show them 'cut-out' against a plain white background, was one of the presentational languages used by *Minotaure* that might be seen as apparently 'aesthetic'. Since its inception, photography had found a natural affinity with 'sculpture' as a means of highlighting the qualities of form and material.[46]

However, as Elizabeth Edwards has pointed out, one of photography's earliest applications was also in the clear visual description of objects.[47] An emphasis on form, texture and materials, a uniform light and the removal of background shadows to create 'floating objects' were all means of construing the object as 'pure specimen'.[48] Nicolas Thomas has analysed the precedent to this, in the eighteenth-century use of engraved or drawn reproductions of isolated and de-contextualised ethnographic objects seen as 'specimens' and sites of scientific enquiry, in an attempt to wrest them from the vagaries of (morally suspect) 'curiosity'.[49] In this way, the 'aesthetic' and the 'scientific' isolation and photographing of the object overlapped. Only through subtle signifiers of a conscious ethnographic context might the object retain its status as 'document', signifiers that in fact would disturb the 'purity' of the specimen. 'All objects should be photographed', Mauss wrote in his *Manuel d'ethnographie*, 'preferably in a natural way' ('sans pose').[50] *Notes and Queries* recommended that: 'an artificial background made of cloth, preferably of a dove grey colour, is stretched between two poles at sufficient distance for the object to be out of focus, but near enough to cover the whole field'.[51] The pieces of plain canvas as backdrops, guiding strings, or bits of museum floor or wall visible in photographs of objects from the Trocadéro's collection, in the *Minotaure* special issue and elsewhere (for example in the images accompanying Rivière's article 'Archéologismes'), might be the only registers dividing the specimen from the art work.

Arguably, the de-contextualised object presented photographically was already too over-determined to serve an 'objective' purpose in the pages of *Minotaure*. More immediately, with regard to the periodical's singling out in 1933 of certain pieces found and acquired by the expedition, the notion of the ethnographic 'masterpiece' had been reinforced with special vigour by Rivière's installation of the so-called 'Treasury' at the Trocadéro in 1932 (figure 18). Aided by sculptor Jacques Lipchitz, who designed special black marble plinths and the lighting scheme, Rivière assembled the 'gems' of the museum's collection: a Hawaiian feathered helmet, a gold Ivory Coast mask, a Marquesan *Tiki*, a Mexican crystal skull, an Aztec 'serpent god', Precolumbian masks, a Benin plaque, and an ivory headrest from the Belgian Congo on loan from Charles Ratton. One journalist described the room in which these were placed as 'chapel-like', and another evoked it as follows: 'A small, long and narrow room, with no windows, it has the air of a secret chamber; but, clothed in white, with narrow and luminous niches with pink backdrops, where each highlighted treasure rests, it also has the most modern of looks'.[52] The pieces which were selected for this installation, by virtue of their special 'artistic' qualities, deserved, according to Rivière, a place apart: 'a little realm where they can enjoy the privilege of extraterritoriality, relieved of scientific apparatus and classification, and brought together for our eyes' pleasure'.[53] While the ethnographers of the Dakar–Djibouti expedition were away in Africa, Rivière was creating a crowd-pleasing display whose values of preciousness and uniqueness contradicted their own disciplinary aims. How to not fall into the trap of encouraging similar values in the presentation of specific, isolated objects was surely one of the implicit goals of the *Minotaure* special issue.

18 The 'Treasury' at the Trocadéro Ethnographic Museum (1932–35), photographed in 1934.

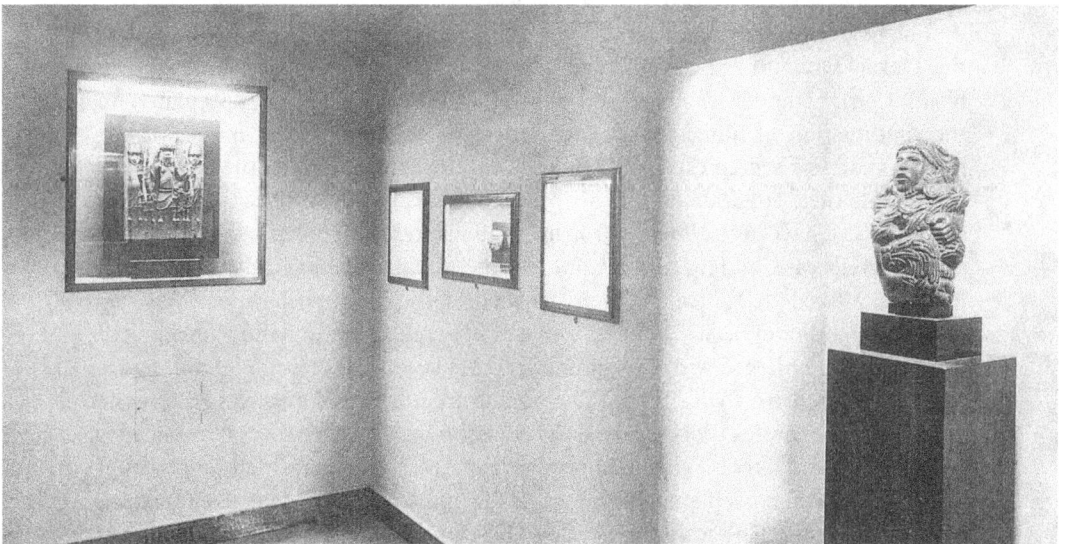

One of the functions the special ethnographic issue of *Minotaure* could have, was to present the expedition's findings in the form of selected artefacts. Like surrealist found objects, when presented in isolation, these could carry with them a special charge. A good example of this was the Bamana *boli* altar figure (known to the expedition as a *kono* figure) (see figure 14). The photograph of it carried in *Minotaure* heightened its tactile qualities: the thick layer of encrusted blood covering and concealing its hidden inner forms. Like the cylindrical graph in Breton's *Nadja*, or the stone found on a beach by Einstein in *Documents*, its immediate appearance was unfamiliar and also sculptural, inviting an imagined bodily encounter with its surfaces and volumes. The Bamana *boli* figure was doubly mysterious because of the impossibility of knowing what it might contain: a real animal skeleton, a constructed form in wood, magical substances or objects, an empty space? Made of mud, wax and blood over wood, the object has a cavity inside it linking its 'mouth' and 'anus', through which meat and water were passed in sacrificial rituals, according to a later account.[54] This object, and others like it, as we have seen in Chapter 3, were stolen from sanctuaries and sacred sites in the then French Sudan, and the fact that they were deliberately withheld from the ethnographers of the Dakar–Djibouti expeditions inevitably heightened their cachet. Particularly in terms of Griaule's police-detective imagery, these figures were *star* 'witnesses', bearing testimony to what was most secret and hidden. Some of the press reviews of the expedition's findings played up the horrific possibilities of these objects. One commentary described 'mysterious objects covered in coagulated blood used for terrible and unknown rituals', while another claimed that the *kono* figure contained in all likelihood, despite its animal appearance, a child's corpse.[55] Leiris himself helped to encourage these associations in an interview for *Paris-Midi* where he discussed the possible continuing practice of human sacrifice amongst the cultures studied by the expedition.[56]

The Dogon 'mothers of masks', some of the most striking artefacts collected by the Dakar–Djibouti expedition, had also been formerly baptised with human blood, Leiris claimed in a press interview.[57] In *L'Afrique fantôme* he speculated on the continuation of human sacrifice amongst the Dogon, having found a fresh human skull in a sacred cave, and reading into the expressions on the faces of his informants their concealment of this practice.[58] Clearly, these sensationalist suggestions must have been aimed at arousing public interest in the expedition, as well as, in Leiris's case, adding to the Conradesque tone of death and danger that his field diary liked to cultivate. One of the photographs published in *Minotaure* showed a 'mother of masks' lying on a pile of human remains, inviting a reading of its austere head pierced with two gaping rectangular holes as a human skull (figure 19). In his extensive 1938 study of Dogon culture in relation to masking, Griaule described the complex process of mask fabrication that involved several animal sacrifices before and after carving, including to the tree itself from which wood would be hewn. An iron hook planted in the mask's front plane had a protective function, having been bathed in sacrificial blood.[59] These masks were stored carefully raised

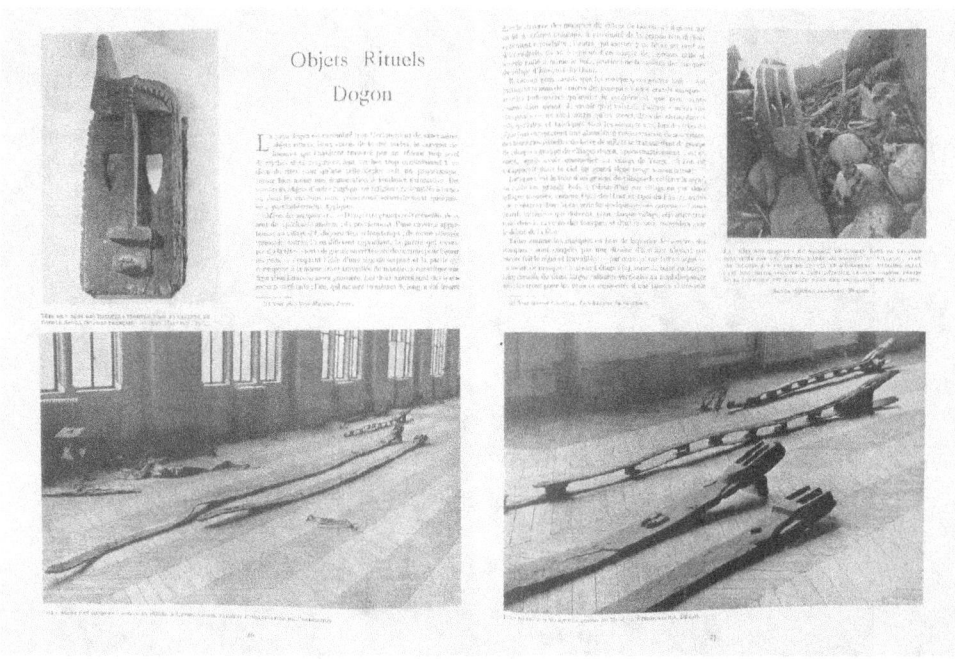

19 Dogon 'mothers of masks', Gogoli, Sanga, and shown at the Trocadéro Ethnographic Museum, *Minotaure*, 1:2 (1933).

on stones or inserted into rock crevices to protect them from termites, usually in special caves near villages that were prohibited to women and children. The question of what these masks might have *seen* while in hidden, sacred places, or while being sacrificially prepared, surely gave them an added gravitas and poignancy.

These giant masks, measuring up to ten metres long and made from the wood of the kapok tree, were some of the most striking artefacts collected by the expedition. Their great size, making them difficult to transport, ensured their impressive impact. Unlike some of the other dance masks collected by the expedition with more familiar bodily proportions, the giant masks had an architectural function, moved in and out of the houses of dead secret-society members during a ten-day ritual, according to Leiris's account in *Minotaure*.[60] Like the so-called 'masks with storeys' (*sirige*), which made explicit architectural reference to tall Dogon buildings, these large masks had openings in their wooden length 'so that the wind could pass through and not knock them over'.[61] Leiris also mentioned an old legend of a giant mask in a mountain cave emerging and retreating of its own accord.[62] The conjunction in these objects of architectural feature, unwieldy dance mask, and a kind of huge zoomorphised snake was a powerful challenge to established categories of non-western artefact. Jean Cassou noted their striking impact in a review of the 1933 Dakar–Djibouti display, where he described them as 'singular creatures that partake of both object and animal, strange snakes loaded with mystery'.[63]

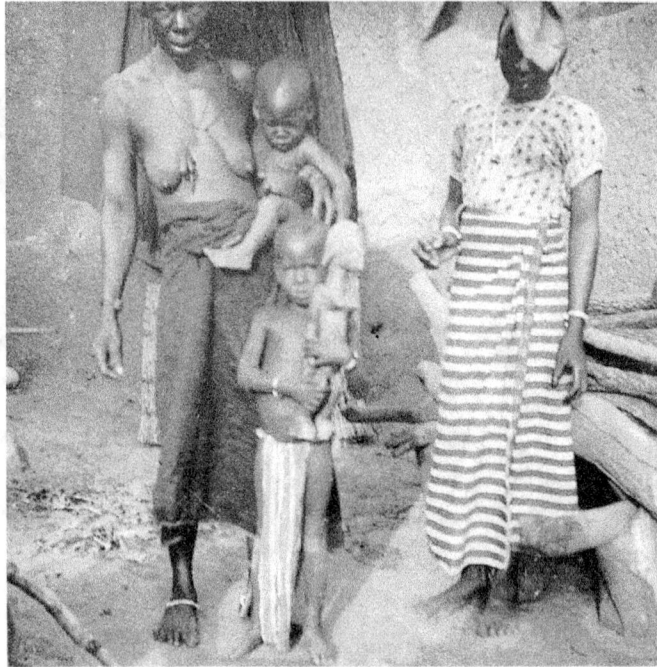

20 *The potter's daughter holding a doll bought from a Sakyu blacksmith*, Bamako, 1931, photograph by Marcel Griaule.

The Dogon 'mothers of masks' clearly fitted the sense of 'spectacle' that Jamin has characterised as a major aspect of the expedition's approach, and that appears to motivate many of the photographs published in *Minotaure*.[64] Photographs taken by the expedition team but not included in the periodical showed objects in much more banal interactions with their human owners and users. In one, a young potter's daughter in Bamako holds a figure acquired by the expedition, her eyes meeting the camera with bewilderment (figure 20). There is nothing to 'see' in this photograph with respect to ritual practices, nothing for the collected object itself to 'witness'. Ironically, however, an image like this comes closer to the kinds of complex and uneasy human transactions described by Leiris in his field diary. One dark photograph used in the periodical does point to these transactions, showing a 'mother of masks' taken out of its cave-sanctuary and apparently propped on the head of the informant, 'Petit Abara', who revealed its secret location to the expedition team.[65]

The presentation of objects collected by the Dakar–Djibouti expedition looked to situate these within the documented rituals and customs of specific groups of peoples. Some objects were shown deliberately both in and out of use: Dogon masks, and the *wasamba* circumcision rattles of the Bamana and Mandigue, shown variously against neutral white backgrounds, throwing dramatic shadows, and also in the hands of young boys undergoing circumcision rituals.[66] However, the collage-like juxtaposition of objects from very *different* cultures which was a feature of *Documents* and also, more prominently, of *Cahiers d'art*, had no place in the special issue of *Minotaure*. We could compare in this respect the presentation of African objects in *Minotaure*'s article 'Variétés du Soudan français' with the illustrations to Zervos's article on contemporary sculpture for *Cahiers d'art* in 1929, which included a Sepik figure from Pierre Loeb's collection (figures 21 and 22).[67] Zervos's plates evoke a principle of universal syncretism. While the *Minotaure* miscellany from the French Sudan brought together objects and a cloudscape with little explanation, their geographical location and the context of the expedition gave them an apparent 'time and place'. The photograph of clouds in the sky, a moment of ephemerality fixed forever, underlined the temporality of the combination of images, albeit tinged with poetic cliché.

'Surrealist ethnography', in Clifford's famous essay, is marked by the collage principle, and 'that moment in which the possibility of comparison exists in unmediated tension with sheer incongruity'.[68] This definition might more readily apply to the collection of things shown in the page from *Cahiers d'art* than to this *Minotaure* double-page spread. Perhaps this is not so surprising, as Clifford's formulation evokes certain broad perceptions of modernist art practice and its effects, rather than a specific surrealist sensibility. Surrealism often had good reason to be drawn towards unified wholes, as Michael Richardson, in his critique of Clifford's essay, has shown.[69] As a humanist discipline in this period, ethnography was geared towards creating comprehensible wholes, the 'total social facts' of Mauss, and not towards

21 Horn with human head, Nyangaso, San, wood, 45h, Bamana sacrificial calabash, Dyabougou, San, 15d, cloudscape, San and Kono ritual mask, Nougna, San, 84h, for 'Miscellany of the French Sudan', *Minotaure* 1:2 (1933).

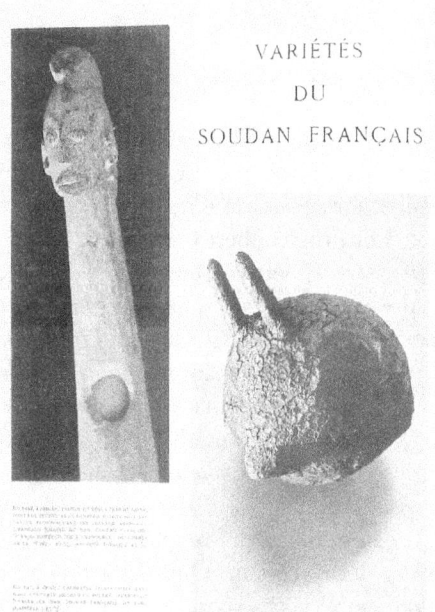
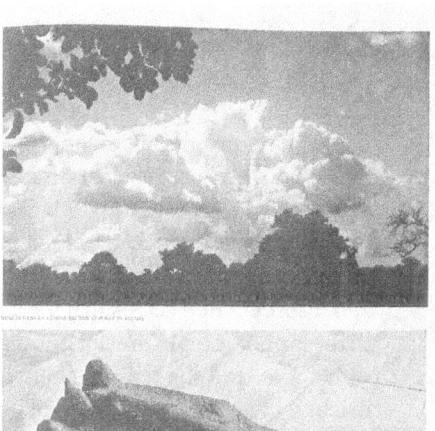

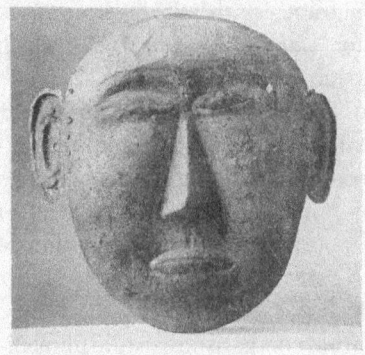
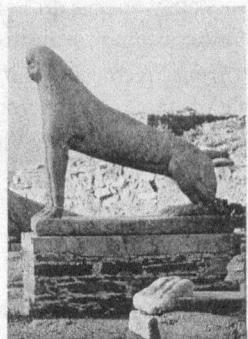
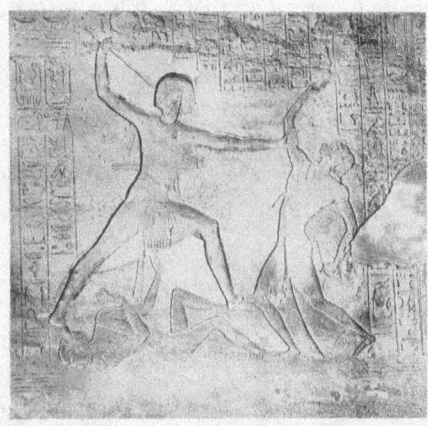
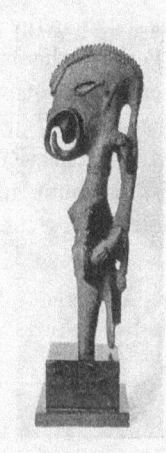

22 Chinese archaic mask, lion, Delos, frieze, Luxor and *Parrot with lizard on its back*, Sepik River, New Guinea, 47h, collection of Pierre Loeb, in *Cahiers d'art*, 4:10 (1929).

deliberately promoting incongruity or the 'unusual'.[70] The archaic Chinese mask, Delos lion, Luxor frieze and Sepik figure brought together by Zervos are 'incongruous', in a way that the Sudanese trumpet for agricultural rites and objects covered in sacrificial chicken's blood, are not. The problem here might lie in Clifford's suggestion of the '*unmediated* tension' [my stress] between epistemological order and disorder, for it seems that mediation precisely is crucial. The objects and scenes in these photographs are not given to us directly but filtered through different visual discourses, and the tensions between them are similarly manipulations of already existing meanings. Clifford's definition implies the immediacy of the 'document' (and, indeed, the supposed 'spontaneity' of surrealist automatism). The interest of the imagery used in the special ethnographic issue of *Minotaure* lies instead in its complex negotiation of apparently banal visual languages.

An obvious appeal of the 'catalogue' to an ethnographic expedition to a wider public could be its inclusion of exotic local colour. One reviewer of the Dakar–Djibouti exhibition and its catalogue praised its lavish photographic illustrations and its inclusion of striking scenes: 'It is no longer, according to the outdated aims of a narrow ethnography, only the *material* specimen but also the poetry of the moment, like a sunset for example, that has a place in the collection of the investigators'.[71] The image of the 'sunset over the Niger', included amongst a discussion of Bani roof finials, like the Sudanese cloudscape, pointed to the travelogue and the guidebook. How could such scenes, examples presumably of the special issue's tendency to run 'dangerously close to the touristic', as Walker has claimed, be reconciled with the ethnographic project?[72] An intriguing example for the Dakar–Djibouti expedition in this respect, especially given Leiris's involvement as 'secretary' and also as the (unnamed) editor of *Minotaure* no. 2, were Gide's travels in the Congo and the publication of photographs from them taken by Marc Allégret.[73] Gide's article 'Architectures nègres' for *Cahiers d'art* in 1927 included striking images of different kinds of dwelling.[74] His text, however, stressed above all the 'beauty' of these buildings. Gide's travel diary, *Voyage au Congo*, published the same year, provided geo-political information, mainly in the form of long footnotes and appendices, and became known for its critiques of the colonial system.[75] Its main text, nevertheless, was marked by the recurrent themes of the picturesque, the exotic and the beautiful, taking the form of interlacing greenery, spectacular sunsets and sunrises:

> The sun rises as we enter the Bolobo pool. On the vast stretching expanse of water, not a ripple … it is like an intact scale, where the very pure reflection of the pure sky sparkles. In the east a few long clouds reddened by the sun. To the west, sky and lake share the same pearly colour … The enchantment of this mystical landscape only lasts a few moments[76]

The mingling in Gide's account of 'documentation' and 'poetry', and the respect he gained for his commentary on colonial mores, blurred the boundaries of travel writing and ethnographic account. Already in his *Voyage au Congo*, the 'picturesque' took its distance from the touristic.

Minotaure's two-page spread 'Variétés du Soudan français' placed its scudding clouds alongside two objects covered in sacrificial blood, disturbing any conventional 'poetic' impulse, particularly as the photographic landscape heightened the sensual tactility of the blood-encrusted surfaces. But one of these photographs also doubly disturbed the cohesion of the spread. While the landscape carried the caption 'Clouds in the San region (French Sudan)', the *kono* mask below it, from the same region, was photographed not in Africa, but lying on the distinctive parquet flooring of the Trocadéro museum. Seen together, these images arguably worked against the principle of indexical 'authenticity', the 'we were there and saw that'. The *kono* mask pictured rather forlornly on the Trocadéro floor evoked precisely not the genuine ethnographic experience but the object in limbo, freefloating and open to interpretation and further interaction with its now western viewers and handlers.

This type of presentation was apparent in the series of amateur-style shots for Leiris's article 'Dogon ritual objects', taken in the Trocadéro's empty rooms,

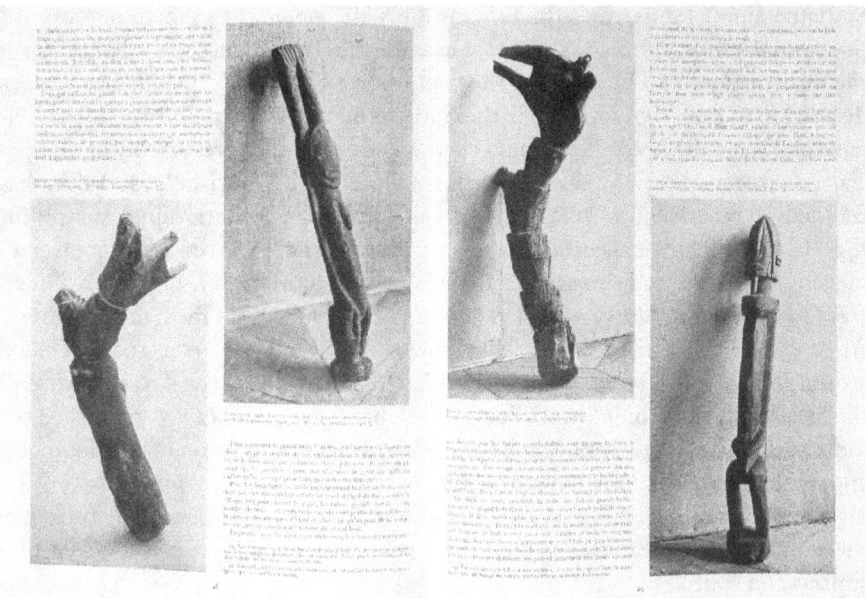

23 *Bazou*, Sanga, 106h, statue with raised arms, Yougo, 45h, *bazou*, Dyamini, Sanga, 110h and anthropomorphic statue, Dyamini, 85h, *Minotaure* 1: 2 (1933).

presumably prior to installation (figure 23). Objects were propped against a wall or in one case held in place by a visible string. These photographs functioned as a documentary record of a moment of transition, where objects were no longer in the field, but had not yet entered the display case. A figure from Dyamini leaning against the museum wall almost had a kind of comic nonchalance, as if resting between 'performances'. The spectacular Dogon 'mothers of masks' were laid out lifelessly on the museum's floor surrounded by random bits of rope, as if they had been hurriedly pressed into the service of the periodical's overall 'display' (see figure 19). These photographs must have been taken partly for pragmatic reasons: to provide plates for the *Minotaure* special issue before the Trocadéro's displays were in place. But in their emphasis on process, rather than the 'finished' arrangement, they gave a partial insight into the messy end of the ethnographic endeavour at the moment of its presentation: what to do with all the awkward, fragile or heavy stuff that needed to be lugged, shifted, propped and put on display.

The vitrine effect: ethnography on display

The Trocadéro Ethnographic Museum in the early 1930s was certainly not immune to the lure of the spectacle, and this concern was largely the responsibility of Rivière as assistant director. Rivière had made his name as a curator with the 1928 exhibition of Precolumbian art at the Pavillon du Marsan in the Louvre. His status there as an enthusiastic outsider allowed for a fresh perspective on works that had had a contested status in European accounts of them.[77] Raoul d'Harcourt, in the preface to the exhibition's catalogue, certainly claimed that it could get away with things a more consciously 'ethnographic' exhibition could not, 'rescuing' certain pieces from the 'dark and dusty lethargy' of the Trocadéro.[78] A photograph from 1928 showed the president, Gaston Doumergue, visiting the Precolumbian show with a top-hatted entourage, ironically echoing Rivière's own image of Aragon visiting Altamira in his 1926 article 'Archéologismes' (figure 24).

It was apparently on the strength of this exhibition that the Trocadéro's director, Paul Rivet, employed Rivière in June 1928, through the recommendation of David-Weill and Charles de Noailles.[79] The latter's role on the consultative committee of the museum in 1928, as another art-world figure with no anthropological training, probably facilitated Rivière's appointment.[80] Rivière could bring his wide range of art world and commercial contacts, put to good use, as we have seen, in the organisation of the Dakar–Djibouti expedition. A letter to him written by Griaule from Africa in August 1931 contained the telling reminder 'Keep *all* your contacts'.[81] Rivière could also bring his knowledge of museums internationally, both ethnographic and art museums (in 1929 he married the American Nina Stevens, the widow of the late director of Toledo Art Museum in Ohio).[82] It is likely that Rivière funded his international travel himself, as someone

24 Gaston Doumergue inaugurating the exhibition *The Ancients Arts of America*, Pavillon de Marsan, Louvre, Paris, May–June 1928.

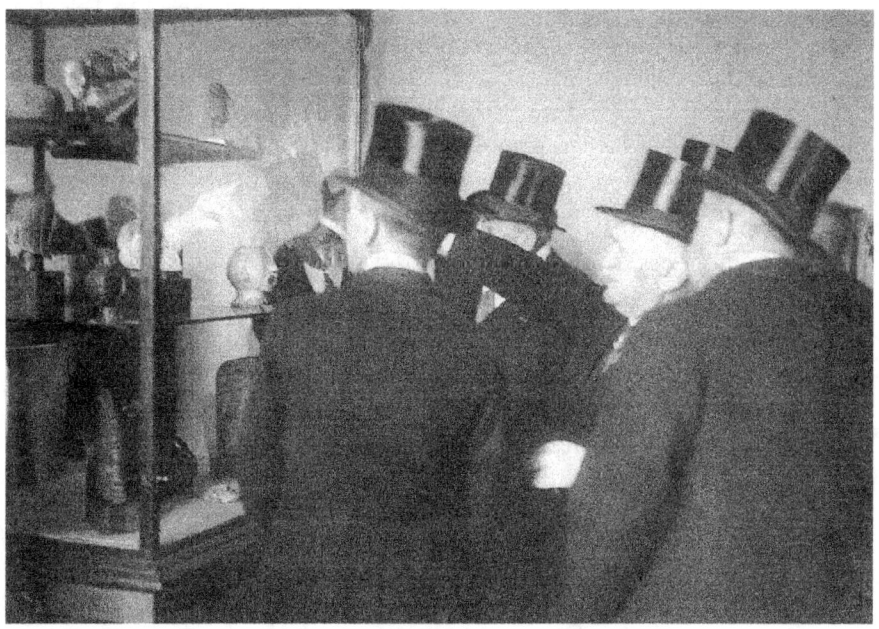

with private means. In one of his memos for the museum in 1932, he claimed that he had contributed 60,000 francs of his own money towards its budget that year.[83] The Trocadéro was certainly heavily dependent upon the private help it received from David and Pierre David-Weill, the de Noailles and Georges Wildenstein, and the work of its friends' society (SAMET). Rivière could use his contacts to enlist practical help, too: in 1930, Leiris was listed in a note as part of the museum's voluntary staff, while Griaule was put in 1929 at the museum's disposition weekday mornings courtesy of the periodical *Documents* (presumably via Wildenstein's funding).[84] Rivière's sister, Thérèse, also worked there as a secretary and research assistant.[85]

The budgetary problems of the Trocadéro over several decades had led to material problems of storage and display. In 1914 the Ethnographic Museum received 25,000 francs, about a tenth of the state support of a comparable institution in Berlin.[86] The museum's former director, René Verneau, had already identified these but was unable to do anything about them.[87] Dust, damp, some harsh natural light, and inadequate security were the main difficulties, along with unwieldy and cramped exhibition spaces. After the appointment of Rivet, who reunited the Trocadéro Ethnographic Museum to the larger body of the Muséum National d'Histoire Naturelle, funding rose to 100,000 francs in 1930, while the Colonial Ministry set up an annual 150,000-franc subvention.[88] This funding did not, in fact, remain stable in the early 1930s – in 1932 Rivière wrote to Griaule in Africa describing the museum as the 'Tracadéro' (dogged by 'tracas', trouble).[89] Nevertheless, substantial improvements were undertaken. One of the first initiatives was to insert a false ceiling dividing the building's central space in two, and allowing for an upper floor where a library and work rooms could be installed. Since the initial planning of the reorganisation of the museum in 1928, Rivet had wanted a kind of 'ethnological centre', where research and collections could come together. The plans for this were published in the first issue in January 1931 of the museum's bulletin.[90] The new organisation of space would allow for two stores, a conservation studio, a *photothèque*, offices and laboratories, and a high-profile library based on the Library of Congress in Washington.[91]

One of the most significant and expensive parts of the museum's transformation, whose overall cost was projected at 4 million francs in 1930, was the acquisition and installation of new, state-of-the-art vitrines. A report on the museum's reorganisation estimated that about 10 per cent of the collection had already been lost.[92] The display of fabrics and feathers in the open had meant damage by moths, while loose display cases had led to worm-eaten wooden sculptures and thefts. Some of these cases were made from the soft wood packing crated objects had arrived in. The stores were a haphazard jumble of unclassified and unprotected things. For display purposes, the answer to these problems was modern metallic cases, at a cost of about 1,400,000 francs, given that roughly 184 were needed.[93] These cases were airtight, shock-resistant and carried their own electrical lighting that could be controlled by visitors. It seems that at least two different companies were used to provide these vitrines: Nord & Alpes, whose advertisement appeared in the Dakar–Djibouti expedition issue of *Minotaure* with a photograph of their installation in the Trocadéro, and Sage, whose advertisements appeared in the catalogue for the Benin exhibition of 1932.

The modernisation of the Trocadéro in the early 1930s set the stage for high-profile displays and exhibitions, like the 'Treasury' that Rivière installed in 1932. The opening of this installation coincided with one of the Trocadéro's most successful shows in the early 1930s, *Bronzes and Ivories from the Kingdom of Benin*. The Benin show was seen as exemplary of what the Belgian art historian Paul Fierens called the 'double museum': dedicated both to art and to research.[94] Divided into two sections, it complemented the 'artistic' with 'documentary' materials (photographs, maps, textual commentaries).[95] The exhibition was an important strategic move, intended to raise the profile of the museum. A report of the National Museum of Natural History of 1935 admitted as much, mentioning 'spectacular manifestations indispensable for attracting a crowd of visitors'.[96] The exhibition could also consolidate links both with other ethnographic museums (from whom it borrowed widely for the show) and with private collectors. Lenders to the exhibition included Baron Robert de Rothschild, Louis Carré, Edgar Worch, Sidney Burney, Derain, Tzara, Eluard and Lipchitz, as well as its organiser Ratton. The prestige of Benin works was very much in keeping with the new high market values for African objects, for which the de Miré sale in December 1931 had set the standard. Alongside the serious anthropological content of the exhibition, whose catalogue referred to research by von Luschan and von Sydow, as well as the recent archaeological work of Frobenius, it had an emphasis on 'art'.[97] Its catalogue, probably written by Ratton as the exhibition's curator and main source of finance, claimed that the Benin show would inaugurate a series of analyses of 'different aspects of ethnology and primitive arts'.[98] This could but sit uneasily with the Trocadéro's scientific rationale. Rivet had deliberately, upon taking up the direction of the museum in 1928, attempted to bring it under the aegis of the Education Ministry, rather than the Ministry for Fine Arts. Further, the discourse of luxury and preciousness that the Benin show seemed to inspire must have been difficult for Rivet with his socialist credentials and popularising mission.[99] More visitors to the museum were certainly welcome, but an elite audience of the rich and fashionable was surely more problematic.

The tensions in the encounter of professional ethnography and the Parisian art world were brought into relief by the Trocadéro's Benin show. Its presentation of what were by the 1930s seen as the most precious African 'art works' did not obviously correspond to the Dakar–Djibouti expedition's aim to collect 'typical' material evidence. We have seen, however, how the presentation of the expedition's findings in *Minotaure* drew attention to certain pieces, 'special' not for their financial value or aesthetic qualities, but because of their significance within the transactions and interactions of the expedition's ethnographic encounter, their 'entanglement', to borrow Nicholas Thomas's phrase.[100] The 'biographies' of some objects, like the Bamana *boli* or the Dogon 'mothers of masks', were more powerful than others, like the objects found by surrealists at flea markets whose meanings were not purely intrinsic, enhanced through their relationships with their finders. The range of photographic material in the *Minotaure* special issue had managed to suggest the lability of the objects collected by the expedition, their shifting status and the creation of new values for them through the contexts of collection, research and display. How to evoke these in the museum was a significant challenge.

The first exhibitions at the transformed Trocadéro to draw directly upon ethnographic expeditions came in 1933. The exhibition of material from the Dakar–Djibouti expedition was in fact pre-empted by a display drawing upon recent fieldwork by Henri Labouret in French West Africa.[101] Labouret was successor to Delafosse as Professor of Ethnography at the Ecole Coloniale and the School of Oriental Languages, and had organised the ethnological section of the Benin exhibition in 1932. As an eminent figure with strong links to colonial administration, it appears that Labouret had the clout to undercut to some degree the Dakar–Djibouti expedition by including some of their objects in his exhibition. This was despite the fact that the Dakar–Djibouti expedition had wanted to protect its findings from reproduction until its return.[102] Some of the Dogon 'mothers of masks', for instance, were included in the Labouret expedition show. This exhibition was based on then current life in West Africa. Unlike the Benin works, or prize pieces in the collection that were little documented, it could directly address the notion of cultural 'wholes', where each artefact was part of a network of practices. A Sudanese dance mask was shown accompanied by its costume, and surrounded by other ritual artefacts including a wooden sword and a drum (figure 25). In fact these pieces did not all belong to one specific location or group, but the overall effect implied the interconnection of carved wooden objects, masks and fibre and fabric costumes. While the old mannequins had been done away with, left to languish in the Trocadéro's store rooms, they were replaced here by a mock-up of a standing figure, arranged vertically to face the visitor. Jean Gallotti, reviewing the Labouret exhibition for *L'Art vivant*, praised the dramatic effect of its installations: 'The way in which they had arranged, in the shadowy entrance hall, a frieze of Bobo ritual costumes, where, for the first time, we could see masks accompanied by kinds of domino made of palm fibres with which dancers cover themselves, partook of the best theatrical artistry'.[103] This arrangement of mask and costume very much played up the spectacular dimension of the ethnographic display, where the suspended ensembles seemed on the point of animation, having just been, or about to be, filled.

The exhibition of the Dakar–Djibouti expedition between 2 June and 29 October 1933 would also use this technique to display Ethiopian clothing and other costumes. This was also a practical solution, enabling one large vitrine to be divided vertically into two and for two separate displays to be mounted inside it. This exhibition included a vast amount of material, shown in the long narrow 'Salle de l'Afrique Noire' at the front of the building on the first floor. For Rivière,

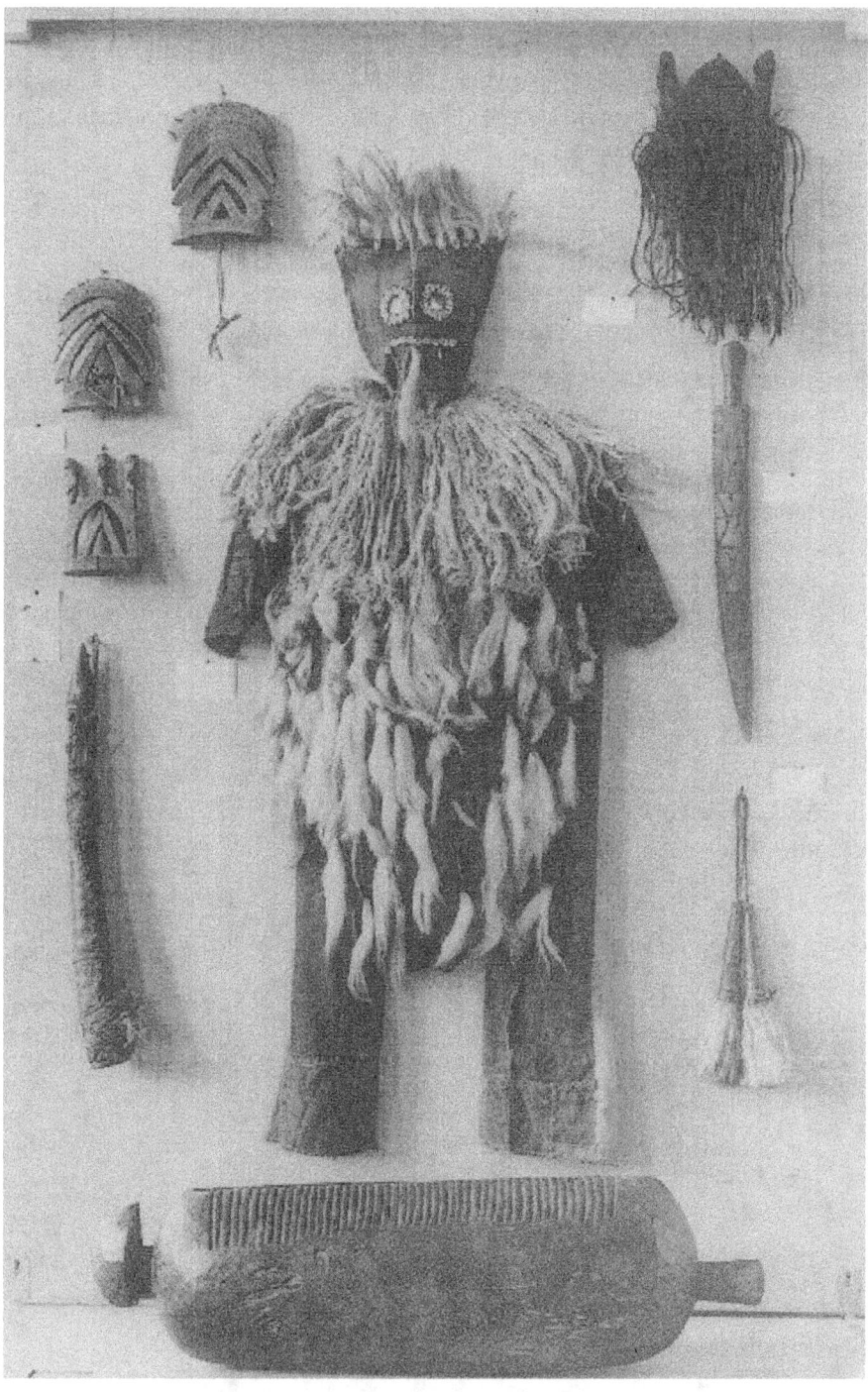

25 *Vitrine of the French Sudan*, Trocadéro Ethnographic Museum, Paris, 1934.

the exhibition of the Dakar–Djibouti expedition material was also an opportunity to put into practice yet another new set of museological principles at the Trocadéro. The way in which he described this in an article for *L'Intransigeant* marked an apparent departure from the rationales of other displays, such as the Benin show, or his 'Treasury'. The new exhibition would be:

> a typical example of the new methods applied to ethnological museography. No jewel-box vitrines, no mountings as art objects or like tie pins; above all a very simple presentation, where each thing is shown in as living as way as possible and surrounded by a maximum of information. It is not a question here of 'art nègre', jewels for antiquarians or even articles in a bazaar; it is a question of *human documents*.[104]

Rivière's commentary is certainly intriguing. The aim of the exhibition of African material at least would be to provide evidence of the use of objects displayed, within their 'living' context. The huge Dogon 'mothers of masks' were displayed within a long, low case placed directly on the floor, like biological specimens, reptiles in a vivarium (like those housed in the new Musée des Arts Africains et Océaniens which opened in eastern Paris in 1933). While for the Benin show in 1932, photographic documentation had been kept apart from the 'art', a year later, for the exhibition of the Dakar–Djibouti expedition, photographs were included within vitrines and provided immediate points of reference. Jean Gallotti, in one of his many articles on the display of the Dakar–Djibouti expedition findings,

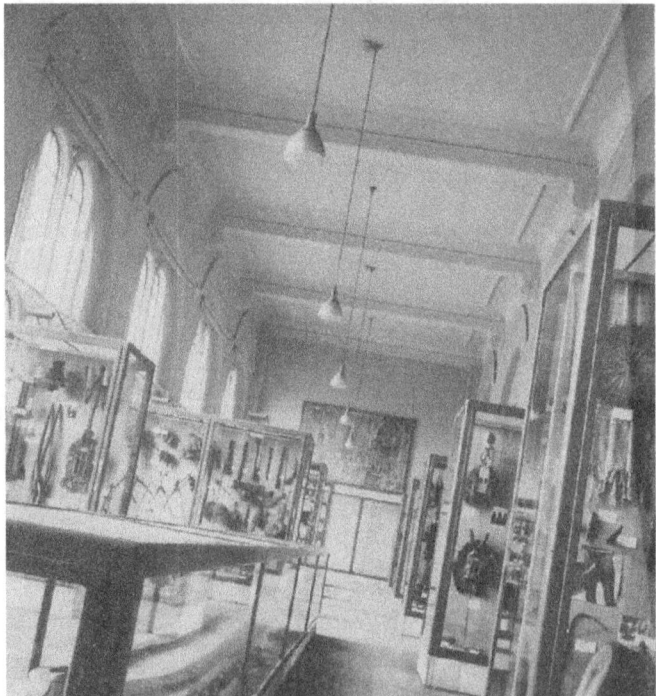

26 *Black Africa Room. Temporary exhibition of the Dakar–Djibouti expedition,* Trocadéro Ethnographic Museum, Paris, 1933 (photograph gift of *Beaux-Arts* magazine).

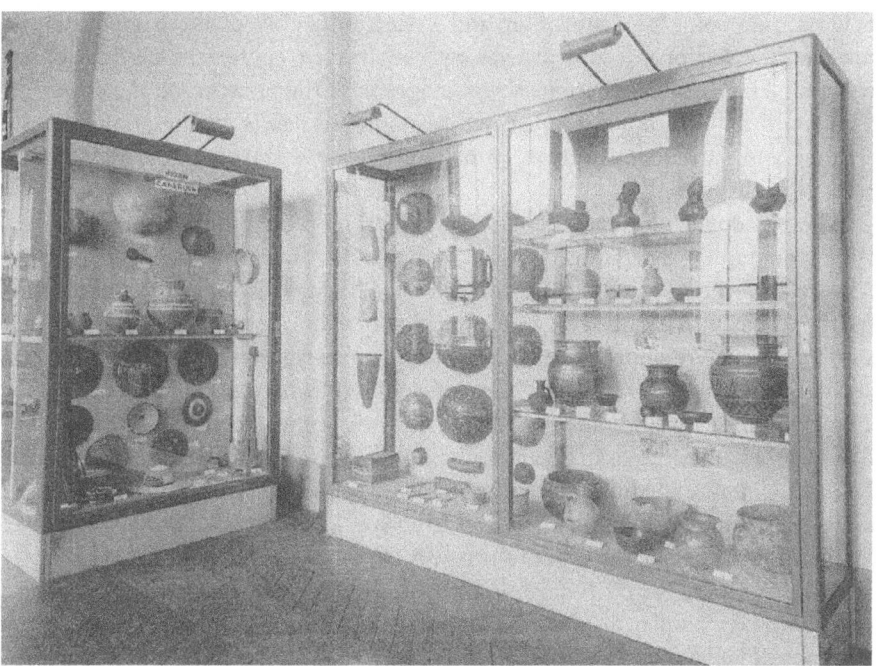

27 *Black Africa Room. Temporary exhibition of the Dakar–Djibouti expedition,* Trocadéro Ethnographic Museum, Paris, 1933.

praised the way in which the strange Dogon 'mothers of masks' were complemented by photographs showing them propped up on skulls in caves.[105] In one installation photograph, we can see the white Ireli monkey mask in the second case on the right accompanied by a photograph of three masked Dogon dancers (figure 26). In the case nearest the viewer, Kirdi penis sheaths are shown next to a photograph of one being worn. A similar photograph taken during the expedition was used to illustrate Leiris's article on Namchi circumcision rites in 1934.[106] These photographs served as 'proof' that these objects had very recently been in contact with living human bodies. Displays of pottery and other small-scale functional artefacts included photographs of different stages of their fabrication, which emphasised their inseparability from techniques and practices (figure 27). In this way, these installations gave both a sense of the object 'in situ' and 'in context', to apply Kirshenblatt-Gimblett's distinction, using photography to show 'more of what was left behind' and creating didactic, classificatory arrangements (a mask like this would *normally* be accompanied by a costume like this).[107] In keeping with Rivière's desire to create a 'museum-laboratory', the use of photography alongside artefacts also gave some sense of the ethnographer's working materials. Rather than staging (the illusion of) a one-to-one confrontation between viewer and objects displayed, it interposed the ethnographer's mediation, showing artefacts captured photographically by someone who had been in the field at the point of acquisition and collection. This could complicate the museum's assertion of control over its constructed contexts, as Edwards has claimed: 'Has the object become the photograph or the photograph the object?'[108] The fact that the Trocadéro presented photographs *within* vitrines, doubling the framing and flattening effects of both, reinforced the staged and artificial character of its displays.[109]

The paradox of the Trocadéro's new 'scientific' principles, however, was that the ethnographic 'encounter' was reconfigured in the museum as distant and removed. Despite Rivière's intention to create 'living' displays of 'human documents', the new, hermetically sealed vitrines the Trocadéro was now using had a sterile and austere appearance. 'More sober, more rigorous, more rigid', Leiris recalled in retrospect.[110] Due to the practicalities of conservation, objects recently animated by touch and human interaction in their original contexts were now held unattainably behind glass. The installation style used for the exhibition of the Dakar–Djibouti expedition became the model for successive shows, such as the large-scale Sahara exhibition in 1934.[111] Much of the Dakar–Djibouti material was left in place to become the core of the new room devoted to 'Black Africa', inaugurated in December 1933. Indeed, the Musée de l'Homme until recently still had cases with very similar displays, including many original (sometimes faded) photographs. The layout of material in the 1933 Dakar–Djibouti display and subsequently certainly enforced the ethnographic principle of the equal status of functional artefacts, figures and masks as part of a cultural whole. In fact, the regular spacing of objects could create an impression of excessive uniformity. If material was not intended to be 'unique' or 'singular', aberration and deviation were not welcome. If Leiris as ethnographer had spoken out of turn in his accounts of the expedition, the object as 'witness' was not expected to. The ethnological aim to provide a consistent picture of a non-western culture was of course part of a very serious project to educate a potentially ignorant and prejudiced western public. But it could also work against the audience's more direct and personal engagement with objects displayed, and could lead to a homogenised museum. Jean Cassou in 1933 expressed reservations in the press about the Trocadéro becoming like the Universal Exhibitions: 'a kind of slightly frightening temple, where an elementary and equal synthetism brings together the most remote arts and the most obscure religions'.[112]

As the Trocadéro transformed itself into a modern ethnographic museum, prior to its more major re-invention in 1937–38 as the Musée de l'Homme, it attracted a wider public, but also moved further away from the artistic avant-garde. Rivière's comment that he did not want displayed objects to look like 'articles in a bazaar' tantalisingly suggested the domain of the surrealist second-hand, of unexpected finds and accidental combinations. René Daumal's 1933 criticism that the Trocadéro had become 'a big luxury store' suggested the difficulties of Rivière's penchant for the vitrine.[113] The coming together of 'scientific value and commodity desire', as Edwards puts it, in the photography of ethnographic objects and the displays of anthropology museums, was hard to resist.[114] The ethnographic principles that the new Trocadéro embodied favoured order and a kind of cultural 'purity', and this was mirrored in the work of some of its key collaborators. While Griaule had picked out the 'impure' motif of the Baoule drum for *Documents* and discussed the appropriation of modern western materials, his subsequent work served to construct Dogon culture as a self-contained and implicitly timeless whole.[115] The 'ragged edges' of the ethnographic object, legible in its interaction with its users and collectors, would find their immediate expression not in the tightening nets of French ethnography as a discipline, but in the production by European artists of unclassifiable and 'irritating' objects.

Notes

1 Leiris, 'Phantom Africa' [1934], in *Brisées* [1966], trans. Lydia Davis (San Francisco: North Point Press, 1989), p. 46.
2 *Ibid.*, p. 46.
3 *Ibid.*, pp. 46–7, my italics.
4 *Notes and Queries on Anthropology*, 6th ed. (London: Routledge and Kegan Paul, 1951), p. 46.
5 Beaujour, 'Qu'est-ce que "Nadja"?', *Nouvelle revue française*, 15:172 (1967), p. 793.
6 *Notes and Queries*, 6th ed., p. 48.
7 Jamin, 'De l'humaine condition de "Minotaure"', *Regards sur Minotaure* (Geneva: Musée d'art et d'histoire, 1987), p. 85.
8 *Bulletin du Musée d'Ethnographie du Trocadéro* [1931–35] (Paris: Jean-Michel Place, 1988), and Jamin, 'L'ethnographie mode d'inemploi', p. 66.
9 This advertisement appears in the prefatory pages of *Minotaure*, 1:1 (June 1933).
10 This advertisement precedes the main content of *Minotaure*, 1:2 (June 1933).
11 Jamin, 'De l'humaine condition de "Minotaure"', p. 81.
12 See Edwards (ed.), *Anthropology and Photography, 1860–1920* (New Haven, CT: Yale University Press, 1992).
13 See Poignant, 'Surveying the Field of View: The Making of the RAI Photographic Collection', and Pinney, 'The Parallel Histories of Anthropology and Photography', in *ibid.*, pp. 42–73 and pp. 74–95.
14 Malinowski, 'Baloma; the Spirits of the Dead in the Trobriand Islands'.
15 Pinney, 'The Parallel Histories of Anthropology and Photography', p. 90.
16 *Ibid.*, pp. 82–91.
17 Walker, *City Gorged with Dreams, Surrealism and Documentary Photography in Interwar Paris* (Manchester: Manchester University Press, 2002).
18 Breton, 'Introduction to the Discourse on the Paucity of Reality' [*Commerce*, No. 3, winter 1924], in *Break of Day* [1934], trans. Mark Polizzotti and Mary Ann Caws (Lincoln: University of Nebraska Press, 1999), pp. 3–20.
19 *Ibid.*, p. 16.
20 *Ibid.*, p. 16.
21 *Ibid.*, p. 16.
22 *Ibid.*, p. 17.
23 *Ibid.*, p. 16.

24 Breton, *L'Amour fou* (Paris: Gallimard, 1937), pp. 38–57.

25 Iversen, 'Readymade, Found Object, Photograph', *Art Journal*, 63:2 (summer 2004), p. 51.

26 *Ibid.*, p. 50.

27 Breton citing Paul Morand's *Clarisse ou l'amitié* in 'Guillaume Apollinaire' [1917], *Les Pas perdus* (Paris: Gallimard, 1924), p. 30.

28 On the surrealists' attitudes towards travel, see the excellent survey by Robert McNab, *Ghost Ships: A Surrealist Love Triangle* (New Haven, CT: Yale University Press, 2004), pp. 1–37. On Roussel, see my 'Sights Unseen: Roussel, Leiris, Cornell and the Art of Travel' in Taylor and Edwards (eds), *Joseph Cornell: Opening the Box* (Oxford: Peter Lang, 2006).

29 See Ford, *Raymond Roussel and the Republic of Dreams* (London: Faber and Faber, 2000), pp. 170–1.

30 Leiris, 'Le voyageur et son ombre', *La Bête noire*, 1 (1 April 1935), p. 8. Desnos had published articles on Roussel in *391* (1924), *Paris-Journal* (1924) and *La Revue européenne* (1925), Leiris in the *Journal des débats politiques et littéraires* (1927), Vitrac in *La Nouvelle revue française* (1928).

31 Caradec, *Raymond Roussel* (1972), trans. Ian Monk (London: Atlas, 2001), p. 179.

32 This rose is reproduced in *Les Magiciens de la terre* (Paris: Pompidou Centre, 1989), p. 60, where it is dated c.1920.

33 *Cahiers d'art*, 1–2 (May 1936), p. 50.

34 Bataille, 'Les mangeurs d'étoiles', in Barrault *et al.*, *André Masson* [1940] (Marseille: André Dimanche, 1993), p. 27.

35 *Ibid.*, p. 27.

36 Bataille, 'The Notion of Expenditure', pp. 173–4.

37 Cited in Poignant, 'Surveying the Field of View', p. 65.

38 *Ibid.*, p. 65.

39 Frobenius, *The Voice of Africa*.

40 *Oeuvres d'Afrique Equatoriale Française, Oubangui-Chari et Tchad de G. Geo-Fourier* (Paris: Musée d'Ethnographie, March 1933).

41 Delafosse, *Haut-Sénégal-Niger*, plate XLI, fig. 80.

42 R.[ené] D.[aumal], 'Au Musée d'Ethnographie du Trocadéro', *Nouvelle revue française* (1 December 1933), p. 942, and 'Des nouveautés au musée ethnographique', *Le Rempart* (25 November 1933), MH/2 AM 1 B5a.

43 Anon, 'Quelques types du nord Cameroun', *Minotaure*, 1:2 (1933), pp. 62–64.

44 On Griaule's subsequent and more sustained filmic work, see Philippe Lourdou, 'The Dawning Commentary in Ethnographic Films: Marcel Griaule's Cinematographic Work', *Visual Anthropology*, 6 (1993), pp. 65–84.

45 Preface to *Minotaure*, 1:2 (1933), [p. xii].

46 See the two anthologies by Frizot and Païni (eds), *Sculpter-Photographier, Photographie-Sculpture* (Paris: Marval/Musée du Louvre, 1993), and Johnson (ed.), *Sculpture and Photography* (Cambridge: Cambridge University Press, 1998).

47 Edwards, *Raw Histories*, p. 51.

48 *Ibid.*, p. 59.

49 Thomas, 'Licensed Curiosity'.

50 Mauss, *Manuel d'ethnographie*, p. 19.

51 *Notes and Queries*, 5th ed., p. 376.

52 Anon, 'Au Musée d'ethnographie du Trocadéro', *L'Europe nouvelle* (25 June 1932), and R. C., 'Le musée d'ethnographie métamorphosée sort de sa gangue', *La Liberté* (16 June 1932), MH/2 AM 1 B4a.

53 Rivière, 'L'Exposition du Benin et les transformations du musée d'ethnographie', *Nouvelles littéraires* (9 July 1932), MH/2 AM 1 B4a.

54 *Chefs-d'oeuvre du Musée de l'Homme*, p. 54.

55 de Roveredo, 'Les nouvelles salles au Trocadéro', *Les Arts* (9–16 June 1933), p. 21, and Diolé, 'Quatre expositions et cinq salles nouvelles seront inaugurées le 1 juin au musée d'Ethnographie', *Le Rempart* (29 May 1933), MH/2 AM 1 B4f.

56 'Bagheera Lakchmi', 'Des taches sanglantes sur les masques étranges exposés au Trocadéro', *Paris-Midi* (4 June 1933), MH/2 AM 1 B4f.

57 *Ibid.*

58 Leiris, *Miroir de l'Afrique*, p. 257.

59 Griaule, *Masques dogons* (1938) (Paris: Institut d'Ethnologie, 1963), pp. 393–418.

60 Leiris, 'Objets rituels dogon', p. 29.

61 *Ibid.*, p. 28.

62 *Ibid.*, p. 29.

63 Cassou, 'Expositions: Au Musée d'Ethnographie', *Marianne* (14 June 1933), MH/2 AM 1 B4 f.

64 Jamin, 'Aux origines du Musée de l'Homme', p. 36.

65 *Minotaure*, 1:2 (1933), p. 8.

66 Eric Lutten, 'Les Wasamba et leur usage dans la circoncision', *Minotaure*, 1:2 (1933), pp. 13–17 and Leiris, 'Masques Dogon', *ibid.*, pp. 45–51.

67 'Variétés du Soudan français', *ibid.*, pp. 22–4, and Zervos, 'Notes sur la sculpture contemporaine', *Cahiers d'art*, 4:10 (1929), pp. 465–72.

68 Clifford, 'On Ethnographic Surrealism', p. 563.

69 Richardson, 'An Encounter of Wise Men'.

70 See Jamin, 'L'ethnographie mode d'inemploi', p. 50.

71 G.-D. Perier, 'L'éternel art nègre, Mission Dakar-Djibouti', *Le Rouge et le noir* (20 September 1933), MH/2 AM 1 B4f.

72 Walker, *City Gorged with Dreams*, p. 193.

73 Allégret, *Carnets du Congo, Voyage avec André Gide* (Paris: CNRS, 1993).

74 Gide, 'Architectures nègres', *Cahiers d'art*, 2:7–8 (1927), pp. 263–5.

75 Georges Sadoul, in a negative review of Leiris's *L'Afrique fantôme*, offered Gide as a model for colonial critique that Leiris ought to have followed, *Commune*, 18 (February 1934), pp. 630–1.

76 Gide, *Voyage au Congo*, pp. 31–2.

77 On the reception of Precolumbian culture, see Williams, 'Art and Artifact at the Trocadéro: *Ars Americana* and the Primitivist Revolution', in George Stocking (ed.), *Objects and Others: Essays on Museums and Material Culture* (Madison: University of Wisconsin Press, 1985), pp. 146–66.

78 *Catalogue de l'Exposition des Arts anciens de l'Amérique* (Paris: G van Ouest, 1928), p. xi.

79 Rivière's contract ran from June 1928 to February 1937, but he did not begin work there until the end of 1929, Gorgus, *Der Zauberer der Vitrinen*, p. 42 and note 3.

80 De Noailles is listed as present at a meeting with Mauss on 30 June 1928, MH/2 AM 1 G2a.

81 Letter from Griaule to Rivière, Bamako, 18 August 1931, MH/2 AM 1 M2 B.

82 His marriage was 'arranged' by mutual friends and ended in divorce in 1935. Gorgus suggests that Rivière benefited financially from the arrangement, while his wife gained an entrée into Parisian society, possibly not realising that Rivière was homosexual, *Der Zauberer der Vitrinen*, p. 26 and note 4.

83 Note of 16 November 1932 on the operation of the MET in 1933, MH/2 AM 1 G2e.

84 Report by Rivet of 23 June 1930, p. 1, and report of 29 June 1929, p. 1, MH/2 AM 1 G2a.

85 Gorgus, *Der Zauberer der Vitrinen*, p. 44, note 9.

86 Dias, *Le Musée d'ethnographie du Trocadéro*, p. 252.

87 Verneau, 'Le musée d'ethnographie du Trocadéro'.

88 Rivet and Rivière, 'La réorganisation du musée d'ethnographie du Trocadéro', *Bulletin du Musée d'ethnographie du Trocadéro*, 1 (January 1931), p. 4. The total budget for 1930 was about 396,000 francs.

89 Letter from Rivière to Griaule, 30 August 1932, MH/2 AM 1 M2d.

90 Rivet and Rivière, 'La réorganisation du musée d'ethnographie du Trocadéro', p. 5.

91 Gorgus, *Der Zauberer der Vitrinen*, p. 46. The librarian Yvonne Oddon made a special trip to the USA in preparation for this.

92 Report on reorganisation of the MET, undated (c.1929–30), MH/2 AM 1 G2b.

93 Budget statement of 11 April 1930, report on metal vitrines 6 June 1930, MH/2 AM 1 G2d.

94 Fierens, 'L'art du Benin', *Feuilleton du Journal des Débats* (26 July 1932), MH/2 AM 1 B4a.

95 *Exposition de Bronzes et Ivoires du Royaume de Bénin* (Paris: Musée d'Ethnographie, 1932), p. v.

96 Rivet, Rivière and P. Lester, 'Le laboratoire d'anthropologie du Muséum', *Archives du Muséum d'Histoire Naturelle*, 6:12 (1935), p. 517.

97 Felix von Luschan produced some of the earliest scholarly analyses of Benin works, see for instance his early article 'Alterthümer von Benin', *Zeitschrift für Ethnologie*, 30 (1898), pp. 146–64.

98 *Exposition de Bronzes et Ivoires du Royaume de Bénin*, p. v.

99 On the museum's links to the Popular Front through Rivet, see Jamin, 'Le musée d'ethnographie en 1930: l'ethnologie comme science et comme politique', in *La Muséologie selon Georges Henri Rivière* (Paris: Dunod, 1989), pp. 110–21.

100 Thomas, *Entangled Objects*, p. 4 and passim.

101 *Mission Labouret, Mission en Afrique Occidentale Française* (Paris: Trocadéro Ethnographic Museum, 28 April–28 May 1933).

102 Letter from Leiris to Trocadéro librarian Yvonne Oddon, Kita, 27 July 1931, reminding her that any reproduction of objects, photographs or documents was forbidden until the expedition's return, MH/2 AM 1 M2b.

103 Gallotti, 'Au Trocadéro l'art de l'A.O.F.', *L'Art vivant* (July 1933), MH/2 AM 1 B4e.

104 Rivière, 'Au Musée d'Ethnographie', *L'Intransigeant* (29 May 1933), MH/2 AM 1 B4f.

105 Gallotti, 'Au Musée du Trocadéro, la mission Dakar-Djibouti', *L'Illustration*, 4721 (26 August 1933), p. 569.

106 Leiris, 'Rites de circoncision namchi', *Journal de la Société des Africanistes*, 4:1 (1934), pp. 63–79, and plate II, 2.

107 Kirshenblatt-Gimblett, 'Objects of Ethnography', pp. 388–90.

108 Edwards, *Raw Histories*, p. 187.

109 On the doubling of the museum display and the photograph, see Jenkins, 'Object Lessons and Ethnographic Displays: Museum Exhibitions and the Making of American Anthropology', *Comparative Studies in Society and History*, 36:2 (April 1994), pp. 242–70.

110 Price and Jamin, 'Entretien avec Michel Leiris', p. 40.

111 *Exposition du Sahara, Guide illustré* (Paris: Musée d'Ethnographie, 1934).

112 Cassou, 'Expositions: Nouvelles salles du Musée d'Ethnographie', *Marianne* (22 November 1933), MH/2 AM 1 B5a.

113 R.[ené] D.[aumal], 'Au Musée d'Ethnographie du Trocadéro'.

114 Edwards, *Raw Histories*, p. 76.

115 See Griaule, *Masques dogons*, and particularly his *Conversations with Ogotemmêli* (1948) (Oxford: Oxford University Press, 1970).

5

Making:
technologies of the surrealist object

Minotaure's first issue, published concurrently in June 1933 with the second special issue devoted to the Dakar–Djibouti expedition, contained a presentation of Picasso's recent work. Among works by Picasso reproduced in the periodical were roughly hewn wooden statuettes made from canvas stretchers, a small figure in twisted steel, and a strange assemblage of a dried-up pot plant, a goat's horn and a feather duster (figure 28). The playfully contingent quality of this combination pointed to the process of its production, rather than the final 'finished' result, a process with inevitable ritual and sacrificial connotations, given the feathers and the horn. For a Belgian reviewer of *Minotaure* for the Brussels-based magazine *Le Rouge et le noir*, a certain 'J. M.', a parallel could be

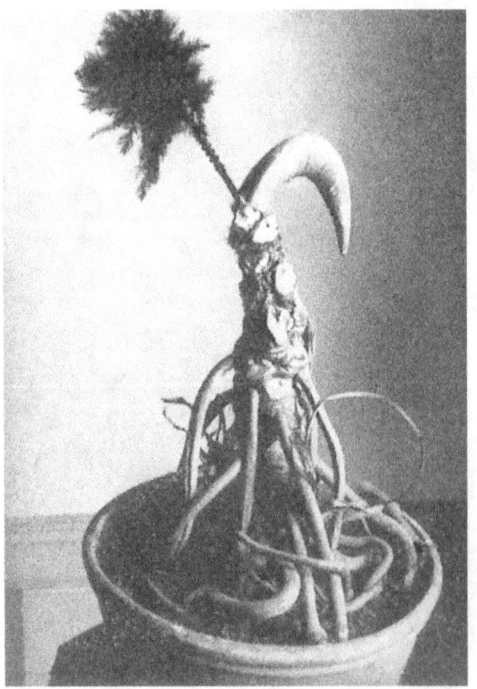

drawn between the 'mystery' of Picasso's work and that of the African cultures studied by the ethnographic expedition, and a religious connection could be made: 'Each object, each painting, has for these populations a more or less religious meaning, and I think that it is this discipline which gives these objects and paintings their great artistic character. Nothing in them is totally gratuitous'.[1] He or she continued by lamenting the lack of 'utility' in current artistic developments in Europe and the USA (beyond the function of decoration), and wondered if Picasso's own Catholic faith had a bearing on the evolution of his art.

The combination of incongruous elements in Picasso's assemblage, and their

28 Pablo Picasso, *Profile*, 1931, flowerpot, roots (fig tree?), horn and red feather duster, dimensions unknown, destroyed, in *Minotaure* 1:1 (1933).

fragile, ephemeral nature aligned it with the surrealist object as it was developing in the early 1930s. The text by Breton that accompanied the reproduction of this work in *Minotaure* reinforced this connection, bringing out Picasso's predilection for perishable and heterogeneous objects.[2] Breton did not mention explicitly the resonances of non-western ritual artefacts in this object, itself a kind of 'European fetish'. But his reading of it did stress its latent animism, while poeticising and sublimating it. The tangled roots for Breton represented 'a supreme convulsion' and 'the grimace of an embrace', while the feather duster (which he described as red) compensated for the now lost foliage of the dead plant.[3] But while these feathers carried allusions of sacrifice and metonymically referred to a (now dead) bird, the feather duster itself also had much more prosaic associations, an everyday domestic object used to control (or not) the dust in Picasso's messy rue la Boétie studio. Compared too to the decorative feather-work of certain Oceanic artefacts, the duster was a debased and throwaway mass-produced household tool. A year later in 1934, Breton would refer to the 'splendid and convulsive cloak made from the infinite repetition of the unique little red feather of a rare bird, worn in the past by Hawaiian chiefs', as one of his instances of 'convulsive beauty'.[4]

Picasso's 1931 now-lost work points to some of the key questions raised by the surrealist object, itself a complex and wilfully varied terrain of artistic activity. The different status of the 'found' and the 'made', and the connotations of different kinds of found thing, were central to this: the serendipitous or unsettling found 'natural' object (repeating to some extent a quasi-Romantic 'pathetic fallacy'), or the 'made' found commodity diverted from its original purpose. The problems of 'use' and 'utility' signalled by Picasso's inclusion of a piece of domestic equipment played a crucial role in formulations of the surrealist object. As the results of deliberately 'anti-art' activity, surrealist objects in all their diversity shared too some of the characteristics of the ethnographic objects sought and collected by the Dakar–Djibouti expedition. Both could be seen as the fragile, ephemeral and obscure fragments of processes and performances. Picasso's own bringing together of things existed only as a photographic record (by Brassaï) of a moment in the context of his studio. For the Belgian critic cited above, it was not a question of whether Picasso's works demonstrated any *formal* similarities with the African objects reproduced in the periodical. Notwithstanding the reactionary connotations of this commentary (the implicit call for a renewal of faith), its use of a comparison between Picasso's work and ethnographic material that went beyond appropriation, suggesting instead an equivalence at the level of outlook and activity, was intriguing. As this chapter will argue, the critical discourses around three-dimensional varieties of art-making in the surrealist milieu (sculpture, objects, assemblage) would also point to ethnographic concepts of bodily engagement and technological function.

Christopher Green has analysed in detail the parallels between issues one and two of *Minotaure* with regard to the construction of Picasso as an 'ethnographic' subject, his series of drawings and private studio spaces becoming available to the viewer and reader.[5] Picasso's conception of his own work as a kind of 'diary' – helped by the presentation of Picasso's work from day to day in Zervos's oeuvre catalogue, and Brassaï's photographs of his working environment – was concurrent with the increasing availability of ethnographic theory to the avant-garde. Picasso in this context, as Green has argued, was made to stand as a 'total social fact', representative of 'creative man' and the modern artist more broadly, his works metonymically referring back to his artistic identity.[6] In the presentation of the Dakar–Djibouti expedition, however, objects themselves provided insights into collective social practices, standing on their own terms in the absence of named artists and makers. This chapter will pursue the implications of these specimens of material culture and the meanings they could bear for French ethnography in the early 1930s for the conception of art-making at the time. It will focus not on the personae of individual artists themselves, but on their works as the embodiment of techniques and practices which engaged both their producers and their subsequent viewers and users.

The objects collected by the Dakar–Djibouti expedition, as we have seen, had several crucial aspects. They were seen as intimately involved in both ritual and everyday practices. Their close ties to social function found a corollary in the new relationships they entered into through their collection by the French ethnographic team. Construed as 'witnesses', they began new 'biographies' of interaction. Alfred Gell has argued for a conception of art which 'considers art objects as persons', and is intended to complicate the distinctions which might be drawn between the 'aesthetic' function of western and non-western material culture.[7] In his terms, art works have 'agency', as art is a 'system of action, intended to change the world'.[8] The relationship that the art object has with those who encounter it is one of 'enchantment' or entrapment, and the means by which this operates is the artwork's technological complexity. Key examples of this for Gell are carved and decorated Trobriand canoe-boards, intended to 'dazzle' their spectators with their technical intricacy.[9] In fact, the Hawaiian feather cloak evoked by Breton in 1934 and the 'war god' feather mask on the postcard sent to Breton by Gide would also be good instances of the assertion of (sacred) power through complex 'artistry'.

Picasso's 'humble' feather-duster assemblage was apparently low on conventional 'technical' skill, but this would be to misread Gell's concept of the 'technology of enchantment', which operates as 'magical' efficacy: 'It is the way an art object is construed as having come into the world which is the source of the power such objects have over us – their becoming rather than their being'.[10]

In Mauss and Henri Hubert's *General Theory of Magic* of 1902–3, magic was similarly conceived as a creative activity on the search for a special new effectiveness.[11] As a kind of 'research', we might say, departing from the tried and tested, magic was potentially inventive, breaking rather than maintaining tradition. The implications of this, in their extraordinary ethnological treatise, challenged a more common conception of the division of western and non-western cultures and 'mentalities' along the lines of innovation (equated with 'art') and tradition (equated with 'artefact'), for instance in the writings of Lévy-Bruhl.[12] Significantly, Mauss and Hubert's theory of magic also described the role of basic, everyday techniques and materials as part of magical activity:

> Magic prepares images from paste, clay, wax, honey, plaster, metal or papier mâché, from papyrus or parchment, from sand or wood, etc. It sculpts, models, paints, draws, embroiders, knits, weaves, engraves ... It makes gree-grees, scapulars, talismans, amulets, all objects that should only be seen as continuing rites.[13]

This chapter will read some of the three-dimensional things produced in the surrealist milieu in these ethnographic terms as 'continuing rites'. In order to bring out the technological possibilities of the surrealist object, it will locate them initially in relation to Giacometti's work, but not the Giacometti of *Suspended Ball* that so excited Breton and Dalí and became an uneasy model for other surrealist objects to follow.[14] Rather, it will return to Leiris's seminal 1929 essay on Giacometti for *Documents*, and follow up some of the implications both of Giacometti's work in the second half of the 1920s, and of Leiris's strikingly 'interactive' reading of it. Leiris's article provided a mode of interpreting contemporary art objects that evocatively emphasised the viewer's involvement with them, bypassing to some degree the thorny problems of the artist's intentions (as a trained sculptor, for example). It also, as we have seen, referred to non-western cultural models and reflected Leiris's nascent ethnographic sensibilities. The ramifications of this approach in surrealist ways of thinking and making in three dimensions point too to the ongoing relevance of surrealist objects, sculptures and assemblages beyond the 1930s. The 1936 exhibition of surrealist objects at Charles Ratton's gallery, himself an important collector of non-western objects and supporter of the Trocadéro, is often seen as the point at which the object was both defined and also killed off and historicised. The problems of the object's continuing potential to involve, implicate, entrap and 'enchant' were central to the fraught encounter of ethnography and art in Paris in the late 1920s and early 1930s.

The found object and its uses

The surrealists looked to found natural and made objects and also to heterogeneous, overlooked or throwaway materials in producing new three-dimensional forms. These things, though, according to most understandings of surrealist activity, were in turn diverted from their original uses. One of the leitmotifs of Breton's writings on the surrealist object was its distance from utility or usefulness, as he argued in the 1936 essay 'Crisis of the Object': 'It is important at all costs to fortify the means of defence which can be set up against the invasion of the tangible world by things that, rather by habit than by necessity, people make use of. Here as elsewhere we need to hunt down the mad beast of *use*'.[15] The surrealist hostility towards 'use' had a specific inflection, however, apparently targeting above all the sphere of bourgeois consumption. In an essay for the first issue of *La Révolution surréaliste* in 1924, 'The Shadow of the Inventor', Aragon railed against the new gadgets he saw at the Concours Lépine inventors' fair: 'those little ingenious contraptions which are of questionable use to housewives. There are tea strainers, spring-loaded candle drip trays that frighten me.'[16] The surrealist found object was intended to provide a way of bypassing this debased realm of mass production. In particular, the found natural object could tap into notions of a lost pre-industrial world, a common trope in modern twentieth-century culture that the surrealist were certainly not immune to (Breton and Eluard's interest in non-western 'art' often suggested this theme). Ethnological and ethnographic theories played an important role in the surrealist approach to the found natural object. But as we will see, distinctions between the natural and the 'man made' were not always clear cut, and the processes of human intervention into these pointed towards technological processes, where the 'use' disdained by the surrealists might find a new articulation as 'practice'.

Found natural objects in the surrealist context can be related to the ethnological concepts of magical 'contagion' and 'similarity', charted in detail in late-nineteenth-century sources like Tylor and James Frazer. Frazer's work was known well to surrealist writers and artists, and both sources served as points of reference for Durkheim, Mauss and Hubert, and Lévy-Bruhl, even if to dispute their findings.[17] Tylor's discussions of animism and the 'Association of Ideas' examined the investment of 'stocks and stones' with special curative powers.[18] Frazer, more specifically, distinguished between what he called 'homeopathic' or 'imitative' magic, based on the 'law of similarity', and 'contagious' magic, based on the 'law of contact'.[19] Both were varieties of what he termed 'sympathetic magic', so called because 'things act on each other at a distance through a secret sympathy'.[20] 'Contagious magic' was attached primarily to body parts and their residues such as hair, nails and teeth, as well as footprints or the imprint of a body on a bed. The principle of similarity pertained, for instance, in the practice of making and then burning wax effigies of one's enemies, objects which Dalí claimed in his 1932 essay 'The Object as Revealed in Surrealist Experiment' were 'the true precursors of articles operating symbolically'.[21]

The workings of the 'law of contact' had featured in a surrealist reading by Leiris of Miró's work in 1926.[22] Leiris picked out metonymic details in Miró's works: a finger, an eyelash, a footprint, a bird's feather, a moustache, the point of a breast.[23] He continued by relating this selection of details to magical practices in non-western societies: 'Formerly, the anxious tribes of men would bury their nail-peelings and their fallen hairs in fear of sorcery; for they believed that these particles of themselves contained their whole vital spirit.'[24] Leiris's use of the term 'fetichism' to describe this echoed Tylor's classic ethnological study, where he had similarly described the act of burying 'cut hair and nails, lest demons and sorcerers should do mischief with them'.[25] An equivalent impulse was manifest, for Leiris, in popular folk art or in sacred relics: 'pictures made with locks of hair snipped from a whole family of brides, or fragments of the martyred bones of saints'.[26] Feathers, head and body hair, footprints and articles bearing traces of bodily contact like gloves were all part of the surrealist object repertory.[27]

'Similarity' as well as 'contagion' pervaded the chance natural occurrences assembled by surrealists: a sprouting potato photographed by Brassaï, strange-shaped stones and bones, anthropomorphic rocks, and mineral formations of unusual appearance.[28] All of these played into a discourse that was not specific to surrealism, where 'objective chance' and 'convulsive beauty' overlapped with more conventional notions of fortuitous artistic 'inspiration'.[29]

While surrealist two-dimensional 'automatic' techniques like drawing, frottage or *grattage* could trace their lineage back to Leonardo's experiments with the accidental shapes in cracked walls or knotty wood (as Ernst did, for instance),

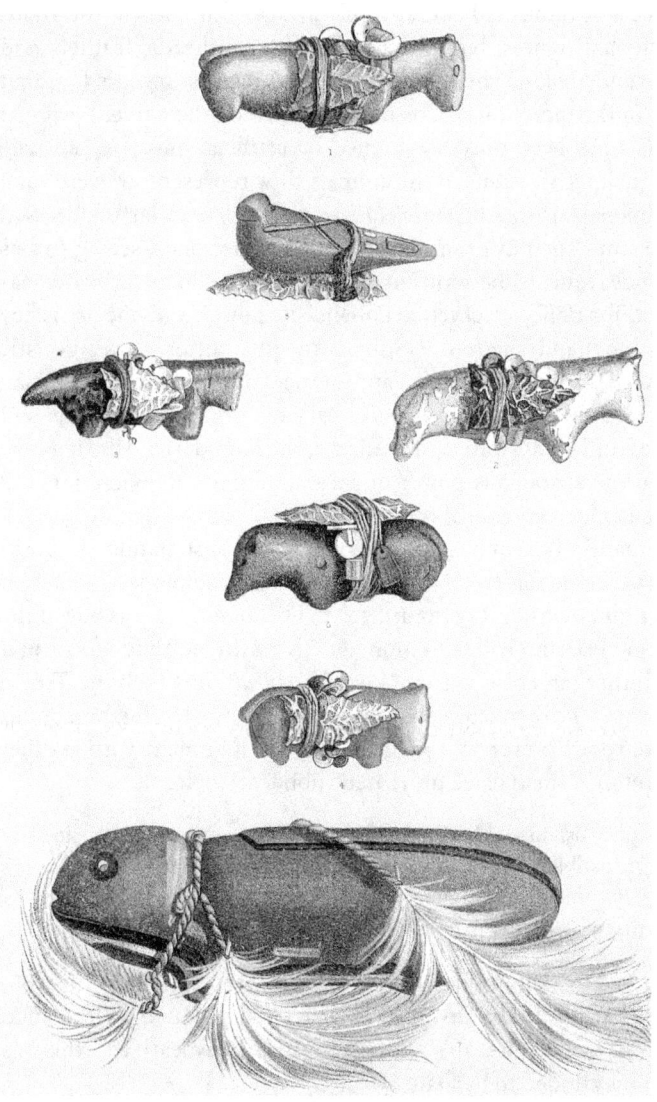

29 *Prey god fetiches*, plate 1 in Cushing, *Zuñi Fetiches* (1883).

three-dimensional forms had no clear tradition to draw upon. Ethnological discussions of art's origins that had what we might call a specific 'sculptural' perspective were rare, as those that did tackle 'art' directly tended to focus on the development of linear designs and mark-making.[30] The use of found natural objects did feature in some late-nineteenth-century ethnological accounts, however, where the enhancement of their unusual appearance was discussed. The 1883 study of Zuñi 'fetiches' by Cushing, the heroic fieldworker and Zuñi initiate admired by the Dakar–Djibouti expedition, included a fascinating examination of the magically 'sympathetic' qualities of these objects (figure 29).[31] Cowling has suggested that the publications of the Smithsonian Institution Bureau of Ethnology, the series in which Cushing's work was published, were widely available in Paris in the 1920s and 1930s.[32] These 'fetish' figures, bound together with flintheads, feathers and bracelets of turquoise and abalone shell, were based on special stones, as Cushing explained: 'either natural concretions ... or objects in which the evident original resemblance to animals has been only heightened by artificial means ... all true fetiches, are either actual petrifactions of the animals they represent, or were such originally.'[33] Balfour in his 1893 *The Evolution of Decorative Art* similarly addressed the harnessing of the animistic power of objects found by accident, seeing this as the origin of artistic endeavour.[34] The addition of marks, incised lines and other features to such an object, for Balfour, served to enhance its power, and one of his key examples of this was the mandrake root.[35] Subject to superstitious and animistic belief, the mandrake's anthropomorphic appearance and magical potential, according to Balfour, was heightened by careful carving while the root was still growing.[36] In both the Zuñi stones and the mandrake, the boundaries were deliberately blurred between the auspicious power of accidental natural concretion and growth, and the carved enhancements of the 'artist'.

Breton included a mandrake root he owned as one of the constellation of significant objects in his 1934 article for *Minotaure*, 'La beauté sera convulsive', where it was photographed for him by Man Ray (figure 30).[37] The mandrake was one of the disquieting objects which Breton had 'summoned to live with me', and he saw in it Aeneus carrying his father (an episode from Virgil's *Aeneid*), in which the Trojan prince fled from a burning Troy, rescuing his elderly father by carrying him on his back.[38] The mandrake root's power was suggested by its alignment with another object collected by Breton, a small black untreated rubber statuette:

> a young, bizarre creature, listening, bleeding at the slightest scratch, as I was able to confirm, with an inexhaustible blood of dark sap, a creature which moves me particularly because I know nothing of its origins nor its purpose and rightly or wrongly decided to see it as a magical charm [un objet d'envoûtement].[39]

If the mandrake described by Balfour had been enhanced through human intervention, Breton's rubber charm was also involved in an activity pursued by its owner: scratching it to make it 'bleed'. Breton's 'ritual' was clearly evocative of the wax effigies pricked with pins alluded to by Dalí.

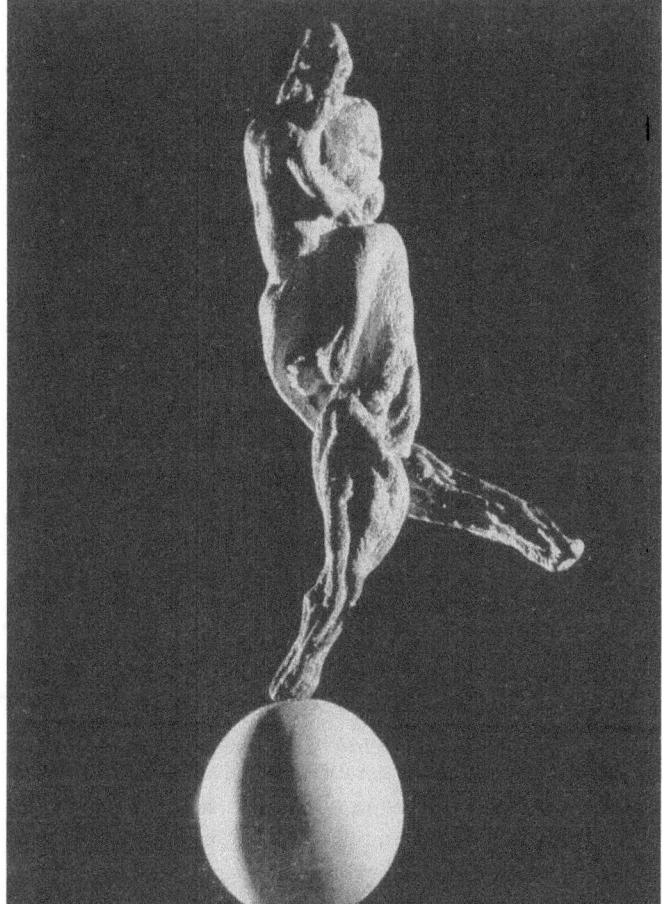

30 Man Ray,
*Aeneus carrying his
father*, in *Minotaure*,
1:5 (1934).

Objects like Breton's mandrake and rubber statue were not just 'found', they
were also 'made' through ongoing processes. If we read them in accordance with
the surrealist contempt for conventional objects of consumption, we could interpret them as a means of bypassing the Marxist division of 'use-value' and
'exchange-value' in the commodity, continuing to be 'produced' with each finder.
If a commodity's intrinsic and extrinsic properties were separated through western
capitalist means of production in Marx's analysis, in an ethnological reading of the
found object in Mauss and Hubert's *General Theory of Magic* such distinctions
were elided:

> In general, magical properties ... are considered to derive from characteristics which
> ... can only be regarded as secondary. This applies, for example, to the accidental
> shape of stones which resemble taros, pig's testicles and pebbles with holes in them
> ... Other characteristics include an object's toughness, its name, its rarity value, its
> mysterious presence in a particular spot (a meteorite, prehistoric stone axes) or the

circumstances of its discovery. The magical properties of an object derive from a kind of convention, a convention which plays the role of a sort of embryonic myth or rite. Anything which possesses magical properties, by its very nature, is a form of rite.[40]

For Mauss and Hubert, the special qualities of the found thing were inseparable from magical practices, and to some extent entirely dependent upon these. This comparison of the commodity and the found object echoes in part the opposition in economic theory of (western) commodity and (non-western) gift, the alienable and the inalienable (for which Mauss's 1923–24 *Gift* is a significant point of reference).[41] However, Mauss and Hubert's earlier 1902–03 study also complicates this dichotomy through its discussion of the creative practice of magic, avoiding any simple equation of non-western societies with traditional and unchanging techniques and technologies. The 'special kind of effectiveness' of magic for them was distinct from 'mechanical effectiveness' controlled by a 'continued perception of homogeneity between cause and effect', an observation aimed surely not only at western 'science' but also at the simplistic theories of magic outlined in Tylor and Frazer.[42]

Surrealism's interest in found objects of different kinds has been related to Walter Benjamin's notion of 'aura', a quality attaching itself, for instance, to 'outmoded' relics of a recent historical past.[43] Hal Foster has compared 'aura' to Marx's 'commodity fetishism', as a reversal of its terms and more positive valorisation of its effects, 'as if aura were the magical antidote to such fetishism'.[44] We have seen how the 'counter-colonial' display for the 1931 Colonial Exhibition, organised by certain surrealists, implied an ambivalent understanding of the function of non-western objects. Breton in particular appeared to invest certain Oceanic objects in other contexts precisely with such an 'aura', like the Easter Island statuette in *Nadja* which elicited declarations of love from him.[45] Benjamin's 'aura' was intimately linked to nostalgia within the context of western modernity, as the imprint of lost techniques: 'If we designate as aura the associations which … tend to cluster around the object of a perception, then its analogue in the case of a utilitarian object is the experience which has left traces of the practiced hand.'[46] The ethnological work of Mauss and Hubert, however, emphasised the ongoing experience of the 'practiced hand', within techniques that were not static and confined to a lost past, but subject to change and experimentation. This can provide us with a different way of reading the surrealist object in relation to processes of human technology, taking the interests of writers and artists affiliated with surrealism in non-western cultures to more sustained conclusions. These would find their seminal articulation within the context of the development of the surrealist object in the pages of the 'dissident' surrealist periodical *Documents*, from the pen of an ethnographer in the making, Leiris.

Objects, equipment and techniques in surrealism

Leiris's 1929 *Documents* article on Giacometti, as well as being the first extensive commentary on the artist's work, can be regarded as one of the first explorations of 'sculpture' in a surrealist context, notwithstanding the difficulties for surrealism of medium specificity.[47] Leiris had already a few years earlier published poetic texts on Miró and Masson, two artists central to surrealist visual production at the time.[48] But in the context of *Documents* and its ethnographic concern with human technology, Leiris would provide an enigmatic and imaginative response to this. His text drew in striking ways upon imagery of domestic objects and activities, such as furniture, utensils, cooking and eating. Leiris's evocation of 'fetishism', one of the most obvious ethnological references in his text, as we have seen, included an extraordinary domestic image:

> that true fetishism, that is to say, that love – really loving – of ourselves, projected from inside to outside and covered with a solid shell which imprisons it in the boundaries of a precise thing and situates it, just like a piece of furniture which we can make use of, in the vast strange room called space.[49]

Leiris's imagery recalled a series of paintings by de Chirico of 1927–28 of chairs and wardrobes in outdoor settings, such as *Furniture in the Valley* of 1927 (he would write a review of de Chirico's 1929 novel *Hebdomeros* for *Documents* in 1930).[50] His reference to furniture implied that Giacometti's sculptures could be read as bodily moulds: the flattened relief heads as pillows, perhaps, bearing the imprints of the face, the *Reclining Woman who Dreams* between two undulating sheets, the rounded hollow of *Woman* as a kind of curving chair. One of the photographs by Marc Vaux accompanying Leiris's article showed a grouping of small works on the floor adjacent to the sculptor's bed, interacting within his living space (figure 31).

Leiris mentioned in his article that he had been able to *feel* Giacometti's sculptures, an experience that was central to him in encountering them.[51] The principle of magical 'contagion' here that probably derived from Leiris's readings of anthropological texts, was a central theme in them, describing the extension of the boundaries of the individual to include their possessions, their tools, weapons, dwelling and food.[52] Losing oneself in the flow of associations sparked by contact with Giacometti's works was also an ecstatic moment, and Carl Einstein's analysis of the work of Masson in the second issue of *Documents* was a clear inspiration to Leiris in this respect.[53] Einstein had discussed Masson's 'totemic identification' with the subjects of his paintings, and the subsequent breakdown of the separation between subject and object.[54] His article, however, bore the title 'André Masson, *ethnological* study' [my emphasis], suggesting the realm of anthropological theory rather than practice: Leiris's 'fieldwork' in Giacometti's studio. This was especially important with regard to Leiris's references to actual physical contact with Giacometti's sculptures, which in the final lines of his account lent themselves to the ultimate consubstantial exchange: 'What we have here, in the end, is stone food' ('Voici enfin des mets de pierre').[55] Beyond the intriguing homoerotic implications of these associations, which are mirrored in the sensuality of Leiris's text, the projected malleability and even digestibility of apparently hard and solid sculptures was a powerful poetic conceit. Leiris's exploration of Giacometti's

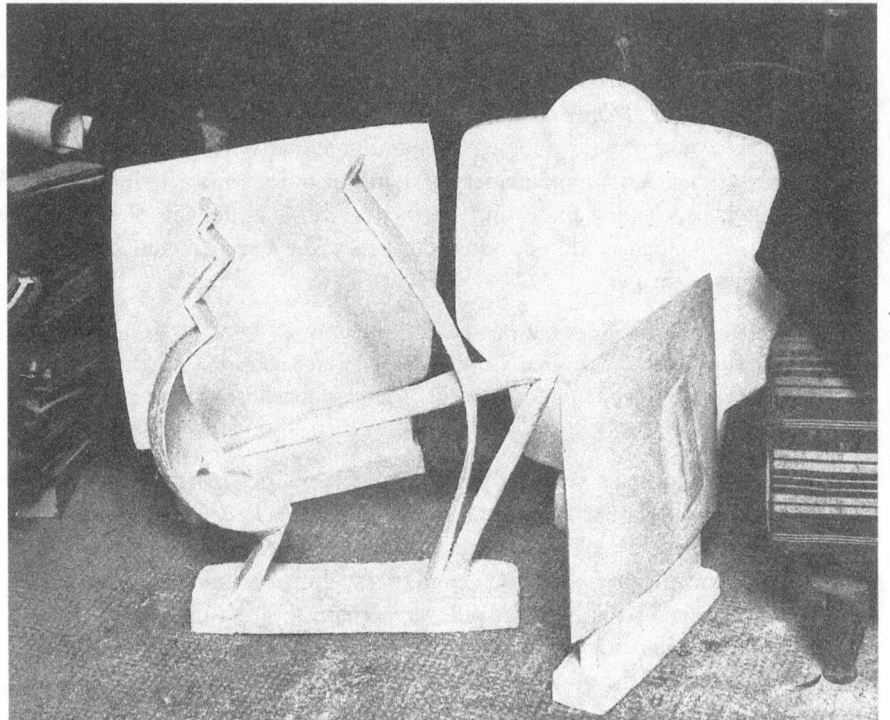

31 Alberto Giacometti, *Man and Woman*, 1929 (front left), *Gazing Head*, 1928 (rear left), *Man*, 1927–28 (rear right) and *Woman*, 1928–29 (front right), in *Documents*, 1:4 (1929), p. 212, photograph by Marc Vaux.

sculptures in these terms was arguably much more significant for early 1930s formulations of the surrealist object than has been acknowledged. Dalí, in his 1932 essay 'The Object as Revealed in Surrealist Experiment' would also refer to eating in the encounter between object and viewer: 'The object tends to bring about our fusion with it and makes us pursue the formation of a unity with it (hunger for an article and edible articles).'[56] Leiris's reading of the dusty qualities of Giacometti's works as nail-filings – 'intangible cinders that a lover should keep like a relic' – also found a counterpart in Breton's account of his own interaction with the sculptor. Breton claimed to have asked Giacometti to make him an ashtray ('cendrier'), in relation to the 'slipper-spoon' found at the flea-market and its fairy-tale owner Cinderella ('Cendrillon').[57]

The erosion of the boundaries of Giacometti's sculptures was played out in Leiris's account with reference to the material processes of their make-up. Plaster as a sculptural material was a key element here (despite Leiris's additional mention of stone and bronze), its grainy texture and friability inspiring a series of poetic associations. The special function of plaster as a studio-based material which could be worked quickly, modelled and carved, which had a contingent status as a traditional preparatory material, and which photographed extremely well, was exploited by Giacometti and other sculptors in the 1920s and 1930s in Paris, as Wood has shown.[58] For Leiris writing about Giacometti, the appearance of his plaster sculptures inspired an extended chain of analogies based on the qualities and properties of salt. Giacometti's works were:

> moulded from the fleeting and sweet salt of snow, the dust that falls from nails when they are filed ... the marvellous salt that so many ancient seekers thought they could extract from the bowels of the earth, the salinity of waves and stars ... the salt of tears ... laden with the salt of frozen skeletons and carcasses ... concrete drops of water resembling that salt which will always stir up our hunger, kitchen salt, bitter salt, salt of cracking joints, salt of teeth, salt of sweat, salt of glances.[59]

Leiris's extended poetic digression on the different associations of salt had clear overtones of Paracelsian alchemy, in which salt was introduced as a new, and strikingly material, element, and also suggested his own background as an organic chemist.[60] The physical transformations that Leiris described, from dry powder, to liquid, and finally becoming solid, suggested the properties of plaster, but also, importantly, emphasised the *process* of making works (albeit with much poetic licence), implicitly equated with other processes like chemical and alchemical experiments, or cooking.

In their analysis of magic, Mauss and Hubert gave a rich description of its affinities with other processes:

> Magic is an art of cooking, preparing mixtures, fermentations and dishes. Its products are ground down, pulverised, kneaded, diluted, transformed into scents, drinks, infusions, pastes, cakes of a special shape, images, to be fumigated, drunk, eaten or kept as amulets. This cooking, chemistry, or pharmaceutics, has not only got as its aim to make magic things usable. It serves to give them their ritual form, which is part, and not the least part, of their efficacy ... What the preparation of the victim is to sacrifice, this cooking is to the magic ritual. It is a moment of the ritual.[61]

If Leiris in his reading of Giacometti's works proceeded to break them down and then reconstitute them in a ritual of poetic interpretation, he also conceived of them as agents of a kind of domestic magic, as a set of tools. Leiris described Giacometti's sculptures as the 'petrifaction' of moments of 'crisis', when external world and internal self met, and compared them to 'poignant grills placed between the inside and the outside', 'spatulas' and 'riddles that the wind erodes'. Sieves or riddles for sorting minerals, spatulas for spreading, griddles, gratings and grills of kitchen equipment ('cribles', 'spatules', 'grillages'): these objects allowed for works like *Man* and *Reclining Women who Dreams*, with their ladle-like heads, to be read as anthropomorphised utensils (figure 32).

Although not named explicitly in Leiris's text or reproduced, one of Giacometti's earlier works that was probably still present in his rue Hippolyte-Maindron studio was surely a crucial precedent here, the 1926–27 *Spoon Woman*

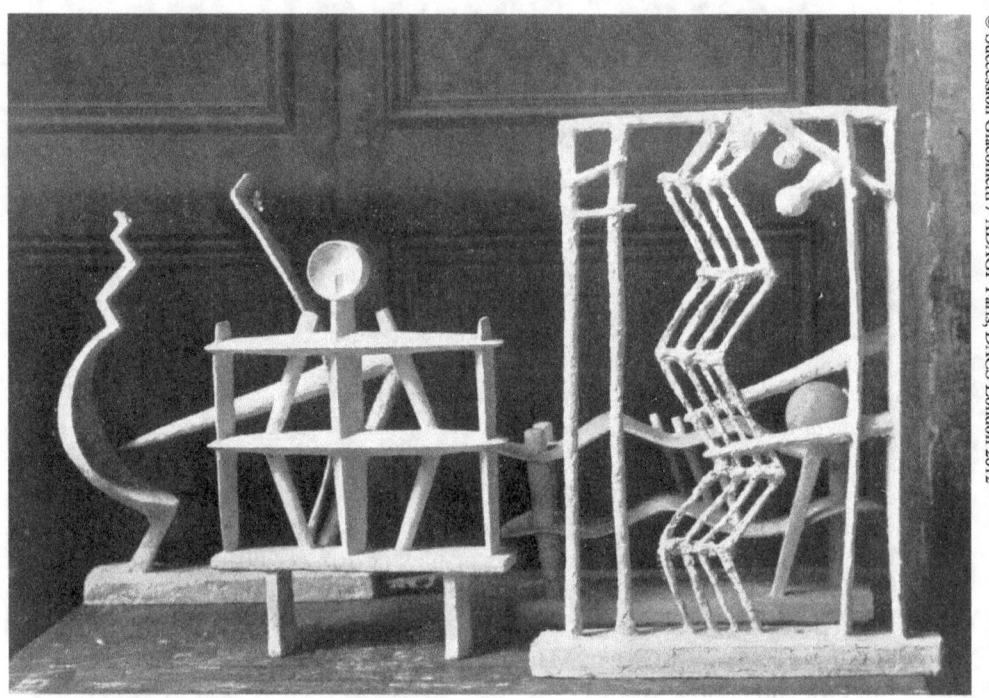

32 Alberto Giacometti, *Man (Apollo)*, 1929 (front left), *Man and Woman* 1929 (rear left), *Reclining Woman who Dreams*, 1929 (rear right) and *Three Figures Outdoors*, 1929 (front right), in *Documents*, 1:4 (1929), p. 214, photograph by Marc Vaux.

(see figure 1).[62] In this work created prior to Giacometti's involvement in surrealism (but not his interest in it), the *détournement* or diversion of the object of utility from its original function was played out.[63] This piece's stylised forms have been compared to the art-deco furniture of Pierre-Emile Legrain and Jacques Ruhlmann, which in turn 'borrowed' the forms and textures of African masks and other artefacts, a phenomenon which Rosalind Krauss has termed 'black deco'.[64] The apparently anthropomorphic spoon in Giacometti's sculpture of 1926 suggested that he knew the example of African decorated spoons, common to parts of West Africa such as Gabon, the Ivory Coast and the Congo. Dan spoons are usually cited as the specific type that the sculptor might have known, through the collection of Guillaume.[65] The decorative complexity and sophistication of African spoons incorporating figures was emphasised by Clouzot and Level in a 1922 article on 'sculptures and objects of use' from French West Africa. For these writers, the delicacy and intricate workmanship of such spoons was a mark of the good taste of the culture that created them, and the fine detail of these objects of modest dimensions (between thirteen and fifteen centimetres high) was of note.[66] In Giacometti's reworking of the motif, on the other hand, the spoon and 'figure' were pared down and simplified. Rather than tapping into the possible anthropomorphic configurations of spoons with heads, whole bodies, or legs, the sculptor's forms were closer to the simpler, geometricised wooden and ivory spoons reproduced for instance in P.-C. Lepage's *La Décoration primitive* of c.1924 (figure 33).[67] This streamlining was suggestive of contemporary industrial design, blurring the distinction between the handcrafted and the mass reproduced. In Giacometti's 1920s sculptures, the combination of (hand) carving and modelling, and casting in bronze in this work and others such as *The Couple* (1926), where the bronze mimicked dark patinated wood, compounded this ambiguity.

Giacometti's figure had a spoon-as-abdomen resting upon a small tapered pedestal, which in turn could be read as its legs continuing below. This re-configuration, which had no obvious African precedent, was significant, as was the transposition of the small decorated, carved, spoon into a larger figure, about three-quarters life size. The spoon's 'use' on this scale could only be ceremonial – if the spoon were put to someone's lips, this 'use' would take on a completely different nature. Giacometti also chose to take up a tapered, oval spoon form common in western societies, but by no means universally common: Leroi-Gourhan's diagram of spoon forms in his 1945 study of human techniques charted their diversity (figure 34).[68] This was subtly modified by the protruding bulge at the top of the spoon's oval, a possible reference to fertility (a swollen abdomen). Giacometti's spoon, which Sieglinde Lemke has described as an 'ethnographic "ready-made"', was certainly diverted from its literal use, but the power or effectiveness of this transposition relied on its complex references to a recognisable utensil.[69]

33 Spoons, Gabon and the Congo, wood and ivory, collections of Moris and Rupalley, in Lepage, *La Décoration primitive* (c.1924), plate XVI.

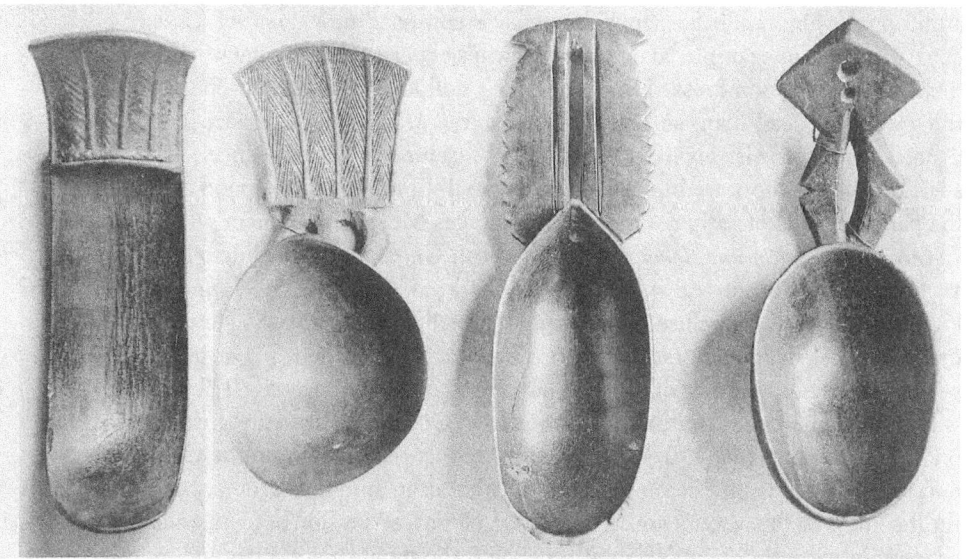

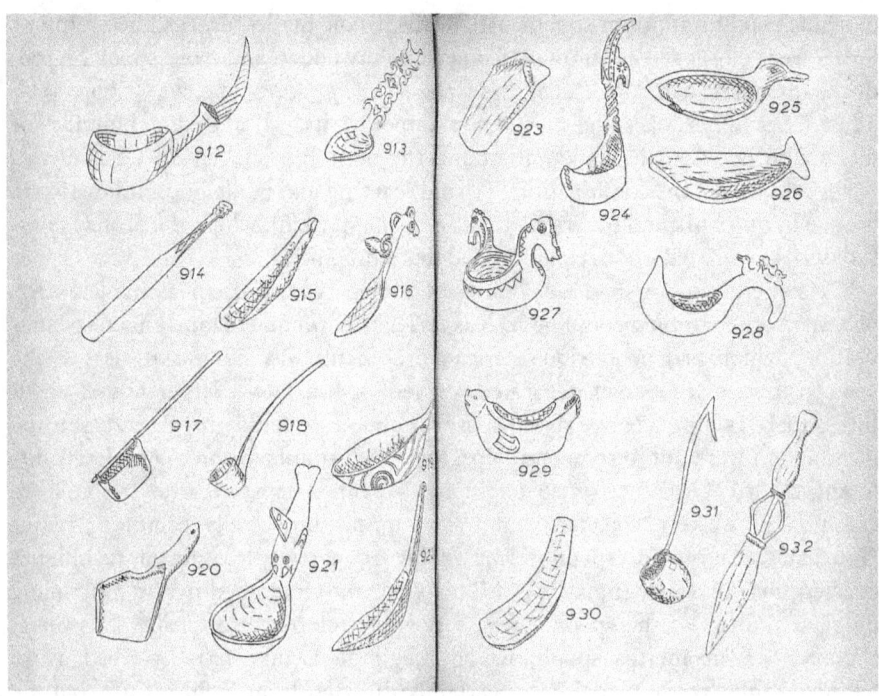

34 Spoon forms in Leroi-Gourhan, *Milieu et techniques* (1945).

Giacometti's 'spoon', like the African decorated spoons that it has been likened to, was made rather than found, unlike other spoons in the surrealist context. Tylor had noted the animistic potential of the spoon as a basic domestic utensil, without anthropomorphic additions, in his extensive compendium *Primitive Culture* of 1871. He cited an example taken from Darwin's experience of Malay women who: 'held a wooden spoon dressed in clothes like a doll; this spoon had been carried to the grave of a dead man, and becoming inspired at full moon, in fact lunatic, it danced about convulsively like a table or a hat at a modern spirit-séance'.[70] Certain surrealist objects appeared to retain the 'normal' function of the spoon as part of the paraphernalia of eating and drinking, such as Meret Oppenheim's 1936 *Fur-Covered Cup, Saucer and Spoon* or Picasso's 1914 *Glass of Absinthe* (included in the 1936 exhibition of surrealist objects). Dalí's 1931 *Object of Symbolic Function* included a 'special spoon used for stirring lead pellets inside the shoe', putting the utensil to work in a pseudo-scientific (or alchemical) experiment.[71] The techniques of the spoon could partake of transformative and magical processes. The so-called 'slipper-spoon' that for Breton was connected to Giacometti's work was decorative, but also drew its meaning from its use, through its relationship to the Cinderella fairytale (figure 35). In Breton's account of what drew him to this object, found at the flea-market, the peasant spoon became an elongated version of Cinderella's lost slipper. Between the spoon's hollow scoop and the small shoe protruding from its handle, Breton traced the progression of Cinderella's fortune, as the wooden spoon 'took on the ardent value of one of the kitchen utensils that Cinderella must have handled before her transformation'.[72] The spoon/shoe juxtaposition and the transposition of the domestic were key here in sparking this object's special charge.

Domestic techniques were alluded to in several of the objects created by surrealist writers as part of the 'anti-art' scope of the object, particularly sewing as a means of combining and binding things. The mechanical, rhythmic piercing of the sewing *machine* clearly held a special charge in surrealist thinking (Lautréamont's famous meeting of the sewing machine and the umbrella on an operating table, Oscar Dominguez's *Electrosexual Sewing Machine* of 1934). But the manual processes of sewing and working with fabrics also played a role, through the hand-stitched seams of ladies' gloves and delicate bindings of fine threads (Valetine Hugo, *Object*, 1931; Jacqueline Breton, *Pour la poche*, 1935; André Breton, *Un bas déchiré*, 1941). One of the objects made by the mentally disturbed collected by Breton set out the paraphernalia of domestic mending in little compartments – half a pair of scissors, buttons, skeins of thread – in a careful but taxonomically unfamiliar arrangement.[73] But sewing was also a significant point of reference in Picasso's work in the second half of the 1920s and early 1930s, one of the most established and 'virtuoso' artists surrealism affiliated itself with. Picasso's series of small 1926 *Guitars* combined scraps of tulle, buttons and string, while the 1930 Juan-les-Pins sand-covered reliefs were sewn onto the canvas. The large 1926 *Guitar* made up of a torn piece of shirt tail has been discussed in reference to the magical functions of the nails holding it in place, on the model of Congo 'nail

35 Man Ray, *From a little shoe that was part of it...*, 1934, in Breton, *L'Amour fou* (1937).

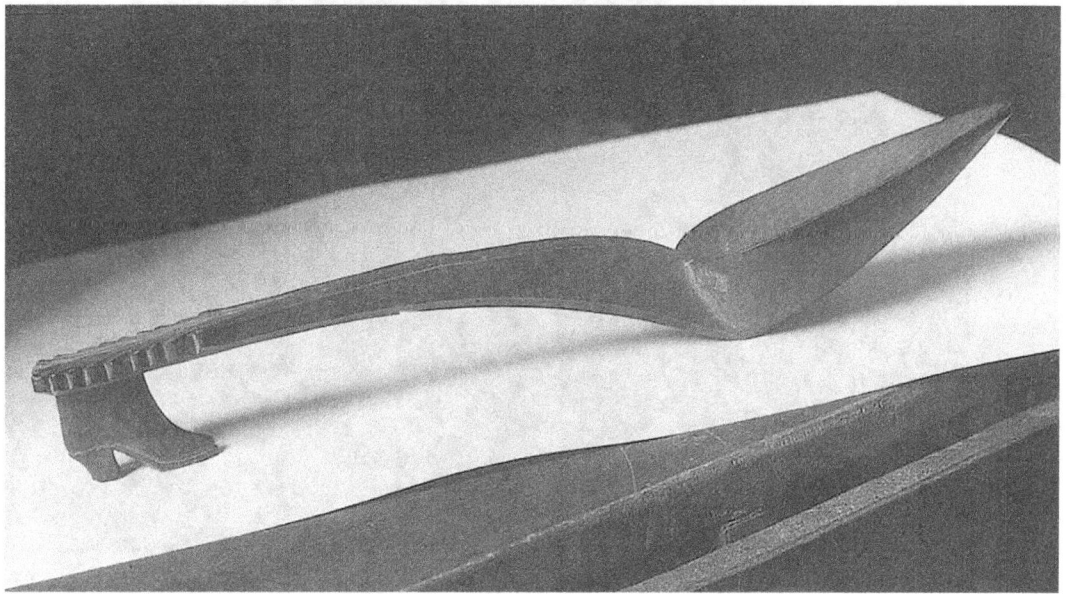

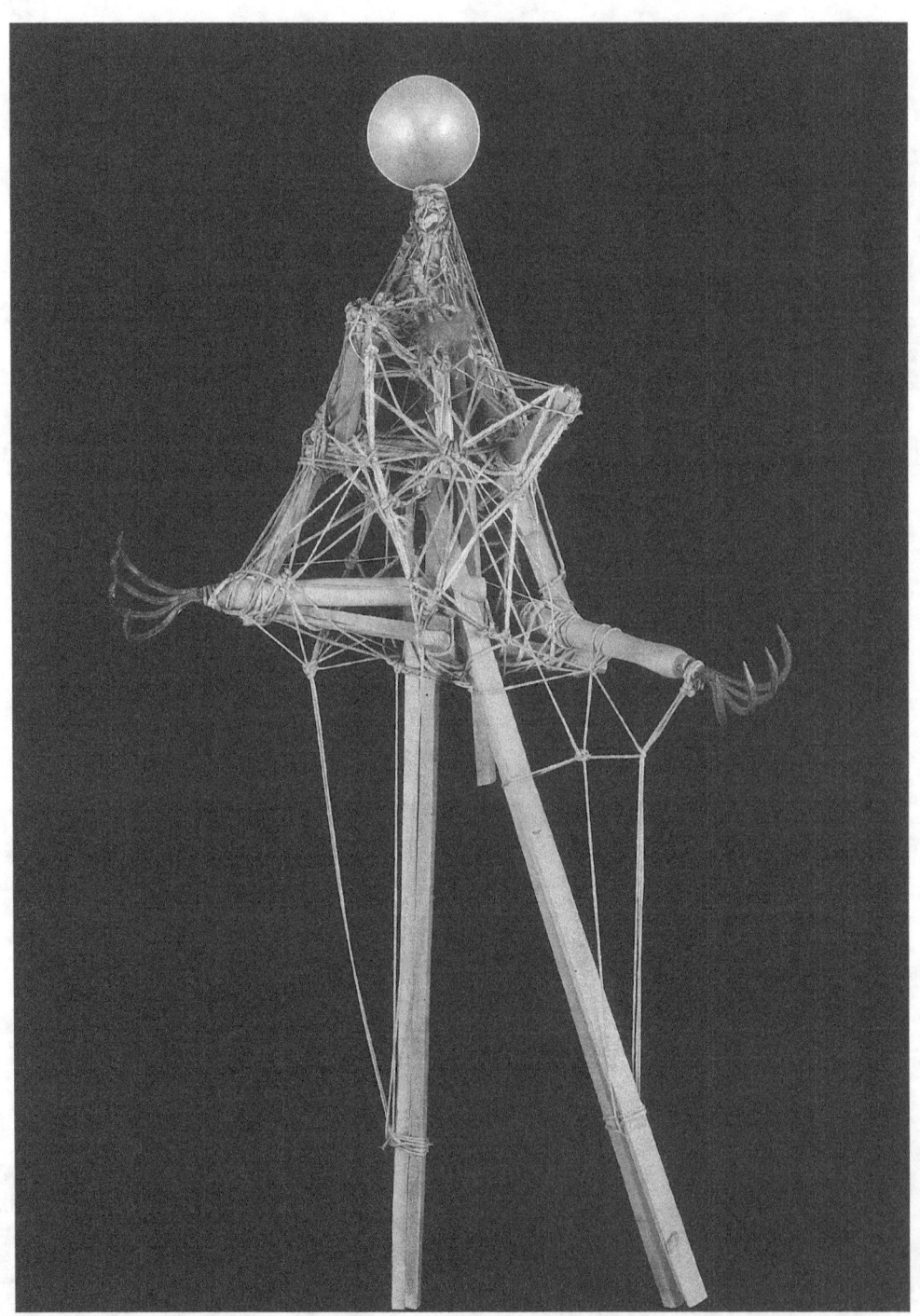

36 Pablo Picasso, *Figure*, 1935, ladle, rakes, wood, string and nails, 112.1 x 61.5 x 29.8, Musée Picasso, Paris.

figures'.[74] It was, of course, additionally sewn to the canvas support, albeit crudely with two large stitches, as was its companion piece. Sewing itself, a technique that Picasso's collages often evoked, was a simple and frequently visible means of attaching things to one another, like nails. But unlike the blunt directness of the action of nailing, or the speed of glueing ('collage'), sewing arguably required greater care and deliberation, and entailed a more extended process or ritual of making. In Picasso's 1937 *Still Life with Mask* he added a series of decorative stitches to the bottom edge of a cardboard 'mask' sewn to the canvas, while a stitched-on red button represented the base of a glass, a tongue-in-cheek throw-back to cubist collages.[75]

In one of the recent works by Picasso included in the 1936 exhibition of surrealist objects at the Ratton gallery, *Figure* (1935), a web of strings held together wooden sticks with household tools: two small rakes and a large ladle (figure 36). Different thicknesses of string from thin ropes to fine threads made up an entangled mass in this piece, forming the figure's 'body', and punctuated by a series of elaborate knots. Knotting and binding have been seen as of special anthropological significance, exemplifying 'the coming together of affective and cognitive processes', and 'the fluid mechanisms of persons and things'.[76] Knotting was another magical practice charted by ethnologists, described, for instance, by Haddon: 'The malevolent tying of a knot brought mischief upon a man, to be averted only by counter-plotting and counter-knotting ... evil spirits had to be exorcised, and the knot of the spell-bound to be loosed'.[77] The process of tying knots could be as complex and loaded as that of cooking (the ladle) or agricultural activity (the hand-held rakes). Picasso's *Figure* had a certain malevolence in its spiked rake hands: Spies has described it as a 'threat-ening scarecrow' symbolically representing greed and insatiability.[78] But its configu-ration of strings holding wooden elements in place also had the air of a trap, with its two outstretched claws ready to spring shut and its mass of entangling strings. For Gell in his 1996 essay on 'traps as artworks', the animal trap in non-western cultures provided an imaginative model for the function of art more generally: 'traps commu-nicate the idea of a nexus of intentionalities between hunters and prey animals, via material forms and mechanisms ... suitably framed, animal traps could be made to evoke complex intuitions of being, otherness, relatedness'.[79] Certain surrealist objects and sculptures that implied the viewer's participation thematised the con-cept of trapping. Ernst's 1936 *Mobile Object Recommended for Families* had a phallic collapsible wooden extension that could pinch the fingers of its curious participant. The cage structures in Giacometti's work of the early 1930s, and his horizontal board works recalling fairground games, like *Caught Hand* and *Point to the Eye*, played out scenarios of physical threat and entanglement. Giacometti's floor piece *Woman with her Throat Cut* (1932), can be read as a large metal man-trap, as well as suggesting the surrealist fascination with the praying mantis. Breton's 1931 *Object of Symbolic Function* supposedly contains a catapult mechanism to send a sugared almond through the air to strike a bicycle bell, but the presence in its centre of a bicycle seat also gave it the appearance of a human snare.

The 'treasury of ideas': worthless objects in precious combinations

The technological processes evoked by Mauss and Hubert in their study of magic had certain characteristic material qualities, often involving the combination of fragile or insubstantial things to create a more firm or stable whole. Techniques of sewing secure the frayed edges of cloth and increase the strength of thread by knotting and binding. The culinary or alchemical shifts of matter evoked in Leiris's 1929 article on Giacometti played out processes of dematerialisation and solidification, mirroring the process of creating plaster sculptures from a dry powdery substance mixed with liquid. The significance of ephemeral and lowly materials in the surrealist object consciously built on the avant-garde legacy of cubist collage through the writings of Apollinaire, whose evocation of the expendable components of 'fetish' figures was borrowed from an ethnological source, as we have seen. But while surrealism shifted its interest in non-western cultures largely away from Africa, the ethnographic principles of the Dakar–Djibouti expedition tallied more closely with notions of surrealist assemblage than might be assumed. The preference of Breton and Eluard for Oceanic over African artefacts has been put down to the fact that the latter had by the later 1920s become 'pure art', subject to formal analysis and the market in luxury items.[80] If Oceanic art was appealing as it was less 'civilised', it was also perceived as less easy to preserve, as some of the most striking figures and masks known and collected in the period were made of wood or vegetable fibre. The Dakar–Djibouti expedition's conscious bias against the 'precious' (echoed in the pages of *Documents*), led it to seek out perishable materials like wood, cloth, raffia or wicker. The masks and costumes of the Dogon, one of the expedition's 'discoveries', were arguably closer to the new 'aesthetic' of Oceanic art than to the prevailing taste in 'fine' African statuettes.

The implications of Apollinaire's discussions of the heterogeneity of collage materials and of non-western objects certainly informed Dada practice, but arguably were only fully taken up within surrealism. Aragon's preface to the 1930 Galerie Goemans exhibition 'La peinture au défi' ('In defiance of painting'), brought out this connection clearly.[81] For Aragon, collage was a way out of an artistic impasse that had seen modern art tamed by the market. Works by Brancusi and Miró were too at home, nowadays, in the Dôme café or in bourgeois apartments:

> Painting is turning comfortable, flattering the person of taste who has paid for it. It is luxurious. Pictures are jewels. But it is possible for painters to liberate themselves from this domestication through money. Collage is poor. For a long time yet its value will be denied.[82]

For artists, using collage could mean recourse to the most humble and devalued materials: paper; bits of string, straws, tooth-picks, safety pins in the work of Picabia; sand and feathers in the work of Masson; nails, corrugated cardboard, bits of rag and netting in the work of Picasso. Picasso in particular, for Aragon, looked to materials which lay at the bottom of any scale of value: 'he wanted the real refuse

of human life, something poor, dirtied, despised'.[83] Not just upsetting artistic hierarchies, the new ways in which artists were using collage, Aragon claimed,
returned art to an older function: 'by bringing it back to the magical practices
which are the origin and the justification for plastic representations, upheld by several religions'.[84] The only non-western cultural form that Aragon made specific
reference to was Peruvian textiles, which he compared to Masson's sand collages;
however, his comments clearly suggested the model of non-western, African and
Oceanic societies. The very ways too in which modern artists were going about
making collages, suggested ritual practices for Aragon, as they behaved 'in a systematic fashion that recalls more the operations of magic than those of painting'.[85]

Aragon's notion of a magical 'system' involving the collage combinations of
feathers, rags, nails and torn bits of paper, set up a tension between the apparent randomness of assembled elements and the sense of their overall fusion. It also pointed
to the significance of the practice of collage, as something ongoing and 'untamed',
rather than finished and ready for exchange. A good counter-example to Aragon's
collage processes was provided by a 1931 article by Zervos on Miró's object-assemblages, works which brought together rough pieces of wood, chains, nails and sandpaper. According to Zervos in *Cahiers d'art*, these 'sculpture-objects' were:

> made from the most humble objects possible, without any intrinsic artistic value.
> They are bits of bone, glass, stone, gathered by Miró according to the whims of his
> wanderings, scraps of string, watch fragments, old bells, little toys. Chosen by
> chance, these objects are not arranged indifferently.[86]

Zervos went on to justify Miró's selection of assemblage elements through reference to his own 'genius', a clear instance of the market-led recuperation of these
'difficult' pieces. By referring to the ways Miró's disparate found objects were
'arranged' and suggesting that this arrangement was intended and definitive,
Zervos put a stop to the 'uncomfortable' activities evoked by Aragon. Once these
humble bits and pieces had been transformed into a distinct and unique surrealist
object, they could leave behind their 'dirty' magic.

The role of the 'humble object' as a key focus for the Dakar–Djibouti expedition
was complex, as we have seen. Its ethnographic rationale had stressed the importance of 'poor' and seemingly insignificant artefacts. At the same time, of course,
the notion of the object as 'witness' to social customs and rituals could lead to the
conscious collection of special things, ceremonial masks, sacred altar figures, things
of great interpretative if not financial value, things worth stealing in spite of the
expedition's counter-colonial sensitivities. In two letters written by Leiris from
Africa to Picasso in Paris, cultural relativism and a concern with ordinary objects
came together. The first of these saw Leiris at his most embittered, complaining to
his artist friend about colonial administration:

> The arrogance of the whites, at all times, seems to be still more stupid than posi
> tively evil. Most of the blacks don't like working, that's their business; they've no
> need at all for morality lessons … I could go on forever carping about the grievances

I increasingly hold against civilisation. I'd rather look at the absurdity that I'm passing through from the angle of amusing madness.[87]

If Leiris's letter set up clearly an inversion of the values of the 'civilised' West versus the 'uncivilised' Africa, a second letter proposed the transformation of everyday things, through a kind of reverse perspective.[88] A letter, he wrote, became suddenly a 'very precious book of spells' ('grimoire') rather than just a scribbled piece of paper, due to its difficulty of delivery. A passport, on the other hand, became just a scrap of paper. These transformations were not metaphorical or idealised. The rain falling as he composed his letter was above all 'a *thing that makes you wet*'. Leiris related his impressions of the power of banal things to artistic debates back in Paris:

> In my opinion, the great mistake of Breton and the surrealists will be always to see something beyond reality instead of a more intense reality. I've thought about this a lot in general, some days when I found myself overjoyed to be squelching in mud, to come back in the evening to the intimacy of a few very simple accessories (camp bed, storm-lamp, jugs, plates, pans) at the same time as I had seen during the day men and women of an astonishing beauty or acquainted with rites of extraordinary poetry.

Leiris's experience, as he relayed it to Picasso, also involved his own physical participation: 'There is also the joy of feeling alive, of touching something simply to touch'. Leiris's letter from Ethiopia in 1932 had a role to play in the 'dissident' surrealist critiques of Bretonian surrealism that had crystallised in *Documents*, particularly around the reception of Picasso. In an article about Picasso's recent work for *Documents*, Leiris had also stressed the role of the *reconfiguration* of reality for the artist, his creation of 'monstrous' forms which were 'creatures unlike us, or rather, the *same*, but with a different form, with a more striking structure'.[89] Leiris related his ethnographic experience in Africa to his own reservations about a transfigured 'sur-reality', comparing his interaction with basic everyday things and the special rituals he observed as part of the same continuum.

Leiris's writings on Picasso and Giacometti, and his responses to the practice of fieldwork would result in a 'materialist' and anthropological reading of surrealism, which he partially shared with Aragon in his 1930 discussion of collage-making. Both of their perspectives implied a resistance to the transfiguration of humble things into a definitive artistic product, but also placed an emphasis on technological activities and processes. In this respect, both could be seen to anticipate the ways in which Claude Lévi-Strauss used surrealism to articulate his theory of *bricolage* in *La Pensée sauvage* of 1962.[90] Lévi-Strauss took surrealism's chance juxtapositions as an example of the processes of 'mythic' thought, producing new structures out of ordinary pre-existing elements: 'using residues and remnants of events, "odds and ends" as the English say, or, in French, scraps and bits, fossil testimonies of the history of an individual or society'.[91] The *bricoleur* too was making use of basic, humble materials and trying out their differing combinations: 'That cube of oak could be a chock to make up for the insufficiencies of a fir plank, or maybe a base, which would allow the grain and the shine of the old wood to be shown off'.[92] Lévi-Strauss's conception of the 'mind in a savage state' was not confined to the ethnological study of non-western cultures but an element too of western thought. Like the creative magic techniques evoked by Mauss and Hubert, the 'structures' of *bricolage* that he proposed were necessarily contingent and disturbed by the workings of individuals, as its result was:

> always a compromise between the structure of the instrumental ensemble and that of the project. Once realised, the latter will be inevitably discrepant in relation to the initial intention ... an effect that the surrealists gave the felicitous term 'objective chance'.[93]

Lévi-Strauss's concept of the *bricoleur* working with the 'heterogeneous objects that make up his treasury' has been related to the surrealist object's combination of humble 'found' elements and to assemblage in modern art more generally.[94] The tensions in this concept between the structures of the 'mythic' system of thinking and the new possibilities that arise through the *bricoleur*'s experimental configurations of things to hand also appear to prefigure Clifford's notion of 'ethnographic surrealism'. Most notably, his definition of the moment when 'the possibility of comparison exists in unmediated tension with sheer incongruity' captures the same ambivalence of experimental openness jostling with interpretative closure.[95] For Clifford, however, Lévi-Strauss's work more generally was marked by over-systematisation, particularly in his reading of Mauss.[96] This may be unjust, especially as the meanings of the things produced by Lévi-Strauss's *bricoleur* resided in the producer him or herself, suggesting a position closer to Clifford's postmodern, self-reflexive ethnographer than might be initially assumed: 'Without ever completing his project, the *bricoleur* always puts into it something of himself'.[97] Nevertheless, the most interesting implications of the theory of *bricolage* lay not in the ways in which it might tell of 'the character and life of its author', but in 'brilliant and unexpected results' of it as a technique.[98]

That the notion of *bricolage* was indebted to Mauss and Hubert was clear from Lévi-Strauss's reference to their description of magic as a 'treasury of ideas'.[99] Poor in content, but rich in thinking, the magic 'treasury' was not a collection of precious objects, like the 'treasury' of special non-western 'masterpieces' installed at the Trocadéro in 1932. The simple bits of wood used by the *bricoleur* had no particular value. In his 1924 essay 'The Shadow of the Inventor', Aragon had posited as the counterpart to the debased contraptions of the inventors' fair his own new inventive uses for everyday objects. Simple things like matches could be made to perform in parlour tricks and take on a new function: 'Thus the match pressed against the friction-strip can be sent in a flick like a comet across the room, thus, with three matches placed in a goal formation on their box, when you light the crossbar in the middle and it flies off, etc'.[100] Aragon's example construed the humble box of matches (something a child might use as a container for its own 'treasury') as a creative 'box of tricks', animated through play and performance, and 'collectable' only as component parts of a changeable whole. The role of the child's imagination in assembling things that were 'not beautiful, but brilliant' would find a key articulation in a 1942 essay 'The Myth of Secret Treasures in Childhood' by Roger Caillois, an important figure in the legacy of surrealism's engagement with both anthropology and science.[101]

By the mid-1930s, surrealist objects, like the ethnographic objects collected by the Dakar–Djibouti expedition, were beginning to be inserted into interpretative systems and fixed in display vitrines. In a 1933 interview with an American writer, Breton used a technological metaphor to justify and unite surrealist objects in a common purpose:

> They seem odd, bizarre, meaningless and ludicrous to the uninitiated. These objects can acquire meaning and purpose only when they are incorporated into the complete picture of a poetic vision ... The old literature is dying because it has become thread-bare. It is like a dress constantly torn up and repaired. It has become colourless, taste-less and lifeless. In our laboratory we are weaving the stuffs for a new poetic dress.[102]

Breton's imagery of weaving would find an echo in one of the major anthropological legacies of the Dakar–Djibouti expedition, the ethnographic study of Dogon cosmology by Griaule and his team of the later 1930s and beyond.[103] Griaule's conversations with the Dogon elder Ogotemmêli described the creation of the 'word' by an ancestor spirit, weaving language in the warp and weft movements of his teeth and tongue.[104] The delineation of a complete Dogon cosmology, like Breton's 'poetic dress' for the initiated, implied a coherent structure of meaning, where what was once inexplicable or unexpected would find a logical place.

Breton's 1933 'mission statement' for the 'difficult' surrealist object found its realisation, arguably, in the 1936 exhibition of surrealist objects at Charles Ratton's gallery (figure 37). The installation used the same type of modern metal vitrine introduced a few years earlier at the Trocadéro, which was unsurprising given Ratton's links to the Ethnographic Museum. Its aping of a 'scientific' mode of display suggested the 'complete picture' was to be made up from disparate parts. This was particularly the case with those objects in glass cases, flattened like the 'floating objects' in photographs and tending towards the 'semiotic homogeneity' described by Bruno Latour: 'mobile ... immutable, presentable, readable and combinable with one another'.[105] The division of these vitrines into relatively evenly spaced shelves and visual compartments through its internal glass partitions very much reinforced this effect. The containment of the object in this way had been imaginatively anticipated and problematised in a drawing by Giacometti for *Le Surréalisme au service de la révolution* in 1931 (figure 38). Giacometti had presented a series of 'Mobile and mute objects' framed in a cartoon-like and captioned strip whose rectangular boxes echoed the vitrine-like 'cages' of his own sculptures. But these boxes included the crucial additions of a schematic drawn hand broaching one frame to touch the phallic *Disagreeable Object*, and what resembled a bent arm holding an eye intruding into another. His drawn objects were a deliberate mixture of realised

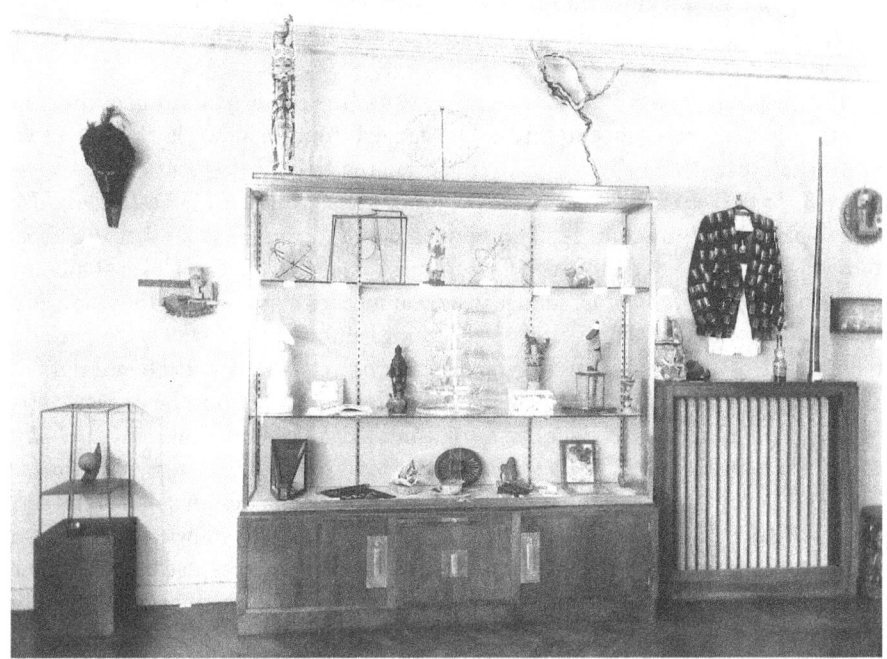

37 Installation photograph of the *Exhibition of surrealist objects*, Charles Ratton Gallery, Paris, May 1936.

OBJETS MOBILES ET MUETS

Toutes choses... près, loin, toutes celles qui sont passées et les autres, par devant,

trois personnes, de quelle gare? Les locomotives qui sifflent, il n'y a pas de gare par ici,

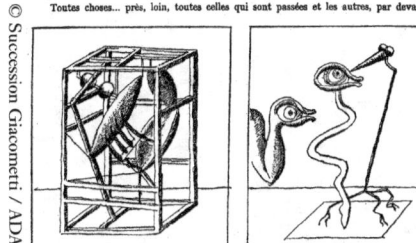 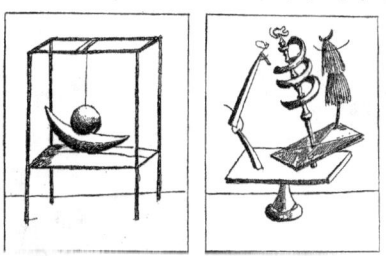

qui bougent et mes amies — elles changent (on passe tout près, elles sont loin), d'autres approchent, montent, descendent, des canards sur l'eau, là et là, dans l'espace, montent,

on jetait des pelures d'orange du haut de la terrasse, dans la rue très étroite et profonde — la nuit, les mulets braillaient désespérément, vers le matin, on les abattait — demain je sors —

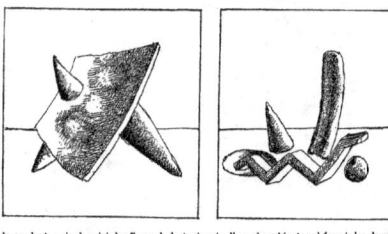 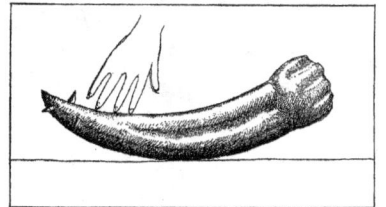

descendent — je dors ici, les fleurs de la tapisserie, l'eau du robinet mal fermé, les dessins du rideau, mon pantalon sur une chaise, on parle dans une chambre plus loin ; deux ou

elle approche sa tête de mon oreille — sa jambe, la grande — ils parlent, ils bougent, là et là, mais tout est passé.

ALBERTO GIACOMETTI.

18   19

38 Alberto Giacometti, 'Objets mobiles et muets', *Le Surréalisme au service de la révolution*, 3 (1931).

and realisable works, and impossible combinations of fragile and unsteady things, like the skeletal form and raffia costume teetering on an unstable de Chiricoesque plaque.

That Giacometti was alert to the complexity of the commodification of the sur-realist object and resistance to this can be gauged from the interplay between two of the sculpture-objects he created in the early 1930s: his *Disagreeable Object to be Thrown Away* (1931) and *Vide-Poche* (1930) (figures 39 and 40). The *Disagreeable Object* played into discourses of the ephemeral and unrepeatable ritual object, thrown away once used (like the Dogon mask collected by the Dakar–Djibouti expedition). The *Vide-Poche*, similar in appearance with its conical protrusion and shallow hollow, mimicked a container for things emptied from pockets, especially money. Giacometti worked producing designer objects for fashionable interiors in the early 1930s, knowing more than many other surrealists about the uneasy com-promises of 'avant-garde' identity with commercial commissions.[106] His *Vide-Poche* was reproduced in *Art et Industrie* in 1936, pictured on top of a dresser designed by Jean-Michel Frank, one of the sculptor's main design collaborators.[107] But his little 'tidy' was not strictly functional, already filled with two plaque forms, one of which resembled an additional shallow receptacle. Its plaster fragility too could not withstand everyday use. Giacometti's objects knowingly

39 Alberto Giacometti, *Disagreeable Object to be Thrown Away*, 1931, wood, 22 x 30 x 30, Scottish National Gallery of Modern Art, Edinburgh.

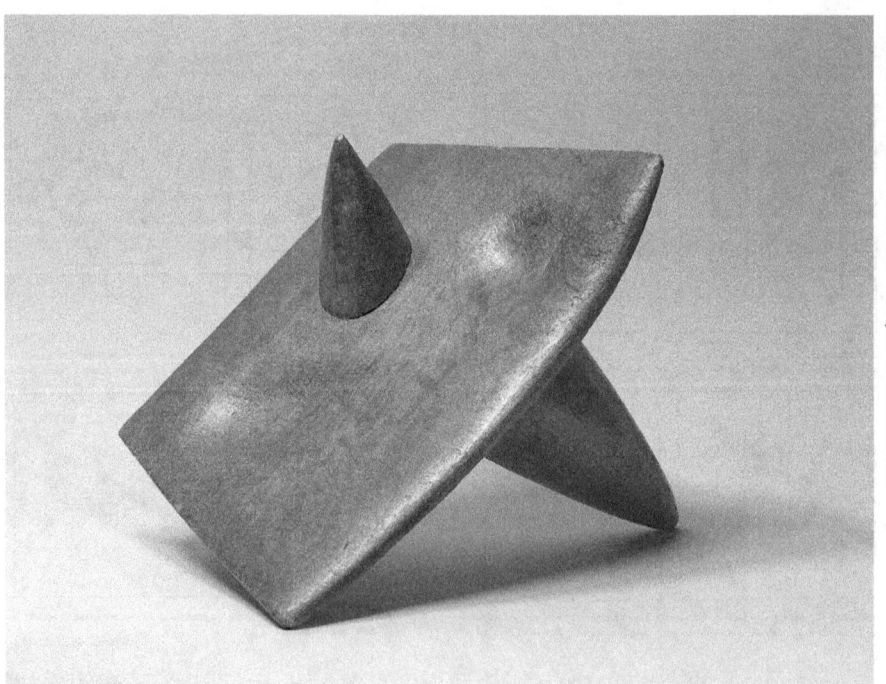

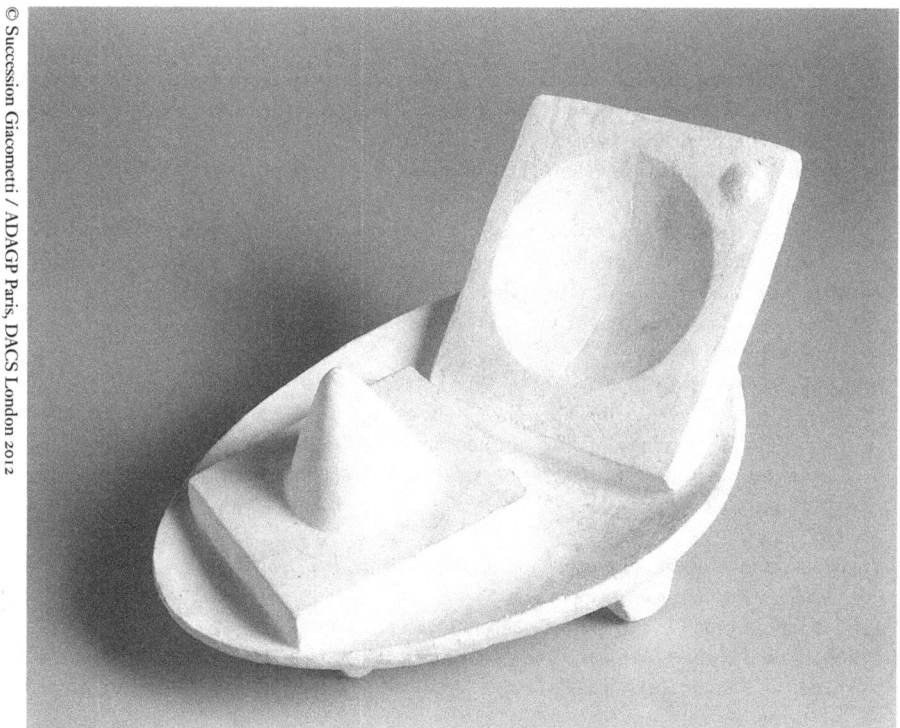

40 Alberto Giacometti, Vide-Poche, 1930/31, plaster, 17.5 x 19.5 x 29.5,Kunsthaus Zürich, Alberto Giacometti Foundation.

blurred the difficult distinctions in surrealist three-dimensional things between everyday pieces of equipment and special, elite collectors' items. His deliberate mobilisation of the viewer as participant and user meant that these tensions could continue to be kept in play.

The 1936 Ratton Gallery show has been seen as the moment of surrealism's 'return to art', marking the abandonment of the attempt to challenge categories of art, while surrealist objects could and can now only serve as the 'fragile mementos' of a lost utopian project.[108] However, this is to underestimate the importance of surrealist objects, in their production and their reception, for later artistic and cultural activities. To begin to read the three-dimensional things produced in the broader surrealist milieu (objects, sculpture, assemblage) as caught up in technological practices from an ethnographic perspective, as this chapter has done, is both to point up their combinations of unruly elements or forms and the processes implied by these combinations. The object becomes both a bundle of messy *stuff*, and a dispersed network of activities, performances and relations. Its power to 'irritate', which *Documents* sought to harness, is also its power to 'entangle': physically, conceptually and imaginatively.

Notes

1 J. M., 'Revues d 'art, Minotaure 1 et 2', *Le Rouge et le noir* (19 July 1933), MH/2 AM 1 B4f. This reviewer may well have been J. Maes, curator of ethnography at the Museum of the Belgian Congo.

2 Breton, 'Picasso dans son élément', *Minotaure*, 1:1 (1933), pp. 10–22.

3 *Ibid.*, p. 16.

4 Breton, 'La beauté sera convulsive', p. 12. Breton had received a postcard from Gide in 1918, showing a Hawaiian feather mask from the British Museum: see *André Breton: la beauté convulsive* (Paris: Pompidou Centre, 1991), p. 93.

5 Green, 'Zervos, Picasso and Brassaï, ethnographers in the field'.

6 *Ibid.*, p. 137.

7 Gell, *Art and Agency*, p. 9.

8 *Ibid.*, p. 6.

9 Gell, 'The Technology of Enchantment and the Enchantment of Technology', in Coote and Shelton (eds), *Anthropology, Art and Aesthetics* (Oxford: Clarendon Press, 1992), pp. 40–6.

10 *Ibid.*, p. 46.

11 Mauss and Hubert, *Esquisse d'une théorie générale de la magie* (1902–3), in Mauss, *Sociologie et anthropologie*, pp. 11–12.

12 See for example Lévy-Bruhl, *Les Fonctions mentales*, pp. 34–5.

13 Mauss and Hubert, *Esquisse d'une théorie générale de la magie*, p. 46.

14 See Dalí, 'Objets surréalistes', *Le Surréalisme au service de la révolution*, 3 (December 1931), pp. 16–17.

15 Breton, 'Crise de l'objet' (1936), in *Le Surréalisme et la peinture* (Paris: Gallimard, 1965), p. 359.

16 Aragon, 'L'ombre de l'Inventeur', *La Révolution surréaliste*, 1:1 (1 December 1924), p. 22.

17 Lévy-Bruhl for instance in *Les Fonctions mentales* took issue with the fact that Tylor and Frazer's conceptions of animism did not distinguish clearly enough between a 'civilised' and a 'primitive' mentality, marking out the latter in his own work as a separate domain with its own 'laws'.

18 Tylor, *Primitive Culture*, Vol. 2, pp. 147–53, Vol. 1, p. 104.

19 Frazer, *The Golden Bough: A Study in Magic and Religion* (London: Macmillan, 1949), p. 11.

20 *Ibid.*, p. 12.

21 Dalí, 'The Object as Revealed in Surrealist Experiment' (*This Quarter*, 1932, trans. David Gascoyne), reprinted in Finkelstein (ed.), *The Collected Writings of Salvador Dalí* (Cambridge: Cambridge University Press, 1998), p. 243.

22 Leiris, 'Joan Miró, *The Little Review*, 12:1 (1926), pp. 8–9.

23 Leiris had owned since 1924 a collage drawing by Miró incorporating a bird's feather, which undoubtedly inspired his article, see *Donation Louise et Michel Leiris* (Paris: Pompidou Centre, 1984), cat. no. 139, p. 163.

24 Leiris, 'Joan Miró', p. 9.

25 Tylor, *Primitive Culture*, Vol. 1, p. 105.

26 Leiris, 'Joan Miró', p. 9. There is an example of an elaborate late nineteenth-century picture made from looped and woven hair in the Musée des Arts et Traditions

Populaires (origin and use unknown), which may have been in the Trocadéro's collection in the 1920s.

27 Examples of this include feathers in Miró's *Un oiseau poursuit une abeille et la baisse* (1927) and *Spanish Dancer* (1928), pubic hair in another *Spanish Dancer* (1928) by Miró and Dalí's *Scatological Object* (1931), footprints in Miró's *The Farm* (1922) and *Dutch Interior I* (1928), a cast of a footprint in Dalí's *Assemblage of Objects* (1936), a hair-fastening in Breton's *Poem-Object* (1937), and the famous bronze glove deposited at the Bureau of Surrealist Research.

28 Brassaï's photograph was published to accompany Breton's article 'La beauté sera convulsive', p. 16, with the title 'Magique-Circonstancielle'. Carl Einstein had reproduced a head-like stone that he found on a beach in *Documents*, 1: 7 (1929), p. 392. The 1936 Galerie Ratton surrealist object show included Transylvanian stibnite and bismuth crystals as well as pebbles and bone fragments selected and decorated by Miró, Hérold, and Victor Brauner. Ernst and Giacometti spent the summer of 1934 in Maloja carving and painting boulders found in a nearby river.

29 Lévi-Strauss related the surrealist interest in the found object to the inspiration that Benventuto Cellini allegedly found in shells and 'objects carved into shapes by the sea' while walking along the beach, Charbonnier, *Conversations with Claude Lévi-Strauss* [1961], trans. John and Doreen Weightman (London: Jonathan Cape, 1970), p. 98.

30 For example, Haddon's *Evolution in Art* (1895), Worringer's *Abstraction and Empathy* (1908), Luquet's *L'Art primitif* (1930).

31 Cushing, *Zuñi Fetiches* (Washington: Smithsonian Institution Bureau of Ethnology, 1883).

32 Cowling, 'The Eskimos, the American Indians and the Surrealists', *Art History*, 1:4 (December 1978), p. 487.

33 Cushing, *Zuñi Fetiches* (Washington: Smithsonian Institution, 1883), p. 12.

34 Balfour, *The Evolution of Decorative Art*, p. 79.

35 *Ibid.*, p. 85.

36 *Ibid.*, p. 86.

37 Breton's interest in the mandrake may also have derived from his knowledge of German Romantic literature, where it is a common motif.

38 Breton, 'La beauté sera convulsive', p. 13.

39 *Ibid.*, p. 16. While rescuing his father, Aeneus lost his wife in the dark burning city.

40 Mauss and Hubert, *Esquisse d'une théorie générale de la magie*, p. 96. I am citing from the translation by Robert Brain (London: Routledge and Kegan Paul, 1972), p. 103.

41 See for example the classic 1982 study by Gregory, *Gifts and Commodities*, but also the more recent questioning and qualification of this distinction in Thomas, *Entangled Objects*, pp. 14–22.

42 Mauss and Hubert, *Esquisse d'une théorie générale de la magie*, p. 20.

43 See Foster, *Compulsive Beauty* [1993] (Cambridge, MA: MIT Press, 1997), pp. 157–64.

44 *Ibid.*, p. 197.

45 Breton, *Nadja*, p. 147.

46 Benjamin, 'On Some Motifs in Baudelaire' [1939], *Illuminations* (New York: Schocken Books, 1969), p. 186.

47 See also Potts, *The Sculptural Imagination*, pp. 118–19.

48 Leiris, 'Joan Miró' and 'André Masson', *The Little Review*, 12:1 (1926), pp. 8–9 and pp. 16–17.

49 Leiris, 'Alberto Giacometti', p. 209.

50 Leiris, 'Hebdomeros', *Documents*, 2:5 (1930), p. 311. While Breton and Aragon had turned against de Chirico's paintings of the late 1920s, they were received positively by Roger Vitrac, one of the allies of *Documents*.

51 Leiris, 'Alberto Giacometti', p. 210.

52 See for instance Lévy-Bruhl, *The 'Soul' of the Primitive* [1927] (London: George Allen and Unwin, 1965), particularly chapter III, pp. 110–27.

53 Einstein, 'André Masson, étude ethnologique', *Documents*, 1:2 (May 1929), pp. 93–102. On the concept of ecstasy in Einstein and Leiris's writings, see Palermo, 'Tactile Translucence: Miró, Leiris, Einstein', *October*, 97 (summer 2001), pp. 31–50.

54 Einstein may well have been inspired by Besson's *Le Totémisme*, available in the *Documents* office.

55 Leiris, 'Alberto Giacometti', p. 210.

56 Dalí, 'The Object as Revealed in Surrealist Experiment', pp. 243–4.

57 Breton, *L'Amour fou* (Paris: Gallimard, 1937), pp. 38–57.

58 See Wood, 'From *vue d'atelier* to *vie d'atelier*: 46 rue Hippolyte-Maindron and the beginnings of Giacometti', in Read and Kelly (eds), *Alberto Giacometti: Critical Essays* (Aldershot: Ashgate, forthcoming).

59 Leiris, 'Alberto Giacometti', p. 210.

60 On the new interest in salt and its properties in seventeenth-century alchemy, see Sherwood Taylor, *The Alchemists* (St Albans: Paladin, 1976), p. 151.

61 Mauss and Hubert, *Esquisse d'une théorie générale de la magie*, p. 46.

62 Although it does not feature in Marc Vaux's photographs for *Documents*, the plaster version of *Spoon Woman* was shown lurking in a corner of Giacometti's studio (to which he moved in 1927) in a photograph by Brassaï published in 1933, and was most likely in the studio when Leiris visited it in 1929 in preparation for his article.

63 Giacometti's knowledge of and interest in surrealism in the mid-1920s can be gauged from the inclusion in his 1926 *Still Life* of Aragon's *Paysan de Paris*.

64 Krauss, 'Giacometti', in Rubin, *"Primitivism"*, p. 507.

65 *Ibid.*, pp. 507–8.

66 Clouzot and Level, 'Afrique équatoriale française, Sculptures et objets d'usage', p. 224.

67 Lepage, *La Décoration primitive: Afrique* (Paris: Calavas, c.1924), plate XVI.

68 Leroi-Gourhan, *Milieu et techniques* (Paris: Albin Michel, 1945), pp. 198–9.

69 Lemke, *Primitivist Modernism: Black Culture and the Origins of Transatlantic Modernism* (Oxford: Oxford University Press, 1998), p. 24.

70 Tylor, *Primitive Culture*, Vol. 2, p. 139.

71 Dalí, 'Objets surréalistes', p. 17.

72 Breton, *L'Amour fou*, p. 49.

73 Reproduced in *La Révolution surréaliste*, 5:12 (15 December 1929), pp. 42–43.

74 Green, 'Humanisms', pp. 233–4.

75 This still life was included in the 1935 'Surrealist Objects and Poems' exhibition in London.

76 Susanne Küchler, 'Why Knot? Towards a Theory of Art and Mathematics', in Pinney and Thomas, *Beyond Aesthetics*, p. 59 and p. 64.

77 Haddon, *Evolution in Art, As Illustrated by the Life-Histories of Designs* (London: Walter Scott, 1895), p. 248.

78 Spies, *Picasso: The Sculptures* (Stuttgart: Hatje Cantz, 2000), p. 208.

79 Gell, 'Vogel's Net', p. 29.

80 Cowling, '"L'oeil sauvage"', p. 181.

81 Aragon, 'La Peinture au défi' [1930], in *Les Collages* (Paris: Hermann, 1975), pp. 35–71.

82 *Ibid.*, p. 57.

83 *Ibid.*, p. 67.

84 *Ibid.*, p. 54.

85 *Ibid.*, p. 42.

86 Editor's note (Zervos), 'Exposition Miró de Sculptures-Objets', *Cahiers d'art*, 6:9–10 (1931), p. 431.

87 Leiris, letter to Picasso from Garoua, Cameroon, 3 February 1932, archives of the Musée Picasso, Paris.

88 Leiris, letter to Picasso from Darasguié, Ethiopia, 5 July 1932, archives of the Musée Picasso, Paris.

89 Leiris, 'Toiles récentes de Picasso', *Documents*, 2:2 (1930), p. 70.

90 Lévi-Strauss, *La Pensée sauvage*. The term 'bricolage' has no adequate translation, denoting 'tinkering about', doing 'odd jobs' or 'makeshift repairs', and most commonly translated as 'DIY', which fails to convey its strong sense of active 'doing'.

91 Lévi-Strauss, *La Pensée sauvage*, p. 32.

92 *Ibid.*, p. 28.

93 Lévi-Strauss, *La Pensée sauvage*, pp. 31–2.

94 *Ibid.*, p. 28. *Bricolage* is referred to, for example, by Guigon, *El objeto surrealista* (Valencia: IVAM/Centre Julio Gonzalez, 1997), p. 277, and by Tosatto (ed.), *L'Ivresse du réel: l'objet dans l'art du XXe siècle* (Nîmes: Carré d'Art, 1993), p. 11.

95 Clifford, 'On Ethnographic Surrealism', p. 563.

96 See *ibid.*, p. 547.

97 Lévi-Strauss, *La Pensée sauvage*, p. 32.

98 *Ibid.*, p. 32, p. 26.

99 *Ibid.*, p. 28, footnote.

100 *Ibid.*, p. 24.

101 Caillois, 'The Myth of Secret Treasures in Childhood' [*VVV*, 1942], *The Edge of Surrealism: A Roger Caillois Reader*, ed. Claudine Frank (Durham, NC: Duke University Press, 2003), p. 255.

102 Breton, 'Conversations with S. A. Rhodes' [1933], in *What is Surrealism?* (1978), ed. Franklin Rosemont (New York: Pluto Press, 1989), p. 88.

103 Deborah Lifchitz, member of the Dakar–Djibouti team, returned to Sanga in 1935 with Denise Paulme. Griaule's *Masques dogon* and *Jeux dogons* were published in 1938, and his *Conversations with Ogotemmêli* in 1948. Germaine Dieterlen and Griaule's daughter Geneviève Calame-Griaule, amongst others, carried on his research into the Dogon.

104 Griaule, *Conversations with Ogotemmêli*, pp. 27–8.

105 Latour, 'Visualisation and Cognition: Thinking with the Eyes and Hands', *Knowledge and Society: Studies in the Sociology of Culture Past and Present*, 6 (1986), p. 7.

106 See the exhibition catalogue *Alberto Giacometti: retour à la figuration 1933–1947* (Paris: Pompidou Centre, 1986).

107 *Art et Industrie* (April 1936), p. 11.

108 Harris, *Surrealist Art and Thought in the 1930s* (Cambridge: Cambridge University Press, 2004), p. 221 and p. 5.

Select bibliography

Ades, Dawn (ed.), *Dada and Surrealism Reviewed* (London: Arts Council, 1978)

Ades, Dawn, 'Surrealism: Fetishism's Job', in Anthony Shelton (ed.), *Fetishism: Visualising Power and Desire* (London: South Bank, 1995), pp. 67–87

Ageron, Charles-Robert, 'L'éxposition coloniale de 1931: mythe républicain ou mythe impérial?', in Pierre Nora (ed.), *Les Lieux de mémoire*, Vol. 1 (Paris: Gallimard, 1984), pp. 561–91

Allégret, Marc, *Carnets du Congo, Voyage avec André Gide* (Paris: CNRS, 1987)

André Breton, *La Beauté convulsive* (Paris: Pompidou Centre, 1991)

Apollinaire, Guillaume, *Oeuvres en prose complètes* Vols 2 and 3 (Paris: Gallimard, 1991 and 1993)

Apollinaire, Guillaume and Paul Guillaume, *Sculptures nègres* [1917] (New York: Hacker, 1972)

Appadurai, Arjun (ed.), *The Social Life of Things: Commodities in Cultural Perspective* (Cambridge: Cambridge University Press, 1986)

Aragon, Louis, 'L'ombre de l'inventeur', *La Révolution surréaliste*, 1:1 (1 December 1924), pp. 22–4

Aragon, Louis, *Les Collages* (Paris: Hermann, 1975)

Archer-Straw, Petrine, *Negrophilia: Avant-Garde Paris and Black Culture in the 1920s* (London: Thames and Hudson, 2000)

Armel, Aliette, *Michel Leiris* (Paris: Fayard, 1997)

Arts primitifs dans les ateliers d'artistes (Paris: Musée de l'Homme, 1967)

Asad, Talal (ed.), *Anthropology and the Colonial Encounter* (London: Ithaca Press, 1973)

'Asterisk' (Robert James Fletcher), *Isles of Illusion, Letters from the South Seas*, ed. Bohun Lynch (London: Constable, 1923)

Attfield, Judy, *Wild Things: The Material Culture of Everyday Life* (Oxford: Berg, 2000)

Baacke, Rolf-Peter, 'Rezeptionsgeschichtliche Anmerkungen zur „Negerplastik"', in Baacke (ed.), *Carl Einstein, Negerplastik* (Berlin: Fannei und Walz, 1992), pp. 153–60

Balfour, Henry, *The Evolution of Decorative Art* (London: Percival, 1893)

Basler, Adolphe, *La Sculpture moderne en France* (Paris: G. Crès, 1928)

Basler, Adolphe, *L'Art chez les peuples primitifs* (Paris: Librarie de France: 1929)

Bataille, Georges, 'Les monnaies des Grands Mogols au Cabinet de Médailles', *Aréthuse*, 4 (October 1926), pp. 133–42

Bataille, Georges, 'Notes sur la numismatique des Koushans et des Koushan-shahs sassanides', *Aréthuse*, 5:1 (1928), pp. 19–35

Bataille, Georges, *Oeuvres complètes*, Vol. 1 (Paris: Gallimard, 1971)

Bataille, Georges, 'Les mangeurs d'étoiles', in Barrault *et al.*, *André Masson* [1940] (Marseille: André Dimanche, 1993)

Baudrillard, Jean, 'The System of Collecting' (trans. Roger Cardinal), in Elsner and Cardinal (eds), *The Cultures of Collecting* (London: Reaktion, 1994), pp. 7–24

Beaujour, Michel, 'Qu'est-ce que "Nadja"?', *Nouvelle revue française*, 15:172 (1967), pp. 780–99

Benjamin, Walter, *Illuminations* (New York: Schocken Books, 1969)

Besson, Maurice, *Le Totémisme* (Paris: Rieder, 1929)

Blake, Jody, 'The Truth about the Colonies, 1931: Art indigène in the Service of the Revolution', *Oxford Art Journal*, 25:1 (2002), pp. 35–58

Blanchard, Marc, 'Visions of the Archipelago: Michel Leiris, Autobiography and Ethnographic Memory', *Cultural Anthropology*, 5:3 (1990), pp. 270–91

Blanchard, Marc, '"N stuff…": Practices, Equipment, Protocols in Twentieth-Century Ethnography', *On Leiris, Yale French Studies*, 81 (1992), pp. 111–27

Blondel, Charles, *La Mentalité primitive* (Paris: Stock, 1926)

Boas, Franz, *Primitive Art* [1927] (New York: Dover, 1955)

Bois, Yve-Alain, 'Kahnweiler's Lesson', *Representations*, 18 (spring 1987), pp. 33–68

Botting, Fred and Scott Wilson (eds), *The Bataille Reader* (Oxford: Blackwell, 1997)

Bounoure, Vincent, *Le Surréalisme et les arts sauvages* (Paris: L'Harmattan, 2001)

Bourdieu, Pierre, *Outline of a Theory of Practice* [1972] (Cambridge: Cambridge University Press, 1989)

Breton, André, 'La beauté sera convulsive', *Minotaure*, 1:5 (1934), pp. 9–16

Breton, André, *L'Amour fou* (Paris: Gallimard, 1937)

Breton, André, *Nadja* [1928] (Paris: Gallimard, 1964)

Breton, André, *Le Surréalisme et la peinture* (Paris: Gallimard, 1965)

Breton, André, *L'Art magique* [1957] (Paris: Adam Biro, 1991)

Breton, André, *Break of Day* [1934], trans. Mark Polizzotti and Mary Ann Caws (Lincoln: University of Nebraska Press, 1999)

Brosses, Charles de, *Du culte des dieux fétiches* [1760] (Paris: Fayard, 1988)

Bulletin du Musée d'Ethnographie du Trocadéro [1931–35] (Paris: Jean-Michel Place, 1988)

Cahn, Walter, 'Focillon's *Jongleur*', *Art History*, 18:3 (September 1995), pp. 345–62

Caillois, Roger, *The Edge of Surrealism: A Roger Caillois Reader*, ed. Claudine Frank (Durham, NC: Duke University Press, 2003)

Cardinal, Roger, 'Collecting and Collage-Making: The Case of Kurt Schwitters', in Elsner and Cardinal (eds), *The Cultures of Collecting* (London: Reaktion, 1994), pp. 68–96

Cardoso, Rafael, 'Putting the Magic Back into Design: from Object Fetishism to Product Semantics and Beyond', *Art on the Line*, 1:2 (2004), pp. 1–21

Cassou, Jean, 'Le Dadaïsme et le Surréalisme', in René Huyghe (ed.), *Histoire de l'art contemporain: la peinture* (Paris: Félix Alcan, 1935), pp. 337–44

Catalogue de l'exposition de la mission au Cameroun de M. H. Labouret (Paris: Musée du Trocadéro, 1935)

Cazeneuve, Jean, *Lucien Lévy-Bruhl* [1963], trans. Peter Rivière (Oxford: Blackwell, 1972)

Certeau, Michel de, *The Practice of Everyday Life* [1974], trans. Steven Rendall (Berkeley: University of California Press, 1988)

Charbonnier, Georges, *Conversations with Claude Lévi-Strauss* [1961], trans. John and Doreen Weightman (London: Jonathan Cape, 1970)

Chauvet, Stéphen, *Les Arts indigènes des Colonies Françaises* (Paris: A. Maloine, 1924)

Chauvet, Stéphen, *Les Arts indigènes en Nouvelle-Guinée* (Paris: Société d'Editions Géographiques, Maritimes et Coloniales, 1930)

Chauvet, Stéphen, 'Objets d'or, de bronze et d'ivoire dans l'art nègre', *Cahiers d'art*, 5:1 (1930), pp. 33–4

Chefs-d'oeuvre du Musée de l'Homme (Paris: Musée de l'Homme, 1965)

Classens, Henri, 'La valeur et le sens des sculptures et des peintures des noirs', *L'Art et les artistes*, 25:118 (June 1931), pp. 313–15

Clifford, James, 'On Ethnographic Surrealism', *Comparative Studies in Society and History*, 23 (1981), pp. 539–64

Clifford, James, 'On Ethnographic Allegory', in Clifford and Marcus (eds), *Writing Culture* (Berkeley: University of California Press, 1986), pp. 98–121

Clifford, James, 'The Tropological Realism of Michel Leiris', *Sulfur*, 15 (1986), pp. 4–18

Clifford, James, *The Predicament of Culture: Twentieth-Century Ethnography, Literature and Art* (Cambridge, MA: Harvard University Press, 1988)

Clouzot, Henri and André Level, *L'Art nègre et l'art océanien* (Paris: Devambez, 1919)

Clouzot, Henri and André Level, 'Afrique équatoriale française, sculptures et objets d'usage', *La Renaissance de l'art français*, 5:4 (1922), pp. 223–7

Clouzot, Henri and André Level, 'L'art indigène des colonies françaises et du Congo Belge au Pavillon de Marsan en 1923', *L'Amour de l'art*, 5:1 (1924), pp. 17–22

Clouzot, Henri and André Level, *Sculptures Africaines et Océaniennes* (Paris: Librairie de France, 1924)

Clouzot, Henri and André Level, 'Caractéristiques de l'art des noirs', *L'Art vivant*, 1:5 (1 March 1925), pp. 11–13

Cohen, Margaret, *Profane Illumination: Walter Benjamin and the Paris of Surrealist Revolution* (Berkeley: University of California Press, 1993)

Coiffier, Christian, *Le Voyage de* La Korrigane *dans les mers du sud* (Paris: Musée de l'Homme, 2002)

Coles, Alex (ed.), *Site-Specificity: The Ethnographic Turn* (London: Black Dog, 2000)

Conley, Katharine, 'Modernist Primitivism in 1933: Brassaï's "Involuntary Sculptures" in *Minotaure*', *Modernism/Modernity*, 10:1 (2003), pp. 127–40

Coombes, Annie E., *Reinventing Africa: Museums, Material Culture and Popular Imagination in Late Victorian and Edwardian England* (London and New Haven, CT: Yale University Press, 1994)

Coombes, Annie E., 'Ethnography, Popular Culture, and Institutional Power: Narratives of Benin Culture in the British Museum, 1897–1992', *Studies in the History of Art*, 47 (1996), pp. 143–57

Coote, Jeremy and Anthony Shelton (eds), *Anthropology, Art and Aesthetics* (Oxford: Clarendon Press, 1992)

Cowling, Elizabeth, 'The Eskimos, the American Indians and the Surrealists', *Art History*, 1:4 (December 1978), pp. 484–500

Cowling, Elizabeth, '"L'oeil sauvage": Oceanic Art and the Surrealists', in Suzanne Greub (ed.), *Art of Northwest New Guinea* (New York: Rizzoli, 1992), pp. 177–89

Crescenzo, Casimiro di, *Alberto Giacometti: Early Works in Paris (1922–1930)* (New York: Yoshii Gallery, 1994)

Cushing, Frank Hamilton, *Zuñi Fetiches* (Washington, DC: Smithsonian Institution, 1883)

Dalí, Salvador, 'Objets surréalistes', *Le Surréalisme au service de la révolution*, 3 (December 1931), p. 16–17

Danto, Arthur *et al.*, *Art/Artifact: African Art in Anthropology Collections* (New York: Center for African Art, 1988)

Delafosse, Maurice, 'Statues des rois de Dahomé au Musée ethnographique du Trocadéro', *La Nature*, 1086 (24 March 1894), pp. 262–6

Delafosse, Maurice, 'Le trône de Béhanzin et les portes des palais d'Abomé au Musée ethnographique du Trocadéro', *La Nature*, 1090 (21 April 1894), pp. 326–30

Delafosse, Maurice, 'Une statue dahoméenne en fonte', *La Nature*, 1105 (4 August 1894), pp. 145–7

Delafosse, Maurice, *Haut-Sénégal-Niger* [1912] (Paris: Maisonneuve et Larose, 1972)

Desplagnes, Louis, *Le Plateau central nigérien: une mission archéologique et ethnographique au Soudan français* (Paris: Emile Larose, 1907)

Dias, Nélia, *Le Musée d'ethnographie du Trocadéro (1878–1908)* (Paris: CNRS, 1991)

Didi-Huberman, Georges, *La Ressemblance informe* (Paris: Macula, 1995)

Documents [1929–30] (Paris: Jean-Michel Place, 1991)

Donne, J. B., 'African art and Paris studios 1905–20', in Michael Greenhalgh and Vincent Megaw (eds), *Art in Society* (London: Duckworth, 1978), pp. 105–20

Durkheim, Emile, *Les Formes élémentaires de la vie religieuse* [1912] (Paris: Presses universitaires de France, 1960)

Durrans, Brian, 'The Future of the Other: Changing Cultures on Display in Ethnographic Museums', in Robert Lumley (ed.), *The Museum Time Machine* (London: Routledge, 1988), pp. 144–69

Edwards, Elizabeth (ed.), *Anthropology and Photography, 1860–1920* (New Haven, CT: Yale University Press, 1992)

Edwards, Elizabeth, *Raw Histories: Photographs, Anthropology and Museums* (Oxford: Berg, 2001)

Einstein, Carl, *Afrikanische Plastik* (Berlin: Ernst Wasmuth, 1921)

Einstein, Carl, *La Sculpture nègre* [1915], trans. and ed. Liliane Meffre (Paris: L'Harmattan, 1998)

Elsner, Jas, 'The Birth of Late Antiquity: Riegl and Strzygowski in 1901', *Art History*, 25:3 (June 2002), pp. 358–79

Exposition de Bronzes et Ivoires du Royaume de Bénin (Paris: Musée d'Ethnographie, 1932)

Exposition du Sahara (Paris: Musée d'Ethnographie, 1934)

Fabian, Johannes, *Time and the Other: How Anthropology Makes its Object* (New York: Columbia University Press, 1983)

Fabian, Johannes, *Out of our Minds: Reason and Madness in the Exploration of Central Africa* (Berkeley: University of California Press, 2000)

Faure, Elie, *Histoire de l'art*, Vol. 5 (Paris: G. Crès, 1927)

Fénéon, Félix, *Iront-ils au Louvre? Enquête sur des arts lointains* [1920] (Toulouse: Toguna, 2000)

Fierens, Paul, 'Pour un musée d'art congolais', *Variétés*, 1:7 (15 November 1928), pp. 375–8

Finkelstein, Haim, *Surrealism and the Crisis of the Object* (Ann Arbor: University of Michigan Press, 1979)

Finkelstein, Haim (ed.), *The Collected Writings of Salvador Dalí* (Cambridge: Cambridge University Press, 1998)

Flam, Jack and Miriam Deutch (eds), *Primitivism and Twentieth-Century Art* (Berkeley: University of California Press, 2003)

Focillon, Henri, *L'Art bouddhique* (Paris: Henri Laurens, 1921)

Focillon, Henri, *L'Art des sculpteurs romans* [1931] (Paris: Presses universitaires de France, 1964)

Ford, Mark, *Raymond Roussel and the Republic of Dreams* (London: Faber and Faber, 2000)

Foster, Hal, 'The Artist as Ethnographer', in *The Return of the Real* (Cambridge, MA: MIT Press, 1996), pp. 171–203

Foster, Hal, *Compulsive Beauty* [1993] (Cambridge, MA: MIT Press, 1997)

Foucault, Michel, *The Order of Things* [1966] (New York: Vintage, 1973)

Frazer, James, *The Golden Bough: A Study in Magic and Religion* (London: Macmillan, 1949)

Freedman, Robert (ed.), *Marx on Economics* (Harmondsworth: Penguin, 1973)

Freud, Sigmund, *Totem and Taboo* [1913] (Harmondsworth: Penguin, 1940)

Frizot, Michel and Dominique Païni (eds), *Sculpter-Photographier, Photographie-Sculpture* (Paris: Marval/Musée du Louvre, 1993)

Frobenius, Leo, *Die Masken und Geheimbünde Afrikas* (Halle: Karras, 1898)

Frobenius, Leo, *Das unbekannte Afrika* (Munich: C. H. Becksche, 1923)

Frobenius, Leo, *The Voice of Africa* [1913] (New York: Benjamin Blom, 1968)

Gallotti, Jean, 'Les arts indigènes à l'exposition coloniale', *Art et Décoration* (September 1931), pp. 69–100

Gallotti, Jean, 'Cinq expositions dans les nouvelles salles du Trocadéro', *Vu*, 272 (31 May 1933), pp. 821–22

Ganay, Solange de *et al.*, *Ethnologiques: Hommages à Marcel Griaule* (Paris: Hermann, 1987)

Geertz, Clifford, *Works and Lives: The Anthropologist as Author* (Stanford: Stanford University Press, 1988)

Gell, Alfred, 'The Technology of Enchantment and the Enchantment of Technology', in Coote and Shelton (eds), *Anthropology, Art and Aesthetics* (Oxford: Clarendon Press, 1992), pp. 40–63

Gell, Alfred, 'Vogel's Net: Traps as Artworks and Artworks as Traps', *Journal of Material Culture*, 1:1 (March 1996), pp. 15–38

Gell, Alfred, *Art and Agency: An Anthropological Theory* (Oxford: Clarendon Press, 1998)

Gendron, Bernard, 'Fetishes and Motorcars: Negrophilia in French Modernism', *Cultural Studies*, 4:2 (1990), pp. 141–55

George, Waldemar, 'Le crépuscule des idoles', *Les Arts à Paris*, 17 (May 1930), pp. 7–13

George, Waldemar, *Profits et pertes de l'art contemporain* (Paris: Chroniques du jour, 1932)

Gide, André, 'Architectures nègres', *Cahiers d'art*, 2:7–8 (1927), pp. 263–5

Gide, André, *Voyage au Congo: Carnets de route* (Paris: Gallimard, 1927)

Gide, André, *The Immoralist* [1902] (Harmondsworth: Penguin, 1986)

Goldwater, Robert, *Primitivism in Modern Art* [1938] (London: Belknap Press, 1986)

Gorgus, Nina, *Der Zauberer der Vitrinen: Zur Museologie George Henri Rivières* (Münster: Waxmann, 1999)

Green, Christopher, 'Zervos, Picasso and Brassaï, Ethnographers in the Field: A Critical Collaboration', in Gee (ed.), *Art criticism since 1900* (Manchester: Manchester University Press, 1993), pp. 116–39

Green, Christopher, 'Humanisms: Picasso, Waldemar George and the Politics of "Man" in the 1930s', *Comparative Criticism*, 23 (2001), pp. 231–54

Green, Christopher (ed.), *Picasso's* Les Demoiselles d'Avignon (Cambridge: Cambridge University Press, 2001)

Gregory, C. A., *Gifts and Commodities* (London: Academic Press, 1982)

Gregson, Nicky and Louise Crewe, *Second-Hand Cultures* (Oxford: Berg, 2003)

Griaule, Marcel, *Le Livre de recettes d'un dabtara abyssin* (Paris: Institut d'Ethnologie, 1930)

Griaule, Marcel, 'Mission Dakar-Djibouti, Rapport général', *Journal de la société des africanistes*, 2 (1932), pp. 229–36

Griaule, Marcel, *Masques Dogons* [1938] (Paris: Institut d'Ethnologie, 1963)

Griaule, Marcel, *Conversations with Ogotemmêli* [1948] (Oxford: Oxford University Press, 1970)

Griaule, Marcel and Michel Leiris, *Instructions sommaires pour les collecteurs d'objets ethnographiques* (Paris: Musée d'Ethnographie, May 1931)

Grossman, Wendy, '(Con)text and Image: Reframing Man Ray's *Noire et blanche*', in Hughes and Noble (eds), *Phototextualities* (Alberquerque: University of New Mexico Press, 2003), pp. 119–36

Guigon, Emmanuel, *El objeto surrealista* (Valencia: IVAM/Centro Julio Gonzalez, 1997)

Guillaume, Paul and Thomas Munro, *Primitive Negro Sculpture* (London: Jonathan Cape, 1926)

Guillaume, Paul and Thomas Munro, *La Sculpture nègre primitive* (Paris: G. Crès, 1929)

Haardt, Georges-Marie and Louis Audouin-Dubreuil, *The Black Journey: Across Central Africa with the Citroën Expedition* (London: Geoffrey Bles, 1928)

Haddon, Alfred, *The Decorative Art of New Guinea* (Dublin: Royal Irish Academy, 1894)

Haddon, Alfred, *Evolution in Art, As Illustrated by the Life-Histories of Designs* (London: Walter Scott, 1895)

Hamy, Ernest-Théodore, *Les Origines du Musée d'Ethnographie* [1889] (Paris: Jean-Michel Place, 1988)

Hand, Séan, *Michel Leiris, Writing the Self* (Cambridge: Cambridge University Press, 2002)

Handbook to the Ethnographical Collections (London: British Museum, 1910)

Hardy, Georges, *L'Art nègre: l'art animiste des noirs de l'Afrique* (Paris: Henri Laurens, 1927)

Harris, Steven, 'Beware of Domestic Objects: Vocation and equivocation in 1936', *Art History*, 24:5 (November 2001), pp. 725–57

Harris, Steven, *Surrealist Art and Thought in the 1930s* (Cambridge: Cambridge University Press, 2004)

Hayes, E. Nelson and Tanya Hayes (eds), *Claude Lévi-Strauss: The Anthropologist as Hero* (Cambridge, MA: MIT Press, 1970)

Highmore, Ben, 'Ethno-Graphics', *Art History*, 24:1 (February 2001), pp. 132–9

Hodeir, Catherine and Michel Pierre, *L'Exposition coloniale* (Brussels: Complexe, 1991)

Hollier, Denis (ed.), *The College of Sociology* [1979], trans. Betsy Wing (Minneapolis: University of Minnesota Press, 1988)

Hollier, Denis, 'La valeur d'usage de l'impossible', *Documents* [1929–30] (Paris: Jean-Michel Place, 1991), pp. vii–xxxiv

Hollier, Denis, 'Surrealist Precipitates: Shadows Don't Cast Shadows', *October*, 69 (summer 1994), pp. 111–32

Hubert, Henri and Marcel Mauss, 'Esquisse d'une théorie générale de la magie', *L'Année sociologique*, 7 [1902–03] (Paris: Alcan, 1904), pp. 1–146

Il Dono, The Gift: Generous Offerings, Threatening Hospitality (Milan: Charta, 2001)

Iversen, Margaret, 'Readymade, Found Object, Photograph', *Art Journal*, 63:2 (summer 2004), pp. 44–57

Jacknis, Ira, 'The Ethnographic Object and the Object of Ethnology in the Early Career of Franz Boas', in Stocking (ed.), *Volksgeist as Method and Ethic: Essays on Boasian*

Ethnography and the German Anthropological Tradition (Madison: University of Wisconsin Press, 1996), pp. 185–214

Jamin, Jean, 'Objets trouvés des paradis perdus: à propos de la Mission Dakar-Djibouti', in Hainard and Kaehr (eds), *Collections passion* (Neuchâtel: Musée d'ethnographie, 1982), pp. 69–100

Jamin, Jean, 'Aux origines du Musée de l'Homme: la mission ethnographique et linguistique Dakar-Djibouti', *Cahiers ethnologiques*, 5 (1984), pp. 7–73

Jamin, Jean, 'L'ethnographie mode d'inemploi' in Hainard and Kaehr (eds), *Le Mal et la douleur* (Neuchâtel: Musée d'ethnographie, 1986), pp. 45–79

Jamin, Jean, 'Tout était fétiche, tout devint totem', in *Bulletin du Musée d'Ethnographie du Trocadéro* [1931–35] (Paris: Jean-Michel Place, 1988), pp. iv–xxii

Jamin, Jean, 'Le musée d'ethnographie en 1930: l'ethnologie comme science et comme politique', in *La Muséologie selon Georges Henri Rivière* (Paris: Dunod, 1989), pp. 110–21

Jenkins, David, 'Object Lessons and Ethnographic Displays: Museum Exhibitions and the Making of American Anthropology', *Comparative Studies in Society and History*, 36:2 (April 1994), pp. 242–70

Johnson, Geraldine (ed.), *Sculpture and Photography* (Cambridge: Cambridge University Press, 1998)

Joyce, Conor, *Carl Einstein in* Documents (Philadelphia, PA: Xlibris, 2003)

Karady, Victor, 'Stratégies de réussite et modes de faire-valoir de la sociologie chez les durkheimiens', *Revue française de sociologie*, 20:1 (1979), pp. 49–82

Karady, Victor, 'Le problème de la légitimité dans l'organisation historique de l'ethnologie française', *Revue française de sociologie*, 23:1 (1982), pp. 17–35

Kelly, Julia, 'Between art and ethnography: Michel Leiris and the sculpture of Alberto Giacometti', *Histoire de l'art*, 50 (June 2002), pp. 123–30

Kelly, Julia, 'Sights Unseen: Roussel, Leiris, Cornell and the Art of Travel', in Stephanie Taylor and Jason Edwards (eds), *Joseph Cornell: Opening the Box* (Oxford: Peter Lang, 2006)

Kirschenblatt-Gimblett, Barbara, 'Objects of Ethnography', in Karp and Levine (eds), *Exhibiting Cultures* (Washington, DC: Smithsonian Institute Press, 1991), pp. 386–443

Kuper, Adam, *Anthropologists and Anthropology: The British School 1922–72* (Harmondsworth: Penguin, 1978)

La Muséologie selon Georges Henri Rivière (Paris: Dunod, 1989)

Lavachery, Henri-A., 'L'exposition d'art africain et d'art océanien du Théâtre Pigalle, à Paris', *Cahiers de Belgique*, 3:4 (April 1930), pp. 111–17

Lavrillier, Carol Marc and Michel Dufet, *Bourdelle et la critique de son temps* (Paris: Paris-Musées, 1992)

Layton, Robert, '*Art and Agency*: A Reassessment', *Journal of the Royal Anthropological Institute*, 9 (2003), pp. 447–64

Lebovics, Herman, *True France: The Wars over Cultural Identity, 1900–1945* (Ithaca, NY: Cornell University Press, 1992)

Lecoq, Dominique and Jean-Luc Lory (eds), *Ecrits d'ailleurs, Georges Bataille et les ethnologues* (Paris: Maison des Sciences de l'Homme, 1987)

Lehuard, Raoul, 'La Vente Tristan Tzara', *Arts d'Afrique noire*, 68 (winter 1988), pp. 13–17

Leiris, Michel, 'Rites de circoncision Namchi', *Journal de la Société d'Africanistes*, 4:1 (1934), pp. 63–79

Leiris, Michel, 'Le voyageur et son ombre', *La Bête noire*, 1 (1 April 1935), p. 8

Leiris, Michel, 'Les statuettes magiques', *La Revue des voyages* (January 1939), p. 22

Leiris, Michel, 'The Sculpture of the Musée de l'Homme', *XXe siècle*, 2:1 (1939), p. 55

Leiris, Michel, *La Langue secrète des Dogons de Sanga* (Paris: Institut d'Ethnologie, 1948)

Leiris, Michel, 'L'ethnographe devant le colonialisme', *Les Temps modernes*, 6:58 (August 1950), pp. 357–74

Leiris, Michel, 'The Ethnographer Faced with Colonialism' [1950], in *Brisées* (San Francisco: North Point Press, 1989), p. 114.

Leiris, Michel, *Cinq études d'ethnologie* (Paris: Denoël, 1969)

Leiris, Michel, *A propos de Georges Bataille* (Paris: Fourbis, 1988)

Leiris, Michel, *Brisées* [1966], trans. Lydia Davis (San Francisco: North Point Press, 1989)

Leiris, Michel, *Journal, 1922–1989* (Paris: Gallimard, 1992)

Leiris, Michel, *"Au-delà d'un regard": Entretien sur l'art africain par Paul Lebeer* (Lausanne: Bibliothèque des Arts, 1994)

Leiris, Michel, *Miroir de l'Afrique* (Paris: Gallimard, 1996)

Lemke, Sieglinde, *Primitivist Modernism: Black Culture and the Origins of Transatlantic Modernism* (Oxford: Oxford University Press, 1998)

Leroi-Gourhan, André, *Milieu et Techniques* (Paris: Albin Michel, 1945)

Lévi-Strauss, Claude, *La Pensée sauvage* (Paris: Plon, 1962)

Lévi-Strauss, Claude, *Tristes Tropiques* [1955], trans. John and Doreen Weightman (London: Jonathan Cape, 1973)

Lévi-Strauss, Claude, *Structural Anthropology* [1958] (Harmondsworth: Penguin, 1979)

Lévy-Bruhl, Lucien, *La Mentalité primitive* (Paris: Alcan, 1922)

Lévy-Bruhl, Lucien, *Les Fonctions mentales dans les sociétés inférieures* [1910] (Paris: Félix Alcan, 1922)

Lévy-Bruhl, Lucien, *The 'Soul' of the Primitive* [1927] (London: George Allen and Unwin, 1965)

Lotringer, Sylvère, 'Leiris et son double', *Gradhiva*, 13 (1993), pp. 43–50

Lourdou, Philippe, 'The Dawning Commentary in Ethnographic Films: Marcel Griaule's Cinematographic Work', *Visual Anthropology*, 6 (1993), pp. 65–84

Lowie, Robert, *The History of Ethnological Theory* (London: Harrap, 1937)

Lubar, Steven and W. David Kingery (eds), *History from Things: Essays on Material Culture* (Washington, DC: Smithsonian Institution Press, 1993)

Luquet, Georges-Henri, *L'Art primitif* (Paris: G. Doin, 1930)

Luquet, Georges-Henri, 'L'art du Bénin au musée du Trocadéro', *La Nature*, 2886 (1 August 1932), pp. 97–101

Luquet, Georges-Henri, 'La Mission Dakar-Djibouti au Musée d'Ethnographie du Trocadéro', *La Nature*, 2915 (15 October 1933), pp. 366–8

Luschan, Felix von, 'Alterthümer von Benin', *Zeitschrift für Ethnologie*, 30 (1898), pp. 146–64

Lyon Universitaire, numéro spécial consacré aux arts indigènes, 101 (April–May 1931)

Maanen, John van, *Tales of the Field* (Chicago: University of Chicago Press, 1988)

Mack, John, *Emile Torday and the Art of the Congo* (London: British Museum, 1990)

Maes, J., 'Aperçu de quelques conceptions d'art sculptural au Congo Belge', *Variétés*, 1:7 (15 November 1928), pp. 347–52

Maes, J., 'Des sources de l'art nègre', *Cahiers d'art*, 5:6 (1930), pp. 307–13

Mâle, Emile, *Religious Art in France. The Twelfth Century* [1922] (Princeton, NJ: Princeton University Press, 1978)

Malinowski, Bronisław, *Magic, Science and Religion* (New York: Doubleday, 1954)

Malinowski, Bronisław, *A Diary in the Strict Sense of the Term* [1967] (Stanford, CA: Stanford University Press, 1989)

Malraux, André, *Picasso's Mask* [1974] (New York: Da Capo Press, 1994)

Marchand, Suzanne, 'The Rhetoric of Artifacts and the Decline of Classical Humanism: The Case of Josef Strzygowski', *History and Theory*, 33:4 (1994), pp. 106–30

Marchand, Suzanne, 'Leo Frobenius and the Revolt against the West', *Journal of Contemporary History*, 32:2 (1997), pp. 153–70

Marcus, George and Michael Fischer, *Anthropology as Cultural Critique: An Experimental Moment in the Human Sciences* [1986] (Chicago: University of Chicago Press, 1999)

Marcus, George and Fred Myers, *The Traffic in Culture: Refiguring Anthropology and Art* (Berkeley: University of California Press, 1995)

Mark, Peter, 'The Future of African Art in Parisian Public Museums', *African Arts*, 33:3 (autumn 2000), p. 1, 4, 6, 8, 93

Markov, Vladimir, 'L'art des nègres' [1919], *Cahiers du MNAM*, 2 (1979), pp. 319–27

Martin, Jean-Hubert (ed.), *Les Magiciens de la terre* (Paris: Pompidou Centre, 1989)

Mauss, Marcel, *Sociologie et anthropologie* (Paris: Presses universitaires de France, 1950)

Mauss, Marcel, *Manuel d'ethnographie* [1947] (Paris: Payot, 1967)

Mauss, Marcel, *A General Theory of Magic* [1902–3], trans. Robert Brain (London: Routledge and Kegan Paul, 1972)

Mauss, Marcel, *The Gift* [1923–24], trans. W. D. Hall (London: Routledge, 1993)

McInnes, Mary Drach, *Taboo and Transgression: The Subversive Aesthetics of Georges Bataille and 'Documents'* (Ann Arbor: University of Michigan Press, 1994)

McInnes, Mary Drach, 'Alberto Giacometti, le féticheur', in Keith Aspley, Elizabeth Cowling and Peter Sharratt (eds), *From Rodin to Giacometti: Sculpture and Literature in France 1880–1950* (Amsterdam: Rodopi, 2000)

McNab, Robert, *Ghost Ships: A Surrealist Love Triangle* (New Haven, CT: Yale University Press, 2004)

Meffre, Liliane (ed.), 'Lettres de Carl Einstein à Moïse Kisling (1920–1924)', *Les Cahiers du MNAM*, 62 (winter 1997), pp. 75–113

Mileaf, Janine, 'Body to Politics: Surrealist Exhibition of the Tribal and the Modern at the Anti-Imperialist Exhibition and the Galerie Charles Ratton', *Res*, 40 (autumn 2001), pp. 239–54

Miller, Charles, '"Mad memorials": Picasso's 1927 Apollinaire Monument Designs and the Politics of Commemoration', *Immediations*, 1:1 (spring 2004), pp. 37–59

Miller, Daniel, *Material Culture and Mass Consumption* [1987] (Oxford: Blackwell, 1994)

Minotaure, 1:2 (1933), special Dakar–Djibouti expedition issue

Morton, Patricia A., 'National and Colonial: The Musée des Colonies at the Colonial Exposition, Paris, 1931', *Art Bulletin*, 53:2 (June 1998), pp. 357–77

Morton, Patricia A., *Hybrid Modernities: Architecture and Representation at the 1931 Colonial Exposition, Paris* (Cambridge, MA: MIT Press, 2000)

Ndiaye, Francine, *L'Art du Pays Dogon* (Zurich: Museum Rietberg, 1995)

Noland, Carrie, 'Bataille Looking', *Modernism/Modernity*, 11:1 (2004), pp. 125–60

Notes and Queries on Anthropology, 5th ed. (London: Royal Anthropological Institute, 1929)

Notes and Queries on Anthropology, 6th ed. (London: Routledge and Kegan Paul, 1951)

Palermo, Charles, 'Tactile Translucence: Miró, Leiris, Einstein', *October*, 97 (summer 2001), pp. 31–50

Parezo, Nancy J., 'Cushing as Part of the Team: The Collecting Activities of the Smithsonian Institution', *American Ethnologist*, 12:4 (1985), pp. 763–74

Penny, H. Glenn, *Objects of Culture: Ethnology and Ethnographic Museums in Imperial Germany* (Chapel Hill: University of North Carolina Press, 2002)

Phillips, Ruth and Christopher Steiner (eds), *Unpacking Culture: Art and Commodity in Colonial and Postcolonial Worlds* (Berkeley: University of California Press, 1999)

Phillips, Tom (ed.), *Africa, The Art of a Continent* (London: Royal Academy, 1995)

Pinney, Christopher and Nicholas Thomas (eds), *Beyond Aesthetics: Art and the Technologies of Enchantment* (Oxford: Berg, 2001)

Pomian, Krzysztof, *Collectors and Curiosities* [1987] (Cambridge: Polity Press, 1990)

Potts, Alex, *The Sculptural Imagination: Figurative, Modernist, Minimalist* (London and New Haven, CT: Yale University Press, 2000)

Pratt, Mary Louise, 'Fieldwork in Common Places', in James Clifford and George Marcus (eds), *Writing Culture* (Berkeley: University of California Press, 1986), pp. 27–50

Price, Sally and Jean Jamin, 'Entretien avec Michel Leiris', *Gradhiva*, 4 (1988), pp. 29–56

Ratton, Charles, 'Les Ventes: Collection G. de Miré. Sculptures d'Afrique et d'Amérique', *Cahiers d'art*, 6:9–10 (1931), pp. 453–4

Ratton, Charles, *Masques africains* (Paris: Librairie des arts décoratifs, 1931)

Regards sur Minotaure: la revue à tête de bête (Geneva: Musée d'art et d'histoire, 1987)

Rheims, Maurice, *La Vie étrange des objets* [1959] (Paris: 10/18, 1963)

Richardson, Michael, 'An Encounter of Wise Men and Cyclops Women: Considerations of Debates on Surrealism and Anthropology', *Critique of Anthropology*, 13:1 (1993), pp. 57–75

Richardson, Michael and Krzysztof Fijałkowski, *Surrealism Against the Current: Tracts and Declarations* (London: Pluto Press, 2001)

Rivet, Paul, P. Lester and Georges Henri Rivière, *Le Laboratoire d'Anthropologie du Muséum* (Paris: Masson, 1935)

Rivière, Georges Henri, 'Archéologismes', *Cahiers d'art*, 1:7 (1926), pp. 177–80

Rubin, William (ed.), *"Primitivism" in Twentieth-Century Art: Affinity of the Tribal and the Modern* (New York: Museum of Modern Art, 1984)

Sadoul, Georges, 'L'Afrique fantôme- Michel Leiris, Gallimard', *Commune*, 18 (February 1934), pp. 630–1

Salles, Georges, 'Réflexions sur l'art nègre', *Cahiers d'art*, 2:7–8 (1927), pp. 247–58

Salmon, André, 'L'art nègre' [1920], in *Propos d'atelier* (Paris: G. Crès, 1922), pp. 115–33

Sauerländer, Willibald, 'En face des barbares et à l'écart des dévots, l'humanisme médiéval d'Henri Focillon', in George Kubler *et al.*, *Relire Focillon* (Paris: Musée du Louvre, 1998), pp. 55–74

Sautier, Albert, 'Exhibition of African and Oceanic Art at the Pigalle Gallery', *Formes*, 3 (March 1930), pp. 12–13

Sautier, Albert, 'The Reorganisation of the Trocadero Ethnographical Museum', *Formes*, 3 (March 1930), pp. 17–18

Schildkrout, Enid and Curtis Keim, *African Reflections: Art from Northeastern Zaire* (Seattle: University of Washington Press, 1990)

Schildkrout, Enid and Curtis Keim, *The Scramble for Art in Central Africa* (Cambridge: Cambridge University Press, 1998)

Sculptures anciennes d'Afrique et d'Amérique, Collection de G. Miré (Paris: Hôtel Drouot, 1931)

Sculptures: Afrique, Asie, Océanie, Amériques (Paris: Réunion des musées nationaux, 2000)

Sculptures d'Afrique, d'Amérique, d'Océanie, Collection André Breton et Paul Eluard (Paris: Hôtel Drouot, 1931, and reprinted New York: Hacker, 1972)

Seabrook, William, *The Magic Island* (London: Harrap, 1929)

Simmel, Georg, *The Philosophy of Money* [1900/1907], ed. David Frisby (London: Routledge, 1991)

Simmons, Sherwin, 'Men of Nails: Monuments, expressionism, fetishes, Dadaism', *Res*, 40 (autumn 2001), pp. 211–38

Slaney, Frances M., 'Psychoanalysis and Cycles of "Subversion" in Modern Art and Anthropology', *Dialectical Anthropology*, 14 (1989), pp. 213–34

Soupault, Philippe, 'A propos de l'art nègre', *Art et industrie* (February 1930), pp. 19–22

Spies, Werner, *Picasso: The Sculptures* (Stuttgart: Hatje Cantz, 2000)

Spies, Werner (ed.), *La Révolution surréaliste* (Paris: Pompidou Centre, 2002)

Stocking, George (ed.), *Objects and Others: Essays on Museums and Material Culture* (Madison: University of Wisconsin Press, 1985)

Stocking, George, *The Ethnographer's Magic* (Madison: University of Wisconsin Press, 1992)

Stocking, George (ed.), Volksgeist *as Method and Ethic: Essays on Boasian Ethnography and the German Anthropological Tradition* (Madison: University of Wisconsin Press, 1996)

Stooss, Toni and Patrick Elliott (eds), *Alberto Giacometti, 1901–1966* (Edinburgh: National Galleries of Scotland, 1996)

Strzygowski, Josef, *Early Church Art in Northern Europe, with Special Reference to Timber Construction and Decoration* [1928] (New York: Hacker, 1980)

Sydow, Eckart von, *Die Kunst der Naturvölker und der Vorzeit* (Berlin: Propyläen-Verlag, 1923)

Sydow, Eckart von, *Handbuch der Westafrikanischen Plastik* (Berlin: Reimer/Vohsen, 1930)

Sydow, Eckart von, 'Les sculptures malgaches au musée du Trocadéro', *Cahiers d'art*, 6:9–10 (1931), pp. 397–8

Taffin, Dominique (ed.), *Du musée colonial au musée des cultures du monde* (Paris: Maisonneuve and Larose, 2000)

Thomas, Nicholas, *Entangled Objects: Exchange, Material Culture and Colonialism in the Pacific* (Cambridge, MA: Harvard University Press, 1991)

Thomas, Nicholas, 'Licensed Curiosity: Cook's Pacific Voyages', in Elsner and Cardinal (eds), *The Cultures of Collecting* (London: Reaktion, 1994), pp. 116–36

Thomas, Nicholas, *Out of Time* [1989] (Ann Arbor: University of Michigan Press, 1996)

Thornton, Robert, 'Narrative Ethnography in Africa, 1850–1920: The Creation and Capture of an Appropriate Domain for Anthropology', *Man*, 18:3 (September 1983), pp. 502–20

Tosatto, Guy (ed.), *L'Ivresse du réel: l'objet dans l'art du XXe siècle* (Nîmes: Carré d'Art, 1993)

Trigger, Bruce, *A History of Archaeological Thought* [1989] (Cambridge: Cambridge University Press, 2000)

Tylor, Edward, *Primitive Culture: Researches into the Development of Mythology, Philosophy, Religion, Art and Custom* (London: John Murray, 1871)

Tythacott, Louise, *Surrealism and the Exotic* (London: Routledge, 2003)

Verneau, René, 'Le fétichisme à travers les âges', *La Nature*, 2221 (22 April 1916), pp. 257–60

Verneau, René, 'Le Musée d'Ethnographie du Trocadéro', *Anthropologie*, 29 (1918–19), pp. 547–60

Williams, Elizabeth A., 'Art and Artifact at the Trocadéro: *Ars Americana* and the Primitivist Revolution', in George Stocking (ed.), *Objects and Others: Essays on Museums and Material Culture* (Madison: University of Wisconsin Press, 1985), pp. 146–66

Wood, Jonathan, 'Gods, Graves and Sculptors: *Gudea*, Sumerian Sculpture and the Avant-garde, c. 1930–1935', *Sculpture Journal*, 10 (2003), pp. 67–82

Wood, Jonathan, 'Ornaments, Talismans and Toys: The Hand-held Sculptures of Henri Gaudier-Brzeska', in *Blasting the Future: Vorticism in Britain 1910–1920* (London: Estorick Collection, 2004), pp. 41–8

Worringer, Wilhelm, *Abstraction and Empathy* [1908], trans. Michael Bullock (London: Routledge and Kegan Paul, 1963)

Zervos, Christian, 'L'art nègre', *Cahiers d'art*, 2:7–8 (1927), pp. 229–46

Zervos, Christian, 'Notes sur la sculpture contemporaine', *Cahiers d'art*, 4:10 (1929), pp. 465–72

Index

Note: page numbers in *italic* refer to illustrations

Abyssinia 31 *see also* Ethiopia
    earth drum 56–8
    spells (Griaule) 78
adventure 78, 81–3
Africa 7, 8, 31, 32, 68, 78, 101, 107,
    142
African objects 3, 12, 18, 19, *19*, 20, *20*, 22,
    23, *24*, 27, 29, 32, 41, *42*, 43, 45,
    49, 50, *51*, 52, *58*, 67, *69*, *74*, *83*,
    99, 102, *103*, *104*, *105*, 107, 108,
    108, 111, 112, *113*, 114, *114*, 115,
    115, 117, 123, 134, *135*, 137, 140
    see also Baga; Bakota; Bamana;
    Baoule; Benin; Cameroon;
    Congo; Dahomey; Dan; Fang;
    Mangbetu; Toucouleur
agency 3, 6, 124
Allégret, Marc 107
Altamira 41, 43, 109
animism 75, 123, 148n.17
antiquarianism 6, 7, 44, 52, 59, 92, 114
Apollinaire, Guillaume 13, 15, 20, 21, 26,
    140
    Sculptures nègres, Les (with Paul
        Guillaume) 20–2
Appadurai, Arjun 6
Aragon, Louis 32, 33, 41, 109, 142,
    150n.50
    Paysan de Paris, Le 150n.63
    'Peinture au défi, La' 140
    'Shadow of the Inventor, The' 125–6,
        143–4
archaeology 7, 33, 40, 41, 45, 46, 48,
    54

Aréthuse 44, 46, 48, 55, 61–2n.16
Arp, Jean
    Isms of Art, The (with El Lissitzky)
        41
art and artefact 21, 124–5
art market 6, 7, 15, 24, 25, 33, 44, 49–53,
    55, 111, 140, 141
art nègre 25, 26, 29
    Salmon on 67
    Zervos on 45
assemblage 122, *122*, 140, 141, 143,
    147
Auduoin-Dubreuil, Louis 71

Baga
    nimba shoulder mask 21, 42, *42*
Bakongo nail figures *see* Congo
Bakota 20
    reliquary 16, 18, 22
Balfour, Henry 67
    Evolution of Decorative Art, The 56, 67,
        128
Bamana 43, 104
    boli altar figure (Musée de l'Homme)
        82, *83*, 102, 112
Baoule 20
    drum (Trocadéro) *58*, 59, 117
    mask (Trocadéro) 30
Basler, Adolphe 29, 55
Bataille, Georges 4, 30, 44, 48, 49, 53, 55,
    77, 97, 98
    'Notion of Expenditure, The' 98
Beaujour, Michel 91
Beaux-Arts 44, 62n.17, *114*

Benin 32
  'bronzes' 13, 15, 23, 101
  1932 Trocadéro exhibition 13, 15, 16,
    26, 33, 111, 112, 114
Benjamin, Walter 130
Besson, Maurice
  Totémisme, Le 5, 15, 150n.54
Blanchard, Marc 85
Blondel, Charles 5
blood 78, 82, 102, 106, 107, 128
Boas, Franz 67, 68
Boiffard, Jacques-André 94, 95
Bois, Yve-Alain 18
bone 126, 127, 141, 149n.28
Bourdelle, Emile-Antoine 28
Bourdieu, Pierre 4
Brancusi, Constantin 140
Braque, Georges 56
Brassaï (Gyula Halász) 123, 124, 127,
    150n.62
Breton, André 1, 30, 72–3, 96, 123, 124,
    125, 128, 129, 130, 132, 136, 140,
    142, 144, 148n.4, 149n.27,
    150n.50
  Bas déchiré, Un 137
  'Beauté sera convulsive, La' 128
  'Crisis of the Object, The' 125
  'Introduction to the Discourse on the
    Paucity of Reality' 94, 96
  L'Amour fou 95, 137
  Nadja 72–3, 91, 94, 95, 95, 102, 130
  Object of Symbolic Function 139
  sale of non-western collection 33
  slipper-spoon 95, 96, 132, 136, 137,
    137
Breton, Jacqueline
  Pour la poche 137
Breuil, Henri 45, 76
bricolage see Lévi-Strauss
bronze 18, 46, 47, 50, 99, 111, 132, 135,
    149n.27 see also Benin
Brosses, Charles de 75
Brown, Al 76, 77

Cahiers d'art 7, 40, 44, 45, 50, 56, 96, 97,
    98, 104, 105, 106, 141
Caillois, Roger

'Myth of Secret Treasures in
    Childhood, The' 144
Cameroon 23, 24, 49, 99
  Crossriver Janus masks 49
Cassou, Jean 8, 13, 103, 116
Certeau, Michel de 4, 6
  Practice of Everyday Life, The 6
Char, René 32
Chauvet, Stephen 21, 50
Chirico, Giorgio de 131, 150n.50
circumcision 69, 104, 115
Clarke, Louis 48
classical tradition 45, 46, 54
  non–classical 40, 41, 43, 46
clay 58, 75, 125
Clifford, James 3, 5, 84, 105–6, 143
  ethnographic surrealism 3, 4, 105–6,
    143
Clouzot, Henri 24, 26, 27, 28, 43, 134
  L'Art nègre et l'art océanien (with André
    Level) 27
  Sculptures africaines et océaniennes (with
    André Level) 27
collage 3, 20, 139, 140, 141, 142
collecting (art) 21, 24, 41, 47, 49, 50, 51,
    53, 55–6, 73, 111, 147
collecting (ethnographic) 72–5
Colonial Exhibition (1931) 26, 31–3, 130
colonialism 6, 30, 32–3, 44, 59, 70
  anti-colonial, colonial critique 82, 107,
    141–2 see also Leiris 'The
    Ethnographer Faced with
    Colonialism'
  colonial art 27, 98
  development of museums 14
  recuperation 74
commodification 1, 55, 146
commodity 6, 16, 55, 72, 97, 129, 130 see
    also fetishism
Congo
  nail figures 20, 21, 27, 137 see also
    fetish
Congo (Belgian)
  Warega mask (de Miré) 50, 51
Conrad, Joseph 79, 88n.65
contagion see magic
Contenau, Georges 46, 48

convulsive beauty 1, 123, 127 *see also*
    Breton
cooking 131, 133
Coombes, Annie 6, 15
counter-colonial exhibition *see* surrealism
Cowling, Elizabeth 128
Crevel, René 14, 32, 33
croisière noire 71, 98
cubism 16, 20, 23, 31, 139, 140
curio 43–4, 67, 98
curiosities, curiosity 7, 15, 20, 44
Cushing, Frank 67, 78, 81, 89n.83, *127*,
    128

Dahomey 15, 20, 24, 27, 32, 85
    Gou god of metalwork 15, 41, *42*, 43
Dakar-Djibouti expedition 2, 7, 14, 31, 43,
    59–61, 68–86, 101, 140–1
    acquisition of objects 59, 68–76, 79–84,
        111, 123–4, 146
    display of material (Trocadéro) 103,
        103, 112, 114–16, *114*, *115*, 144
    funding 74, 76, 78
    object as witness 76, 80, 85, 92, 102,
        116, 124, 141
    police ethnography 80–1, 85, 99, 102
    publication of findings 100, 102, 104,
        111, 122, 124 *see also Minotaure*
    'Summary Instructions for Collectors
        of Ethnographic Objects' *see*
        Griaule
    use of photography 99, 104, *104*, 106,
        114–15
Dalí, Salvador 13, 125, 128, 149n.27
    'Object as Revealed in Surrealist
        Experiment, The' 126, 132
    Object of Symbolic Function 136
Dan spoons 18, 134
Daumal, René 16, 73, 116
David-Weill, David 41, 52, 64n.61, 77,
    109, 110
    collection *47*, 50
David-Weill, Pierre 52, 64n.61, 64n.63,
    110
Delafosse, Maurice 15, 26, 29, 68, 99, 112
    Haut-Sénégal-Niger 99, *99*
Derain, André 13, 111

Desnos, Robert 96
Desplagnes, Louis 26, 68–9
diffusionism 55
disciplines 43–4, 46, 59–60
Documents 2, 5, 7, 30–2, 43–61, *47*, *57*, *58*,
    71, 78, 92, 94, 100, 102, 104, 117,
    125, 130–1, *132*, *134*, 142, 147,
    150n.50, 150n.54
Dogon 26, 68, 74, 78, 80–1, 83, 85, 102,
    117, 140, 151n.103
    bazou 68–9, 108
    cosmology 144
    dance mask 74, *74*
    funeral 85, 99
    masks 102, 104, *114*, 115, 146, 151n.103
    mothers of masks 102–3, *103*, 104, 108,
        112, 114, *114*, 115
    Ogotemmêli 144, 151n.103
    ritual objects 85–6, 107, *108*
    Sanga 83, 85, *103*, 151n.103
    sculpture (de Miré collection) 51
    sirige (masks with storeys) 103
domestic 24, 123, 131, 133, 137
Doumergue, Gaston 109, *109*
Durkheim, Emile 6, 26, 30, 33, 54, 67, 70,
    126

earth drum *see* Abyssinia
Edwards, Elizabeth 5, 100, 116
Ehl, Heinrich 54
Einstein, Carl 4–5, 46, 50–2, 102, 131,
    149n.28
    Afrikanische Plastik (1921) 23, *24*
    Negerplastik 22–3, 52
Elsner, Jas 54
Eluard, Paul 31, 33, 111, 140
    sale of non-western collection 33
Epstein, Jacob 16, 36n.66
Ernst, Max 13, 127, 149n.28
    Mobile Object Recommended for Families
        139
Ethiopia 78, 84, 99, 142
    zar 84
Ethnological Institute *see* Institut
    d'Ethnologie
ethnology 5, 10n.23, 67, 131
    development in France 70–1

everyday 14, 20, 24, 55, 59, 61, 69, 72,
        123–5, 142–3, 146
evidence (ethnographic) 6, 73–4, 84, 91,
        94–6, 98–9
evolutionism 26, 40, 44, 48, 54, 67, 71
    in art 48
exchange-value 49, 129

Fabian, Johannes 84
Fang 20, 21, 24, 25
    head (Guillaume) *19*, 21
Faure, Elie 24–5
    Histoire de l'art 24
feather, feathers 22, 82, 101, 110, 122–4,
        126, 128, 140–1, 148n.4,
        148n.23, 149n.27
Fénéon, Felix 25, 43
fetish 12, 20, *20*, 21, 25, 27, 28, 32, 82, 123,
        127, 128, 140 *see also* Bamana
        boli; kono
    European fetishes 32 *see also* counter-
        colonial exhibition
fetishism 8n.7, 18, 55, 68, 94, 126, 130, 131
    commodity fetishism 6, 33, 130
fieldwork 2, 4–5, 31, 67, 70, 76, 80–1, 85,
        131, 142 *see also* evidence; infor-
        mants
Fierens, Paul 15, 111
flea-market 6, 12, 72–3, 94, 95, *95*, 96–8,
        112, 132, 136
Fletcher, Robert James 79
Focillon, Henri 25, 27, 28, 30, 31, 54
    L'Art bouddhique 25, 28
Foster, Hal 5, 130
    artist as ethnographer 5
Foucault, Michel 4, 75
found object 6, 72, 94, 95–6, 102, 112, 123,
        125–30, 143 *see also* surrealist
        object
Frank, Jean-Michel 146
Frazer, James 126, 130, 148n.17
Frobenius, Leo 21, 23, 26, 27, 45, 55, 80,
        98
    Masken und Geheimbünde Afrikas, Die
        21–2, 22
    unbekannte Afrika, Das 26
functionalism 54, 60, 65n.83, 65n.84

Gallotti, Jean 32, 112, 114
Geertz, Clifford 85
Gell, Alfred 6, 7, 124
    agency in art 6, 124
    enchantment 124
    traps as artworks 7, 139
George, Waldemar 13, 29, 31
Germany
    ethnographic expeditions 21, 26
    ethnographic museums 14, 21
Giacometti, Alberto 16–18, 25, 28, 46, 52,
        125, 130, 131, 132, 133, 134, 135,
        136, 142, 144, 146, 149n.28,
        150n.62
    Caught Hand 139
    Couple (1926) 18, *19*, 135
    Disagreeable Object 144
    Disagreeable Object to be Thrown Away
        146, *146*
    Gazing Head 52, *132*
    Man (1927–28) *132*
    Man and Woman (1929) *132*, 134
    Man (Apollo) (1929) *134*
    'Mobile and Muet Objects' 144, *145*, 146
    Point to the Eye 139
    Reclining Woman who Dreams 131, *134*
    Spoon Woman 17, 18, *19*, 133, 150n.62
    Suspended Ball 125
    Three Figures Outdoors 134
    Vide-Poche 146, *147*
    Woman (1928–29) 131, *132*
    Woman with her Throat Cut 139
Gide, André, 84, 107, 119n.75, 124, 148n.4
    'Architectures nègres' 107
    L'Immoraliste 84
    Voyage au Congo 1, 79, 107
gifts, gift theory 6, 11n.42, 52–3, 55, 84,
        97, 98, 130
Goldwater, Robert 15
Grebo mask 18, 22, *22*
Green, Christopher 30, 123–4
Griaule, Marcel 14, 30, 31, 32, 53, 56, 57,
        58, 59, 68, 70, 71, 76, 78, 79, 80,
        81, 82, 85, 93, 99, 102, *104*, 109,
        110, 117, 144, 151n.103 *see also*
        Dogon (cosmology); (masks);
        (Ogotemmêli)

rift with Leiris 85, 90n.105
'Summary Instructions for Collectors
        of Ethnographic Objects' 68,
        71–6, 79, 82, 86
Grousset, René 47, 48, 63n.35
Guillaume, Paul 24, 25, 29, 134 see also
        Apollinaire
    Primitive Negro Sculpture (with
        Thomas Munro) 21
    Fang head 19

Haardt, Georges-Marie 71
Habbé see Dogon
Hackin, Joseph 41, 48, 63n.36
Haddon, Alfred 67, 139
hand-held 24, 37n.71 see also touch
Hardy, Georges 14, 26, 28, 29
    L'Art nègre 29
Hérold, Jacques 96, 149n.28
Hodeir, Catherine and Michel Pierre 32
Hoffman, Malvina 99
Hollier, Denis 1, 4, 49, 55
Hubert, Henri 126, 130 see also Mauss
Hugo, Valentine
    Object 137
humanism 28, 30, 40, 55, 93, 105

Iacovleff, Alexandre 71, 98
idol 23–5
informants 76, 80–1, 85, 98, 104
Institute of Ethnology (Paris) 5, 30, 31, 32,
        53, 70, 88n.49
Ipek 44, 62n.16
Iversen, Margaret 95–6
ivory 50, 51, 101, 135

Jacobsthal, Paul 46, 62n.33
Jamin, Jean 4, 76, 80, 86, 92–3, 104
Joyce, Conor 46

Kahnweiler, Daniel-Henry 13, 18
Karady, Victor 14
Keim, Curtis 6
Kirschenblatt-Gimblett, Barbara 73,
        115
Kisling, Moïse 5
knotting 139

kono 82, 107 see also Bamana boli
Kossinna, Gustaf 41
Kota see Bakota
Krauss, Rosalind
    black deco 134
Kühn, Herbert 44
kula see Trobriand

Labouret, Henri 112
Lascaux 41, 65n.98
Latour, Bruno 144
Lavachery, Henri-A. 31
Lebovics, Herman 32
Leiris, Michel 1, 2, 4–5, 7, 32, 46, 49, 54,
        60, 66n.111, 72, 73, 76, 78–86,
        88n.49, 89n.77, 91–3, 98, 100–4,
        107, 110, 115–16, 125, 130,
        132–3, 141–2, 148n.23
    'Dogon Ritual Objects' 107
    'Ethnographer Faced with
        Colonialism, The' 7
    'Eye of the Ethnographer, The' 60, 78
    L'Age d'homme 79, 84
    L'Afrique fantôme 5, 7, 78–9, 80–2,
        84–6, 91, 98, 102, 119n.75
    Langue secrète des Dogons de Sanga, La
        85
    on Giacometti 18, 25, 52, 125, 130–3,
        142, 150n.62
    on Miró 126
    rift with Griaule 85, 90n.105
    'Summary Instructions for Collectors
        of Ethnographic Objects' see
        Griaule
    'Traveller and his Shadow, The' 96
Leiris, Zette (Louise) 81, 84, 89n.77
Lemke, Sieglinde 135
Lepage, P.-C.
    Décoration primitive, La 135, 135
Leroi-Gourhan, André 135
    Milieu et techniques 136
Level, André see Clouzot
Lévi-Strauss, Claude 4, 142–3
    bricolage 4, 142–3, 151n.90
    Pensée sauvage, La 4, 142–3
Lévy-Bruhl, Lucien 5, 13, 24, 30, 33, 70,
        125, 126

*Fonctions mentales dans les sociétés
        inférieures, Les* 148n.17
Mentalité primitive, La 5, 25
Lifchitz, Deborah 76, 151n.103
Lipchitz, Jacques 16, 101, 111
Lissitzky, El *see* Arp
Loeb, Pierre 52, 105, *106*
Loti, Pierre 5, 96
Louis-Roux, Gaston 76
Louvre
    Ecole du 41, 48, 63n.37
    museum 15, 41, 45–6, 48, 108
Lowie, Robert 5–6
Luquet, Georges-Henri 56
Lurçat, Jean 41
Lutten, Eric 76, 82

Maar, Dora 96, *97*, 98
magic 1, 8n.7, 12, 23, 124, 128, 130, 133,
        141, 143
    contagion 23, 25, 97–8, 126–7, 131
    law of participation 24
    practices 20, 130, 133, 141
    similarity, principle of 126–7
    sympathetic 126, 128
Mâle, Emile 28
Malinowski, Bronisław 2, 67, 76, 81, 84,
        89n.77, 93, 98
Malraux, André 12
mana 52, 97 *see also* Mauss; magic
mandrake root 56, 128–9, *129*, 149n.37
Mangbetu
    harp 56
Man Ray (Emmanuel Radnitzky) 13, 77,
        128, *129*, *137*
Marchand, Suzanne 54
Marcus, George and Michael Fischer 3, 6,
        84
Marin, Louis 32, 70
Marx, Karl 6, 33, 55, 129–30
Masson, André 52, 64n.63, 97, 131, 140–1
material culture 3–4, 14, 44, 68, 74
Mauss, Marcel 3, 6, 13, 30–1, 69–71, 77,
        84, 97, 105, 126, 130, 143
    General Theory of Magic (with Henri
        Hubert) 2, 70, 124–5, 129–30,
        133, 143

Gift, The 52–3, 70, 130
gift exchange 6, 52–3, 55, 84, 97,
        130
Manuel d'ethnographie 70, 72, 100
    total social fact 105, 124
medieval art 27–8
metal 18, 20–1, 27, 125
Métraux, Alfred 56
Minotaure 1, 2, 74, 80, 85–6, 92–3, 100–1,
        122, 128, *129*
    special Dakar-Djibouti issue 7, 92–3,
        98–108, *105*, 111, 112, 122
Miré, Georges de
    collection 50–2, *51*, 111
    Fang figure 24
Miró, Joan 13, 64n.66, 77, 126, 131, 140–1,
        148n.23, 149n.27, 149n.28
modernism 3, 7, 14, 105
Moore, Henry 46
Mueller, Valentin 46, 62n.33
Mühlestein, Hans 45
Musée de l'Homme 5, 8, 12–13, 16, 76, 93,
        116
Musée des Arts Africains et Océaniens
        114
Musée des Arts et Traditions Populaires 5,
        93
Musée Guimet 41, 47–8

Noailles, Charles de 13, 52, 64n.61, 77, 79,
        109–10
non-western objects
    as art 20–3, 25–30, 33, 52, 67, 68–9,
        71–2, 101
    definitions of 3, 6, 15, 20–1, 25, 29,
        40–1, 43–4, 48–9, 59, 68, 71, 100,
        103, 114, 124, 128, 130 *see also*
        curio; curiosities
    prejudice against 26, 29–30, 53
    purity of 33, 59, 71, 117
    and western art and artists 16–18, 29,
        45, 56, 122–3 *see also*
        'primitivism'
Nordenskiöld, Erland 55, 57
Northwest Coast America 8
    art 31
    Kwakiutl objects 53

potlatch 52 *see also* Mauss *Gift*; gift
    exchange
Notes and Queries on Anthropology 70, 75,
    91–2, 100

object as witness *see* Dakar-Djibouti expe-
    dition
objects, properties of
    edible 25, 131, 132
    ephemeral 20, 123, 140, 146
    heterogeneous 20, 123, 125, 140, 143
    humble 14, 53, 56, 57, 58, 59, 72, 124,
        140, 141, 142, 143
    perishable 123, 140
    throwaway 59, 123, 125
objective chance 4, 127, 143
'Occidental' 28, 31, 54
Oceanic objects 3, 8, 12, 23, 27, 31, 32, 41,
    45, 48, 50, 52, 67, 105–6, *106*,
    140 *see also* Solomon Islands;
    Trobriand
Ogotemmêli *see* Dogon
Oppenheim, Meret
    Fur-Covered Cup, Saucer and Spoon
        136

Pahouin *see* Fang
Pelliot, Paul 49, 63n.49
Penny, H. Glenn 14
Péret, Benjamin 32
performance, the performative 1, 57, 76,
    108, 143, 147, 123
Pinney, Christopher 93
photography 1, 7, 56, 67, 92, 93, 94, 95, 96,
    98, 107, 115, 116
    ethnographic 92–4, 98, 114–16
    of isolated objects 94–6, 100–1, 115
    surrealist 94, 98
physical anthropology 26, 99
Picabia, Francis 140
Picasso, Pablo 12, 13, 16, 20, 52, 64n.60,
    122–4, 137–9, 140, 141
    Demoiselles d'Avignon, Les 12
    Figure (1935) *138*, 139
    Glass of Absinthe 136
    Guitar (1912) 18
    Guitar (1926) 137

Guitars (1926) 137
    Profile (1931) 122, *122*
    Still Life with Mask (1937) 139
plaster 99, 125, 132–3, 140, 146
Poignant, Roslyn 98
Pratt, Mary Louise 79
preciousness, the precious 23, 30, 49, 50,
    52, 53, 68, 69, 71, 73, 92, 101,
    111, 140, 142, 143
Precolumbian art 41, 50, 101, 108, 109, *109*
prehistory 33, 46, 56
'primitivism' 2, 3, 15
Pudelko, Georges 45

raffia 22, 140, 146
Ratton, Charles 22, 25, 33, 52, 111, 125,
    139, 144 *see also* surrealist object
Révolution surréaliste, La 31, 44, 125
Richardson, Michael 5, 105
Rivet, Paul 14, 30, 32, 54–5, 70, 71, 109,
    110, 111
Rivière, Georges Henri 2, 4, 14, 15, 16, 32,
    40, 41, 43, 44, 48, 50, 52, 64n.61,
    76, 92, 93, 101, 108, 109, 110,
    111, 112, 114, 115, 116, 120n.82
    'Archéologismes' 40, 41, 43, 46, 100,
        109
Romanesque art 27, 28, 53–4
Roussel, Raymond 77, 78, 96, 97
    Impressions d'Afrique 60
    star-shaped biscuit 96, 97, *97*, 98
rubbish 59, 71, 72, 74

sacred 4, 28, 29, 52, 82, 83, 84, 85, 102,
    103, 124, 126, 141
sacrifice 69, 99, 102, 122
Sadoul, Georges 32, 119n.75
Salles, Georges 41, 45, 48
Salmon, André 67
Sanga *see* Dogon
Schaeffner, André 32, 56–7, 76
Sheherazade 79
Scheltema, F. Adama van 54
Schildkrout, Enid 6
sculpture *see also* African objects; found
    object; objects, properties of;
    Oceanic objects; surrealist object

autonomy 19, 23, 25
  ethnographic 99
  in France (Basler) 29
  Kafir 47–8
  monumental 28 *see also* Romanesque art
  origins of 56, 128
  and photography 100
  Sumerian 46, 48
  surrealist 130–2, 146–7
Seabrook, William 60, 78
  Jungle Ways 78
  Magic Island 78
second-hand 73 *see also* flea-market; found
  object
self-reflexive ethnography 5, 61, 84–5, 143
Seltman, Charles Theodore 46, 62n.33
sewing 137–9, 140
Simmel, Georg 12, 16
Skira, Albert 92
Smithsonian Institution, Washington 71,
  128
Solomon Islands 48–9
  shield (Trocadéro) 50
Sorbonne 27, 30, 48, 54, 59, 70
Soustelle, Jacques 32
spoons 133–7, *135*, *136 see also* Breton;
  Giacometti
Stocking, George 6
stone, stones 56, 76, 126–9, 131–2, 141,
  149n.28
Strzygowski, Josef 53–4, 57, 60, 75
Sudan (French) 26, 68, 79, 82, 105, *105*,
  113
'Summary Instructions for Collectors of
  Ethnographic Objects' *see*
  Griaule
surrealism 1, 4–8, 27, 31–3, 59, 72, 94–6,
  98, 112, 123, 130, 134, 137, 139,
  140, 142–4, 146–7 *see also* photography
  automatism 106, 127
  counter-colonial' exhibition 31, 32, 33,
  130
  dissident 44
  Ratton Gallery exhibition (1936) 136,
  139, 144, *145*, 147, 149n.28
  slipper spoon *see* Breton

star-shaped biscuit *see* Roussel
surrealist ethnography *see* Clifford
  ethnographic surrealism
surrealist object 7, 8, 94–8, *95*, *97*, *122*,
  123, 125–6, *129*, 130, 132, 136–7,
  137, 139, 140–1, 143–4, *145*,
  146–7
Surréalisme au service de la révolution, Le
  32, 44
Sydow, Eckart von 23, 45, 49, 111

Tanguy, Yves 32, 33
technology, techniques (human) 7, 8, 53,
  57, 59, 115, 123, 125, 130, 131,
  135, 137, 140, 142, 147
Tériade (Stratis Eleftheriades) 92
theft 81–84 *see also* Bamana *boli*; Dakar-
  Djibouti expedition acquisition
  of objects
Thomas, Nicholas 6, 7, 100, 111
tools 19, 56, 131, 133
totemism 15, 67 *see also* Besson
touch 16, 19, 21, 23, 25 *see also* magic contagion
Toucouleur
  dolls 79–80
tourism 81, 107
  tourist art 56
toys 56, 67, 141
travel writing 79, 92, 94, 107 *see also* Gide
  Voyage au Congo
Trobriand
  baloma 93 *see also* Malinowski
  canoe boards 124
  kula 52–3 *see also* Mauss (*Gift*); (gift
  exchange)
Trocadéro Ethnographic Museum 2, 5, 7,
  12–13, 29–32, 43, 45, 52, 68, 93,
  107–8, 110, 116–17
  *Bulletin du Musée d'Ethnographie du
  Trocadéro* 92
  collections 41–2, 50, 56, 68, 70, 100
  exhibitions and displays 32, 77, *77*, 98,
  103, *103*, 111–12, *113*, 114–16,
  114, *115*, 144 *see also* Benin;
  Dakar-Djibouti expedition
  finance 110

negative accounts 12, 13
renovation 14, 16, 30, 42–3, 50, 92, 110, 111
SAMET (Société des amis du musée d'ethnographie du Trocadéro) 64n.61, 110
Treasury 16, 101, *101*, 111, 114, 143
'Truth about the Colonies' *see* surrealism counter-colonial exhibition
Tylor, Edward, 126, 130, 148n.17
   Primitive Culture 75, 136
types, the typical 53, 55, 59, 80, 99, 111
Tzara, Tristan 32, 36n.64, 111

use 24, 55, 72, 123, 125, 126, 135, 146
use-value 55, 129
utility 122, 123, 125, 134

Vad, Mamadou 79-80
Vaux, Marc 131, *132*, *133*
Verneau, René 20, 27, 110
Vignier, Charles 41
Vitrac, Roger 96, 150n.50
vitrines 13, 92, 110–11, 116, 144
Vlaminck, Maurice de 14
voodoo 60, 78

Walker, Ian 94, 107
wax 68, 102, 125–6, 128
weaving 144
Wildenstein, Georges 13, 44, 52, 64n.60, 64n.61, 92, 110
wood 18, 20–1, 23, 48, 53–4, 56–7, 59, 68–9, 94, 102–3, 110, 112, 122, 125, 127, 135–6, 139–41, 143
Wood, Jonathan 133
Worch, Edgar 52, 111
Worringer, Wilhelm 12, 16
   Abstraction and Empathy 12, 45, 48

Yoruba 25, 43

Zayas, Marius de 45
Zervos, Christian 44, 45, 105, 124, 141
Zuñi 67, 78, 81, *127*, 128

EU authorised representative for GPSR:
Easy Access System Europe, Mustamäe tee 50,
10621 Tallinn, Estonia
gpsr.requests@easproject.com